The Soviet Union and Eastern Europe are moving away from a centrally planned economy toward integration within the global economy. How did this transition begin? Is this an aim which all the countries can afford? What conditions are to be met so that the countries will achieve a level of development comparable with the average level of their industrial partners?

In this timely volume, leading international political economists from both the East and West provide an in-depth analysis of these questions. In doing so they explore the three main challenges that currently face the Soviet Union and Eastern Europe. First, the contributors analyze how the Communist bloc is redirecting its economic relations away from the political privileges of trade and cooperation with the CMEA and the Third World toward the West, in particular Western Europe. Secondly, they examine how the Soviet Union and Eastern Europe are eager to overcome their development lag and implement a restructuring policy, which implies increasing involvement of Western capital. Finally, the authors assess how the transition to the market requires liberalizing foreign trade, introducing convertibility, transforming property structures, all of which are also part of the ongoing domestic reform.

The Soviet Union and Eastern Europe in the global economy provides a comprehensive understanding of the international dimensions and domestic constraints of changing East–West economic relations. It will be widely read by students and specialists of Soviet and East European studies, economics, and political science.

The Soviet Union and Eastern Europe
in the global economy

Selected papers from the Fourth World Congress
for Soviet and East European Studies
Harrogate, July 1990

Edited for the
INTERNATIONAL COMMITTEE
FOR SOVIET AND EAST EUROPEAN STUDIES

General Editor
Stephen White
University of Glasgow

The Soviet Union and Eastern Europe in the global economy

edited by

Marie Lavigne

Professor of Economics, University of Pau, France

CAMBRIDGE
UNIVERSITY PRESS

CAMBRIDGE UNIVERSITY PRESS
Cambridge, New York, Melbourne, Madrid, Cape Town, Singapore,
São Paulo, Delhi, Dubai, Tokyo, Mexico City

Cambridge University Press
The Edinburgh Building, Cambridge CB2 8RU, UK

Published in the United States of America by Cambridge University Press, New York

www.cambridge.org
Information on this title: www.cambridge.org/9780521172356

© Cambridge University Press 1992

First published 1992
First paperback edition 2010

A catalogue record for this publication is available from the British Library

Library of Congress Cataloguing in Publication data

World Congress for Soviet and East European Studies (4th: 1990: Harrogate,
England)
    The Soviet Union and Eastern Europe in the global economy/edited by
Marie Lavigne.
    219p.   cm.
    "Selected papers from the Fourth World Congress for Soviet and East
European Studies, Harrogate, July 1990" – P.
    ISBN 0 521 41417 2 (hardback)
    1. Soviet Union – Foreign economic relations – Congresses. 2. Europe,
Eastern – Foreign economic relations – Congresses. 3. Soviet Union –
Economic integration – Congresses. 4. Technology transfer – Soviet Union
– Congresses. 5. Technology transfer – Europe, Eastern – Congresses.
6. Joint ventures – Soviet Union – Congresses. 7. Joint ventures – Europe,
Eastern – Congresses. I. Lavigne, Marie, 1935–. II. Title.
HF1557.W67   1992
337.47 – dc20   91–30816 CIP

ISBN 978-0-521-41417-3 Hardback
ISBN 978-0-521-17235-6 Paperback

Contents

Figures

Tables

Notes on contributors

WOJCIECH BIENKOWSKI is Assistant Professor at Main School of Commerce in Warsaw, Poland (formerly Central School of Planning and Statistics). His academic career includes several years at the University of Rochester (NY), Harvard University, and Nagoya City University in Japan. He has contributed to many academic journals and books published in the USA, England, Italy, and Japan, in addition to publications in Poland. He is co-owner and Director of the "NEST"-Art Division Company Ltd., based in Warsaw.

W. DONALD BOWLES is Professor of Economics at American University in Washington, DC, where he previously served as Chairman of the Economics Department, Dean of the College of Arts and Sciences, and Vice-President for Academic Affairs. He has published on the Soviet economy in, among other places, *International Economic Review*, *Journal of Forestry*, *Soviet Studies*, *Slavic Review*, and *World Politics*. During 1983–85 he was an economist with the US Agency for International Development, and served as consultant with the Agency in 1985–89, publishing extensively on various aspects of foreign economic assistance.

MICHAEL J. BRADSHAW is a Lecturer in the School of Geography, and Associate Member of the Centre for Russian and East European Studies, University of Birmingham, England. He is the editor of *The Soviet Union: A New Regional Geography?*, published in 1991 by Belhaven Press and the author of the Economist Intelligence Unit Report *Siberia in a Time of Change*. His research interests include East–West trade and regional development in the Soviet Union and the economic development of Siberia and the Soviet Far East.

HORST BREZINSKI teaches economics at the University of Paderborn. His research mainly focuses on comparative economic systems and international economic relations. He is also the co-editor (together with Wladimir Andreff and Bruno Dallago) of *Convergence Theory and Systemic Change* which is to appear in 1992.

PATRICK GUTMAN is an economist at the University of PARIS-I (Pan-théon–Sorbonne) and member of the ROSES research team (URA 1417 of CNRS) where he coordinates the working group on Foreign Direct Investment in USSR and Eastern Europe. He has published widely on East–West Industrial Cooperation, East–West–South Tripartite Industrial Cooperation and East–South technology transfer, in Europe as well as the United States. He has been a consultant for DGRST, JETRO, OECD, and UNCTAD.

MASUMI HAKOGI has been Professor of Economics since 1982 at the University of Fukushima in Japan. He has written many articles on East–West economic relations, Soviet–Japanese trade relations, and EC–Japan economic relations. He is joint editor with J. S. Berliner and H. G. J. Kosta of *Economics of the Socialist Countries*, published in 1989.

ERIK P. HOFFMAN is Professor of Political Science at the State University of New York, USA. He published numerous articles and books on international relations and foreign policy of the Soviet Union.

MARIE LAVIGNE is Professor of Economics at the University of Pau in France. From 1973 to 1990 she was Director of the Center for International Economics of Socialist Countries at the University of Paris-I and in 1991 Director of the IEWSS European Studies Center in Czechoslovakia. Marie Lavigne has published extensively on the political economy of socialism and the international economic relations of the Soviet Union and Eastern Europe, including, as editor, *East–South Relations in the World Economy*, and *International Political Economy and Socialism*.

JAN MACIEJEWICZ is Professor at the Institute for International Economic Relations, Main School of Commerce, Warsaw (formerly Central School of Planning and Statistics), and has published on questions of foreign trade and investment.

HARRIET MATEJKA is Professor of International Economics at The Graduate Institute of International Studies in Geneva, Switzerland. Her research focuses on the planned economies in transition, as well as the remaining centrally planned economies, and their relations with the developed West. Her most recent publication is *La Perestroika et ses conséquences économiques en Union Soviétique et en Europe de l'Est* (Berne: Conseil Suisse de la Science, 1991), 70pp.

JOZEF MISALA is Professor at the Institute for International Economic Relations, Main School of Commerce, Warsaw (formerly Central

School of Planning and Statistics), and has published on questions of industrial policy and foreign trade.

JOSEPH PELZMAN is Professor of Economics at the George Washington University, Washington DC, USA. He is currently a Visiting Scholar at the Russian Research Center, Harvard University. During 1984–85 and 1990–91 he was a Lady Davis Visiting Professor at The Hebrew University, Jerusalem, Israel. His most recent article in the Soviet area is "The New Soviet–East European Economic Relationship: Post CMEA," in *Economic Systems*, 15, no. 2, October 1991.

ISTVAN SALGO has taught at the Budapest University of Economics and worked as researcher with the Institute of Planning in Budapest. He is now International Director of the Financial Research Corporation, a consulting company in the field of international trade and investment.

SIEGFRIED SCHULTZ is a senior economist at the German Institute of Economic Research in Berlin. His academic work is focused on Third World policy (aid, sectoral studies, project evaluation), trade policy (protectionism, export promotion, trade in services), and debt problems. He has also advised the federal government and para-statal agencies and participated in various evaluation missions to Asia and Africa.

DENIS J. B. SHAW is a Lecturer in the School of Geography, and Associate Member of the Centre for Russian and East European Studies, University of Birmingham, England. He is co-author of *Planning in the Soviet Union* and *Landscape and Settlement in Romanov Russia, 1613–1917* and has written many articles on the historical, urban, and economic geography of the Soviet Union.

KRYSTYNA SZYMKIEWICZ is a researcher at the CNRS (Centre National de la Recherche Scientifique) and a member of the ROSES (Reform and Opening up of the Socialist Economic Systems) team at the University of Paris I Panthéon-Sorbonne. She graduated in 1964 from the Central School of Planning and Statistics in Warsaw, Poland. She took her PhD in Paris in 1975, at the University of Paris I. She has published widely on subjects related to Polish international economics, including a book on Polish foreign trade.

HEINRICH VOGEL was Research Fellow, Osteuropa-Institut, Munich (1966–69), Deputy Director, Osteuropa-Institut, Munich (1969–76), and is Director and Professor, Bundesinstitut für ostwissenschaftliche und internationale Studien, Cologne (1976–). He was Guest Lecturer, University of Oklahoma, Munich Program (1971–73), Assistant Professor, University of Munich (1972–75), and Visiting Professor, Free University, Berlin (1975). He has published monographs and articles on political and economic relations between East and West, the Soviet and East European economies, and European security.

Introduction: The USSR and Eastern Europe opening to the world

Marie Lavigne

The chapters collected in this volume were presented at the IVth World Congress for Soviet and East European Studies (Harrogate, England, July 1990) organized by ICSEES (International Council for Soviet and East European Studies). They focus on the recent developments in the international economic relations of the countries which were part of the Communist bloc, and on the international dimension of the domestic reforms and revolutions occurring in this area.

The countries in transition to the market are faced with three challenges. First, they want to become a part of the world economy, which means above all redirecting their economic relations toward the West, and particularly toward Western Europe, at the expense of other politically privileged areas in the past directions of trade and cooperation, especially with the former CMEA area and the Third World. Second, they are eager to overcome their development lag and to implement a restructuring policy, which implies increasing involvement of Western capital. Third, the transition to the market encompasses the foreign trade sector as well. Opening up to the world requires liberalizing foreign trade, introducing convertibility, transforming property structures, all of which is part of the domestic reform.

The contributions assembled in Part I look at the new international relations of the East. The whole philosophy of what was once called East–West relations is changing. While in the past the East used to highlight the concept of cooperation – "between different economic and social systems" as was the usual wording of United Nations organizations on this matter – the West paid lip-service to cooperation so as to benefit from access to Eastern markets or to Eastern (mainly Soviet) sources of supply, but sought ways to protect itself against undue competition or to avoid politically undesirable technology transfer. Now the very notion of "East–West" relations becomes questionable as there is no longer any systemic basis for differentiating the "East" otherwise than as a geographical area concept. The title of the first article by *Harriet Matejka* exemplifies this by referring to East–West integration, which is ultimately to blur the distinction between East and West in Europe. As is strongly stated in Central Europe, i.e. in Czechoslovakia – the CSFR or Czech and Slovak Federal Republic – Poland, and Hungary, the final aim of these countries is to join the European Community in a move "back to Europe" from which the mentioned countries have been artificially estranged for forty-five years. Since the article was written the drafting of the new "European agreements" has indeed moved forward but complete integration is still far from being completed, and the transition period during which CMEA links are being severed proves much more difficult than expected. This is why the traditional concept of East–West trade is still relevant, the more so where the Soviet Union is concerned. *Heinrich Vogel* stresses the political as well as economic dimensions of this trade and pleads for bolder moves from the West. The deterioration of the economic situation in the USSR as well as the stalemate of Soviet perestroika increase both the challenge and the risk of such an approach. In any case Western cautiousness in dismantling COCOM barriers shows that the East–West divide is still there and that the "normalization" of East–West relations is still ahead when security and national policy considerations come to the fore. In a different field, that of trade protection, *Joseph Pelzman* also has to deal with political conditions in the shift to "normalcy" for US–Soviet relations, though he basically focuses on the expected benefits of the granting of most favored nation (MFN) status to the USSR. Indeed the provisional granting of this status occurred later in 1990, following the expectations presented in the chapter, but the author has been very wise in stressing that the uncertainties about perestroika in the USSR strongly constrained any economic estimates. *Wojciech Bienkowski* and *Masumi Hakogi* show how these uncertainties explain the cautious approach of Japan toward expanded trade with the East.

While East–West trade is on the rise, be it with many difficulties, East–South trade is clearly on the decline. As for economic assistance, Eastern Europe (the USSR excluded) has never been a significant contributor, except for the GDR. The burden of assistance was borne by the USSR and East Germany. In the Soviet case, critique of the aid program has developed among the Soviet population which feels that domestic needs are now a priority. *Donald Bowles* shows how these new attitudes, as well as the reform process itself, should alter Soviet foreign aid practice. There is a fundamental contradiction here between the former political goals of Soviet assistance to the Third World and the economic interests of the USSR as a whole and of the enterprises involved in cooperation with the Third World. Thus aid flows are to be reduced drastically in the future, even though some political considerations are still to remain as the concessionary agreement concluded with Cuba at the beginning of 1991 has shown. The German case is quite fascinating as *Siegfried Schultz* shows. The same trends as in the Soviet Union were already noticeable in the foreign aid policy of the GDR, i.e. a growing consciousness of national economic interests. In the transition period following the fall of the Wall the political justification of an aid policy shifted from the desire to support socialist regimes to a broader concept of the North–South dialogue; unification has integrated East and West German policies in the South, while making East Germany the "south" of the Western part.

The revolutions in Eastern Europe have deeply altered the significance of East–West technological transfer. As before, such a transfer is seen as a most powerful engine for growth. But Western involvement in this transfer is now to become much greater as it increasingly takes the form of joint ventures rather than standard trade-channeled supplies of technology. *Michael J. Bradshaw* and *Denis J. B. Shaw* look at the technology transfer to the Soviet Union from the point of view of a regional perspective, a very timely approach indeed as the regional dimension of Soviet economic development is becoming more important through the disintegration of the Union. They also underline the very small contribution of joint ventures to such transfers. The Eastern European dimension is presented by *Jan Maciejewicz* who dwells at more length on the Polish case. As he underlines in his conclusion, COCOM restrictions are not yet overcome even as regards Eastern Europe, and their lifting is crucial to the development of such sectors as telecommunications or the computer industry which is a prerequisite to economic growth in the region. Long-term Western assistance programs should help in the technological upgrading of the Central European countries but are still marginal in this field. Foreign investment might become an important channel of technology transfer as the Polish case shows.

The issue of foreign capital involvement in the modernization and systemic change process is tackled in three contributions of which the first, by *Patrick Gutman*, derives interesting conclusions from the comparison between the policy of concessions during the NEP period in the twenties and the joint ventures under perestroika. Poland is again the focus of the two following chapters. *Jozef Misala* analyzes current joint venture law in Poland and its impact on the domestic economy from a Polish perspective and ends with rather gloomy conclusions. The opportunities provided by foreign investment regulations are quite extensive but the domestic economic situation is constraining the willingness of foreign partners to invest in Poland. More is said about the attitudes of these partners in the following chapter by *Horst Brezinski* who explores the determinants of their actions through the analysis of a poll conducted with more than 300 joint ventures. This analysis is developed using the framework of transaction costs theory and concludes that transaction costs are not seen as excessive by most of the foreign partners. It also shows, as do other contributions, that the main way to economic development is a true market-oriented reform, of which Western investment is just one component.

Thus the successful implementation of such reforms is a major condition for the expansion of trade and economic relations at large. *Erik P. Hoffman* elaborates on this in a political economy approach to the Soviet case. *Krystyna Szymkiewicz* highlights the Polish experience of decentralization and liberalization with a very detailed study of Polish foreign trade reform. Her final remarks dwell on the very important problem, common to all Eastern European countries, raised by the collapse of the CMEA and particularly of Soviet trade with Eastern Europe. These countries are now caught between two fires in their foreign economic relations, and *Istvan Salgo* does not hesitate to state that the present situation is untenable: the Eastern governments want to shift away from their Eastern trade but the premature reform of CMEA trade introduced in January 1991 could well lead to a downturn in overall trade and negatively influence domestic reform.

It would certainly not be fair to conclude on such a note. This volume on the prospects for a (re-)integration of the East in the global economy highlights a whole range of opportunities, mostly yet to be developed. An obvious missing aspect is the impact of Western assistance, and readers may be surprised not to find it here. This is due to the fact that in 1990 Western assistance was just beginning to be deployed, and no in-depth assessment was available. As for CMEA developments, everyone could feel that the year 1991 would be crucial, but no one could have predicted to what extent. More generally, all the authors have proceeded with many caveats and felt constrained in their projections by the uncertainties of the reforms, and of the international setting. These warnings were certainly needed; the subsequent evolution of the situation has mostly confirmed the expectations of the authors.

Part I

Integration: The East in the world economy

1 East–West European integration

Harriet Matejka

The creation and integration of the European Economic Community (EEC) has been the driving force behind Western European integration, Eastern European cooperation, and, most recently, the proposals for pan-European integration. In Western Europe, at the outset, the creation of the Community in 1957 by Belgium, Luxembourg, the Netherlands, France, Italy, and the Federal Republic of Germany on the basis of the Treaty of Rome prompted the foundation, in 1959, of the European Free Trade Area (EFTA) uniting Austria, Denmark, Norway, Portugal, Sweden, Switzerland, and the United Kingdom. The same year in Eastern Europe, the Council for Mutual Economic Assistance (CMEA) adopted its charter, and then the Principles of the International Socialist Division of Labor in 1962.

In 1968, the EEC's completion of its customs union, its members' acceptance of a common commercial policy in 1970, and the extension of the Community to include the United Kingdom, Ireland, and Denmark in 1973 was followed, in the West, by free trade agreements between the EEC and the remaining EFTA countries,[1] and by a free trade agreement between the EEC and Finland which, until 1985, was only an associate member of EFTA. In the East, the Community changes were followed by the CMEA's publication of the Comprehensive Programme for Socialist Economic Integration,[2] and, as the EEC sought to conclude trade agreements with CMEA member countries, by the Council's proposal, which failed, for a joint agreement between the two organizations, and for a joint commission to supervise not only the agreement but also the transactions between the EEC and individual CMEA countries.

Most recently, the decision of the Community in 1985 to create the Single Market by 1 January 1993, and to add Portugal and Spain to its members, has led to the EFTA–EEC proposal to create the European Economic Area (EEA), negotiations for which began on 20 June 1990. The EEA is intended to extend to services, labor, and capital the freedom of trade first introduced for industrial products between the

7

EEC and EFTA, and thus to create, as the appended table shows (1.3), a market encompassing nineteen Western and Central European countries.

The initial response of the CMEA to this new stage in Western European integration was the recommendation adopted at its 44th session in 1988 itself to create a single integrated market between member countries. But the proposal was effectively dropped with the recommendations of the 45th session in January 1990 to resort to world market prices and convertible currency settlements for mutual trade as from 1 January 1991. This puts intra-CMEA transactions on the same basis as trade with the developed market economies.

Intra-CMEA integration has in fact been overtaken by East–West European integration following the Joint EEC–CMEA Declaration of 25 June 1988, the signature of which was also precipitated by the Community's decision to establish the single market. The Declaration led to the conclusion of "first generation" agreements between the EEC and the European CMEA member countries between June 1988 and November 1990, and to the announcement of a "second generation" of agreements to be based on article 238 of the Treaty of Rome, which relates to association. Thus, fear of being excluded from Community prosperity has integrated Western Europe, has conjured up the EEA, and, as the Community thrusts eastwards into the vacuum left by the disappearance of the CMEA, promises to create a unified pan-European market.

This chapter sets out to see, in section 1, how East–West economic integration is developing; in section 2, what are the systemic conditions for its realization and how extensive it should be and, in section 3, what can be said of the transition schemes being proposed to assist in the achievement of a single East–West trading area. Conclusions are set out in section 4.

1   Unification

The economic reunification of the European continent from West to East around the Community did not begin on 25 June 1988. Instead, it has taken place gradually as the countries in the eastern part of the continent have slowly reoriented their trade toward the EEC. This is reflected in Table 1.1, which shows that the trade of the European members of the CMEA, and particularly of the smaller countries, with the twelve members of the Community has gained in importance in the thirty years from 1958 to 1988. Their trading interests, in turn, have obliged the CMEA countries to conclude agreements with the Com-

Table 1.1. *The share of the Community*[a] *in the total trade of the member countries of the Council for Mutual Economic Assistance (CMEA)*[b] *(percentages)*

	Exports[c]		Imports[c]	
	CMEA 7	CMEA 6	CMEA 7	CMEA 6
1958	12	13	11	13
1960	13	14	12	13
1965	14	15	11	14
1970	15	16	15	17
1975	16	17	19	20
1977	17	17	17	18
1978	17	18	17	19
1979	19	19	18	19
1980	20	20	17	19
1981	18	16	15	16
1982	18	15	13	15
1983	16	14	13	13
1984	17	15	12	12
1985	16	14	12	13
1986	14	15	13	14
1987	15	17	13	16
1988	17	21	15	21

Notes: [a] France, Belgium and Luxembourg, Netherlands, Federal Republic of Germany, Italy, United Kingdom, Ireland, Denmark, Greece, Portugal, Spain.

[b] As the ruble is overvalued, ruble-dominated trade is overvalued in the total trade of the CMEA countries, and the share of the Community in this total appears smaller than if the Rb/$ rate, and cross-rates, were equilibrium rates.

[c] Including intra-German trade.

CMEA 7: Bulgaria, Czechoslovakia, German Democratic Republic, Hungary, Poland, Romania, USSR.

CMEA 6: CMEA 7 less USSR.

Source: Eurostat: *Foreign Trade Yearbook*, various years, Tables 1 and 9.

UN/ECE Common Data Base.

munity as it has achieved integration in one sector after the other. Thus, the introduction of the common agricultural policy (CAP) in 1964 meant that, between 1965 and 1975, Bulgaria, Hungary, Poland, and Romania concluded eighteen agricultural arrangements with the Community instead of with its member countries as had been the case before.[3] When the Community extended its common commercial policy to the East on 1 January 1975, these four countries and Czechoslovakia found themselves having to conclude sectoral agreements on textiles and steel, in addition. By June 1988, the Eastern countries had thus concluded over

Table 1.2. *"First generation" agreements between the EEC and the East*

Eastern partner	Sector	Type of agreement	Date of signature
1. Hungary	All products[a]	Trade and cooperation	26 September 1988
2. Czechoslovakia	Industrial products[a]	Trade	16 December 1988
3. Poland	All products[a]	Trade and cooperation	19 September 1989
4. USSR	All products[a]	Trade and cooperation	18 December 1989
5. Czechoslovakia	All products[a]	Trade and cooperation	7 May 1990
6. GDR	All products[a]	Trade and cooperation	8 May 1990
7. Bulgaria	All products[a]	Trade and cooperation	8 May 1990
8. Romania	All products[a]	Trade and cooperation	22 October 1990

Note: [a]Excepting steel and textiles. Agricultural products are included, except for those falling under sectoral agreements on agriculture.
Source: Official Journal of the European Communities (OJ) and EEC Press Releases.

forty agreements with the Community, although they still withheld diplomatic recognition from it.

But, with one exception, the Community refused to conclude general trade agreements with the Eastern countries before the Joint Declaration and diplomatic recognition in 1988. The single exception was the agreement concluded between the Community and Romania in 1980 on industrial products, excluding steel and textiles, which proved to be a mistake. In all other cases, general trade agreements between the EEC and Eastern countries were concluded after the Joint Declaration. The first was the trade and cooperation agreement with Hungary which was signed in September 1988. There followed agreements with all the other Eastern countries as Table 1.2 shows.

The trade and cooperation agreements are referred to as "first generation" agreements. "Second generation" agreements, based on article 238 of the Rome Treaty relating to association and which, it has been proposed, are to be known as "European agreements," have already been announced.[4] They are to cover trade in goods, services, and factors, as well as cooperation, and their content is to be adapted to the stage in the transition to the market that each Eastern partner has reached and to the special features of its economy. The objective is to be free trade in industrial goods, services, and factors and is to be achieved in two stages, the schedule of which is to be negotiated with each Eastern partner. In the first stage, the Community will reduce its barriers on industrial imports without expecting reciprocity and will grant technical assistance to promote a services sector and capital and labor markets in the Eastern countries. Only in the second stage will free trade in industrial products be achieved on a reciprocal basis, and Community rules be applied gradually to trade in services and to the flows of capital and labor. Agricultural trade will be subject to special arrangements.

The European Commission has made plain that there is no connection between association as described above and membership of the Community under the provisions of article 237 of the Treaty of Rome. Negotiations toward the conclusion of association agreements with Poland, Czechoslovakia ånd Hungary began at the end of 1990.

EFTA is also establishing closer ties with the East, its thirtieth anniversary having been the occasion for the signature, on 13 June 1990, of joint declarations of cooperation with Hungary, Czechoslovakia, and Poland. Modeled on the Bergen declaration with Yugoslavia of 1983, each foresees the negotiation of a free trade agreement between the signatories. A sub-committee to examine the possibility of concluding such an agreement between Hungary and EFTA was established in September 1990, and was followed by the creation of similar sub-committees for Poland and Czechoslovakia in October and November 1990. Thus, while all three countries have signed association agreements with the Community and have declared their desire to adhere to it, they consider collaboration with, and perhaps even accession to, EFTA, to be a stepping stone in that direction or, at least, in the direction of the EEA.

In Eastern Europe, meanwhile, the economic transformation of Western Europe, and the need for its suppliers and clients to adjust to it alone, without even a semblance of CMEA support, has led to proposals for new integration areas, and so new alliances. One such is the proposed economic integration of Hungary, Poland, and Czechoslovakia. The benefit which this might bring has not yet been explored, and it appears to be something of a tactical move to put the three countries in a better position for negotiating with the Community. Like the Central European Payments Union (CEPU), which has also been proposed as a transition scheme, it will therefore be considered in section 3.

The emerging economic organization of Europe thus appears to be a multitier construction. The first tier is formed by the economic union of the twelve Community members, united Germany being one entity, the second tier by the nineteen countries of the EEA which, in due course, are joined by the Eastern countries which conclude association agreements with the Community. The third tier is composed of countries, or groupings, which sign free trade agreements with EFTA. There seems little doubt that Hungary, Czechoslovakia, and Poland will in due course belong to the EEA, or at least have free trade agreements with

Table 1.3. *Member countries of Western European integration areas*[a]

Year	EEC	EFTA	EEC–EFTA Free Trade Agreements	EEA
1957	Belgium, Luxembourg, Netherlands, France, Italy, FRG			
1959		Austria, Denmark, Norway, Portugal, Sweden, Switzerland, United Kingdom		
1970		Iceland		
1972		(Denmark, United Kingdom)		
1973	Denmark, Ireland, United Kingdom		ECE/Austria, Switzerland, Portugal, Sweden, Iceland, Norway	
1974			ECE/Finland	
1981	Greece			
1985	(Greenland)[b]	Finland[c] (Portugal)		
1986	Spain, Portugal			
1990	GDR			
1993[d]				19 EEC and EFTA countries[e]

Notes: [a] Parentheses signify departure from an area.   [b] Becomes overseas territory of the EEC.

[c] Associate member from 1961 to 1985.   [e] Including Lichtenstein.

[d] Intended date of entry into force of the treaty constituting the EEA.

Symbols: EEC – European Economic Community; EEA – European Economic Area; EFTA – European Free Trade Area.

EFTA. What is more doubtful is the place of Bulgaria and Romania in the new scheme of things because of the lack of economic reform there. The same, so far, is true of the USSR, whose future relations to the pan-European market have, additionally, to be defined. For the Soviet Union is not only a European, but also an Asian and Pacific power. Its representatives have, however, expressed the wish that it be included in the EEA.[5]

But just as the agreement between the EEC and the CMEA helped to dissolve the CMEA, so it is being suggested that the thrust of the EEC eastward will overtake the laborious efforts to construct the EEA and make it superfluous. The process could develop as follows. The accession of Austria and Sweden, which have already formally applied for membership, would be followed by that of Finland, with Norway hard on its heels. With these four EFTA countries gone, Switzerland and Iceland would find it difficult to stay out of the EEC. Thus, instead of there being a multitier organization of Europe, the Community would include the Central and Northern European countries, and so extend eastward and northward to the Soviet border. In doing so, it might fully integrate certain associated Eastern economies. Whether this will in fact be the shape of European things to come depends on the Community. But Hungary, it should be noted, has already announced its hope of becoming an associate member of the EEC by 1992, and a full member by 1995.

2   Systemic conditions and size

The extension of the EEC eastward raises the question as to whether, and under what conditions, integration between market and centrally planned economies or, as the Eastern economies are decentralizing, semi-centralized economies, is possible.[6] As the answer has already been given in the mid-seventies, when free trade agreements were concluded between Finland and five Eastern European countries, and other agreements were proposed between some of these and the European neutrals,[7] it need not detain us long. The answer is that while in theory integration between centrally planned and market economies is possible, in practice it is not, because of the lack of transparency of central planning. The argument in outline is the following and stresses the need for decentralization in the planned economies if these are effectively to take part in integration schemes.

Integration may be defined as free trade between a limited number of countries. Free trade, in turn, may be defined as a policy in which the government abstains from intervening in trade, leaving traders to respond to differences in domestic and foreign prices, and so to determine the level, direction, and composition of trade. If this definition of free trade is adopted, it follows that a centrally planned economy in which every economic operation is determined by central instruction, that is central intervention, cannot pursue such a policy. It further follows that integration which involves centrally planned economies is impossible.

But free trade is not only the description of a policy in which the central authority abstains from intervening in trade. It also refers to a particular allocation of resources which is characterized by the equation of domestic and foreign prices. Clearly, such an allocation, described for a single importable product in the following system of equations, is attainable by a planned economy and so, consequently, is integration which would require it to equate its prices with those of its partner countries.

Let

$$S_D = \text{domestic supply}$$
$$S_F = \text{foreign supply}$$
$$D = \text{demand}$$
$$P_D = \text{domestic price}$$
$$P_F = \text{foreign price}$$

Then

$$S_D = S_D(P_D), \quad \frac{dS_D}{dP_D} > 0 \quad (1)$$

$$S_F = S_F(P_F), \quad \frac{dS_F}{dP_F} > 0 \quad (2)$$

$$D = D(P_D), \quad \frac{dD}{dP_D} < 0 \quad (3)$$

$$P_D = P_F, \quad (4)$$

$$SD + SF = D \quad (5)$$

The problem therefore is not a conceptual but a practical one, and lies with the implementation of the integration agreement. For its partners can never ascertain in practice whether the centrally planned economy has met its obligations to equate its prices to theirs. This will be grasped by recalling the operation of a market and of a centrally planned economy, and by comparing the implementation of an integration agreement in both.

In a market economy, the policy authority is separate from the other economic decision makers, that is producers, consumers, and traders. The instruments at its disposal to implement its policies are price-mechanism devices, that is, in so far as the allocation of resources is concerned, taxes and subsidies which are published both because of the separation of the policy authority from the other economic decision makers, and because of the generally high number of the latter. The taxes and subsidies are levied on, or disbursed to, producers, con-sumers, and traders who are autonomous and whose consequent need to earn a profit means that they respond to price variations and so to any tax or subsidy change. Thus, in a market economy, a lowering of tariffs taken as a step toward integration will be published. Moreover, the ensuing price change will prompt a fall in domestic import-competing production, an increase in consumption, and an increase in imports from the partner country, as the following system of equations, where t stands for tariff, describes. The reallocation of resources which integra-tion implies can be expected to take place.

$$S_D = S_D(P_D), \quad \frac{dS_D}{dP_D} > 0 \qquad (1)$$

$$S_F = S_F(P_F), \quad \frac{dS_F}{dP_F} > 0 \qquad (2)$$

$$D = D(P_D), \quad \frac{dD}{dP_D} < 0 \qquad (3)$$

$$P_D = P_F(1+t), \qquad (4)$$

$$S_D + S_F = D \qquad (5)$$

In a centrally planned economy, by contrast, the policy authority and the other economic decision makers coincide, for there is, in the limit, only one decision maker which is the central authority. The producers, traders, and, conceivably, even the consumers, are central agents acting upon instruction from the center. Being neither autonomous nor, conse-quently, intent on covering costs and seeking a profit, they do not respond to price and, hence, to tax and subsidy, changes. Thus, published prices and price-mechanism devices are redundant in a centrally planned economy. Moreover, as in order to maintain the coincidence between central policy making and economic decision tak-ing, central agents are few, the directives they receive, and which determine the level of production, consumption, and trade, are generally not published either. Thus, in a centrally planned economy, the convergence of domestic and foreign prices taken as a step toward economic integration need not be visible. If changes in prices are published, no observable economic mechanism will ensure that the associated reallocation of resources takes place. All economic change will be at the discretion of the central authority which can always choose to act in secret.

This lack of transparency means that it is difficult, if not impossible, to verify the implementation of any international agreement, including integration treaties, in which one partner is centrally planned, and which involve price, and therefore tax and subsidy, obligations. This being so, the partner to an integration agreement which includes a centrally planned economy has the choice between refusing the agreement on the grounds that its implementation cannot be monitored, or of taking it on trust without any assurance that integration will be realized. Integration in practice thus requires that the centrally planned partner decentralizes sufficiently for policy measures to need to be published. For the reallocation of resources, which it implies, to occur will further require that producers and traders be profit seeking.

If this analysis is accepted, it follows that the Community's extension eastward must be very gradual. It will be a function of decentralization and of the introduction of an operating market system in Eastern Europe,[8] and this will mean that not all Eastern countries will be in a position to achieve either associate status or, *a fortiori*, membership of the Community, at once. The obstacle to marketization which CMEA trade has always constituted, however, will lessen in all these countries as the transition to world prices and settlements in convertible currencies is implemented as from January 1991.

The second question which East–West integration raises relates to the size of the proposed pan-European free trade area. Will it extend from Lisbon to Vladivostock, or should it fall short of this? Here only guidelines suggested by the theory of economic integration can be offered. These are two.

The first concerns the gains to be expected from economic integration and follows from the central proposition of the theory of customs unions. This asserts that, as integration describes the passage from one second-best allocation of resources to another, and as there is no presumption that one second-best situation is better than another,[9] integration need not bring gain. This is as true of the creation of a new integration area as it is of the extension of an already existing one. Applied to East–West integration, this proposition means that it may be gainful for the Community to absorb the GDR, but not gainful for it to extend further to integrate with Poland. Or it may be gainful for the EEA to absorb Hungary, but not to include Czechoslovakia or Poland. As theory provides no certain prediction, every integration has thus to be examined on its merits, and there is no ready-made answer to the question of the optimal size of the pan-European free trade area.

Nevertheless, there is a probability established by the analysis of integration that the larger the area, the greater the gains. The assumption is that the larger the area, the higher the share of world production and consumption it comprises, and the more likely it is therefore that trade creation will outweigh trade diversion. Applied to East–West integration, this would seem to justify the largest possible pan-European area, perhaps even spilling over into Asia to include Vladivostock. But a probability is not a certainty, and the case for such an area would again have to be examined on its merits.

Thus nothing definite can be said about the ultimate size of the pan-European area without a close study of resource reallocation, but also of the growth, prompted by integration. What does seem clear, however, is that the gain may be very different for the two partners, the EEC, the EEA or EFTA, on the one hand, and the Eastern countries, on the other. The EEC, EEA or EFTA may find that the addition of Hungary or Czechoslovakia to its market will bring only modest economic gain, while the two countries will, on the contrary, come to the conclusion that the inclusion of their economies into the Western market will bring immeasurable benefits. The urgency of economic association may thus be very different in East and West.

One final word of a political nature may be added. It is that integration areas which require only the reduction of national barriers to the free flow of goods, services, and factors, would appear to be easier to establish than those that require the transfer of national sovereignty to a new integration authority. Preference areas, free trade areas, and areas like the EEA that provide for the free flow of products, services, labor, and capital are, for this reason, likely to be easier to establish than customs or economic unions. Thus East–West economic integration may at first partially or fully free trade in products, services, and factors rather than create a new customs union.[10]

3   Transition

The disappearance of the CMEA has meanwhile brought forth proposals for new Eastern integration areas designed to assist their members in their transition to the market or their inclusion in the Western market. The three examined below concern the creation of an integration area between Hungary, Czechoslovakia, and Poland, the Central European Customs Union, and the proposal for a Central European Payments Union (CEPU).[11]

The proposed integration area between Hungary, Czechoslovakia, and Poland and the Central European Customs Union need not detain us long. For its realization runs up against the same obstacles as association between the EEC and the Eastern countries, or free trade between them and EFTA, namely those resulting from central planning. This being so, integration between the three countries will be a function of the introduction of an operating market system in each of their economies and cannot, for this reason, serve to promote their transition to it. Since, moreover, achieving the market will put each country in a position to choose between association with the EEC or EFTA, mutual integration, or both, mutual integration cannot be considered either as a stage in the process of achieving association with a Western integration area. Rather it constitutes another integration option once the systemic conditions for this are fulfilled. When they are, the option should be assessed on its merits like any other integration project.

The CEPU proposal also brings systemic issues to the fore. It is an attempt to work, for Eastern Europe and under very different conditions, the miracle which the EPU worked for Western Europe in the 1950s. The EPU, established in 1950 and brought to an end in 1959, enabled the Western European economies to go from bilateralism to convertibility in, for the majority of cases, less than ten years. Members' balances of payments were recorded multilaterally with all other EPU members and expressed in a unit of account equal to the dollar. In the event of a deficit, members settled a part of what they owed in gold or convertible currencies, and received a credit for the rest. To finance imbalances in which payments of gold or convertible currencies due to creditors exceeded payments of gold or convertible currencies made by debtors, a fund of working capital was provided by the United States. When a member's deficit widened, the amount it was obliged to settle in convertible currency increased, and so did the interest on the credit granted. Deficit countries thus had an incentive to correct their imbalances, and this was achieved by expenditure-reducing policies or by devaluation.[12] Progressive adjustments, and the dismantling of exchange controls and trade restrictions which they permitted, enabled most countries to restore the external convertibility of their currencies on 1 January 1959. Full convertibility according to article VIII of the IMF Charter followed in 1961.

Table 1.4. *Share of partner's exports in total exports, 1988*
(percentages)[a]

Partner	Czechoslovakia	Hungary	Poland
World	100	100	100
Czechoslovakia	0	5	6
Hungary	4	0	2
Poland	8	3	0

Note: [a]Calculated on values expressed in national currency units.
Source: UN/ECE Common Data Base.

The CEPU is intended to achieve convertibility for the Central East European countries, and possibly the USSR, on the basis of the ECU and an ECU fund set up by the EEC. A weaker argument for it is that it will maintain intra-CMEA trade during the Eastern countries' transition from the plan to the market, and from CMEA-oriented to Western-oriented trade. Both justifications assume, however, that the share of trade involved in Western Europe in the 1950s and in Central–East Europe in the 1990s is similar. The first argument assumes, in addition, that the economic systems in Western Europe in the 1950s and in Eastern Europe in the 1990s are the same. Yet neither assumption holds.

In the first place, the EPU achieved the settlement of the major part of its members' transactions. The liberalization of intra-EPU settlements was thus tantamount to satisfying the necessary condition for convertibility according to article VIII of the IMF Charter, which stipulates that a currency be bought and sold for current transactions at a single exchange rate and in the absence of restrictions. But, as Table 1.4 shows, in the case of the CEPU which, now that the GDR is a part of the FRG, would embrace Hungary, Czechoslovakia, and Poland, the trade covered by the scheme would vary between some 8 and 12 percent of any member's total trade. The liberalization of the associated payments would thus not enable the countries concerned to fulfill the necessary condition for the convertibility of their currencies. Nor, given the magnitude of the flows involved, could the scheme serve to sustain total trade during the three countries' period of transition. Given the geographic structure of their trade, only an extension of the arrangement to the USSR would ensure this. Yet, even if the trade and payments covered by the scheme were important enough to allow the members of the Union to sustain the level of their total trade and to achieve convertibility, their economic systems would not permit the latter, as a comparison of the EPU adjustment mechanism and of the Eastern correction process makes plain.

The EPU adjustment mechanism, it will be recalled, enabled the members of the Union to correct their imbalances and so both to avoid the emergence of permanent deficits and surpluses which would have paralyzed the system, and to lift the restrictions impeding the multilateralization of their payments and progress toward convertibility. The mechanism functioned because, if the economies which composed it were emerging from over five years of central planning during wartime, their underlying organization was nevertheless the market. There existed independent enterprises which would respond to price signals, a monetary system which would affect investment through the interest rate, and a fiscal apparatus which would influence aggregate demand through taxation, once the controls were abolished. Thus expenditure-reducing policies introduced by a deficit country and operating through the monetary and fiscal systems, would affect domestic demand and, through changes in the price level, foreign demand, while devaluation would affect demand abroad and also demand and supply domestically.

This, however, is not the case in relations between the Eastern countries in which central planning prevails and where, consequently, there is no comprehensive market network or price mechanism, and where the fiscal and monetary apparatus, if it exists, is in its infancy. Peel off the planning and no functioning market system emerges underneath. This being so, neither expenditure-reducing policies nor devaluation can correct an external deficit. This will continue despite them and, as disequilibrium becomes permanent, the CEPU mechanism will be blocked. The only effective instrument available to the centrally planned economy to adjust its deficit is the directive which, like other direct controls is incompatible with multilateral payments and convertibility. Under central planning, therefore, the CEPU will cease to operate and turn into another IBEC.

In sum, the functioning of the CEPU requires its members to have market systems. Like the two other Eastern integration areas already discussed, its creation therefore depends on the Eastern countries first having achieved their transition to the market.

4   Conclusion

This chapter has reviewed the evolution of East–West economic integration, and has examined the systemic conditions of its realization, its possible dimensions, and the schemes for transition which are constituted by integration between certain Eastern countries and the Central European Payments Union. It has argued that the Community has been, and is, the driving force behind both Western and pan-European integration, that it is the EEC that will determine whether it expands eastward to the Soviet border, and whether there will be free trade all the way from the Atlantic to the Pacific. The chapter singles out central planning as the chief obstacle to integration, and concludes that the creation of a single East–West trading area will depend on central planning being dismantled, will be gradual, and will encompass Eastern countries not as a group, but individually as they successfully decentralize. Specifically, East–West economic integration will only reach the Soviet Union, or a part of it, once marketization is introduced and has sufficiently progressed there. The probable immediate outcome is thus for East–West integration to extend outward from the Community to certain reforming countries of Central Europe, although this does not preclude free trade from Lisbon to the Baltic states, Byelorussia, the Ukraine, or even the Russian Republic and Vladivostock, in the future.

Notes

1. Namely Austria, Sweden, Switzerland and Lichtenstein, Norway, Portugal, and Iceland, which had joined in 1970.
2. Comprehensive Programme for the Further Extension and Improvement of Cooperation and the Development of Socialist Economic Integration by CMEA Member Countries (Moscow, CMEA Secretariat, 1971).
3. The obligation under which the smaller European countries of the CMEA found themselves is reflected in the fact that, more often than not, the agricultural arrangements were not international agreements but internal EEC regulations which laid down the conditions of supply and designated the foreign trade organization in the exporting country which was to be responsible for delivery.
4. "Accords d'Association avec les Pays d'Europe Centrale et Orientale: Cadre Général" (Communication de la Commission Européenne au Conseil et au Parlement Européen), *Europe Documents*, no. 1646/47, 7 September 1990.
5. See, for instance, the declaration of Vladimir Chematienkov, Soviet ambassador to the EEC, before the Dublin Summit of 25–26 June 1990, *Journal de Genève*, 23–24 June 1990.
6. Integration between two or more economies operating under different systems should not be confused with the take-over of one economy operat-

22   *Harriet Matejka*

ing under one system by a second operating under another system as has occurred in the case of the GDR and the FRG.

7. Harriet Matejka, "A note on free trade areas between market and centrally planned economies," *Policy Responses to the Changing International Environment*, I. Dobozi and H. Matejka (eds.), Budapest, Hungarian Scientific Council for the World Economy, 1981, pp. 125–38; Harriet Matejka, "Szabakereskedelmi övezetek piacgazdasagok és központi tervezésü gazdasagok között," *Kösgazdasagi Szemle*, December 1981, pp. 1470–80.

8. Tibor Palankai suggests that the association of the Eastern countries to the EC could take between five and twelve years, and stresses that trade liberalization between the partners would first require the marketization of the Eastern economies. Tibor Palankai, "Integration of Central and Eastern Europe into the European economy with special emphasis on EC–Hungarian relations," Institute for East–West Security Studies, New York, 24 May 1990, Draft, pp. 16–17.

9. R. G. Lipsey and K. Lancaster, "The general theory of the second-best," *Review of Economic Studies*, vol. 24, 1956–57.

10. Tibor Palankai proposes that: "Mutual, but asymmetric elimination of tariffs and other trade barriers on industrial goods" should characterize the initial stage of association with the EEC. See "Integration of Central and Eastern Europe into the European economy," p. 18.

11. *Etude sur l'économie mondiale 1990* (New York, United Nations, 1990), pp. 118–19. *Economic Survey of Europe in 1989–1990* (New York, United Nations, 1990), pp. 147–75. See also Jozef van Brabant, "On reforming the trade and payments regimes in the CMEA," Draft, 16 March 1990, and Marie Lavigne, "The CMEA's transition from the transferable rouble," Radio Free Europe, *Report on Eastern Europe*, pp. 34–47.

12. For a summary of balance of payments' adjustment through explicit devaluation resorted to by five countries in particular on several occasions, see Leland B. Yeager, *International Monetary Relations: Theory, History and Policy*, New York, Harper and Row, 1966, pp. 374–75. Member countries could also be authorized to reintroduce controls for balance of payments' reasons.

2 East–West trade: what is it good for?

Heinrich Vogel

East–West trade – what is it good for? This appears to be a silly question, if approached in terms of David Ricardo's theoretical framework. Comparative advantage offers a good guideline for assessing the benefit of economic trans-border interaction for any country, be it East, West, North, or South. Yet, there is little doubt that political reason interfered with economics pure and simple not only in our days. Ricardo's contemporaries, too, debated issues of ideology (Christianity versus heathendom). But they had to care less than we do about the consistency of preaching the gospel to the heathens and at the same time trading with them. Superior arms ensured the military and political supremacy of colonial powers. On the other hand, it stood to reason that rival Christian countries also should be denied the advantages of economic exchange and technology transfer. It is the privilege of the twentieth century to have created a kind of controversy on trade among nations which is characterized by a specific and inextricable mix of ideological arguments, economic reason, and power politics.

The seemingly endless debate of some forty years has come to an end. To the surprise of all participants in the West it can no longer be denied that the main opponent in East–West tension, the Soviet Union, has changed. The opening of the Berlin Wall is the last evidence that the Soviet empire has collapsed. The myth of final superiority of communism over capitalism as a social system on a global scale has been abandoned. And the deepening crisis of the Soviet economy has shown that the USSR lacks the necessary economic, political, and technological strength of a veritable great power, i.e. to hold the internal empire together, to maintain control over Eastern Europe, to support client countries in the Third World, and to challenge the Western world militarily. Even at home, the CPSU's reputation as the heroic vanguard of historical social progress has been destroyed by comparative glasnost.

From the very beginning in the early fifties, the critical issue in debates on economic relations was about political aspects, about weighing the advantages and risks of the East–West relationship. Perestroika in the Soviet Union and systemic change in Eastern Europe with their undeniable implications for the international system in Europe and for East–West relations at large now call for a thorough reassessment of premises, paradigms, and policy lines. Clearly, both schools of thought – the believers in the paradigm of totalitarianism as well as those who subscribed to consistent incrementalism – are facing a new reality in the East. The complex structure of contradictory aspects arguing in terms of security, commercial interest, and political (no longer systemic) competition has to be sorted out anew. The public debate has been moving rapidly from "To help or not to help" to "How much," and "Who should be helped first."

Today, general agreement has been reached in NATO that the former military allies of the USSR in the Warsaw Pact should be granted normalized conditions in their economic relations with the West, that they even deserve economic aid. But what about the Soviet Union? Western leaders now acknowledge serious efforts of the new leadership in Moscow at modernization of state and economy and a new approach in foreign policy. More than any of the impressive programmatic statements of a new leadership in Moscow it was the change in military posture (withdrawal of forces from Afghanistan, unilateral concessions in arms control, negotiations, and a cooperative attitude of Soviet diplomacy working for the resolution of regional conflicts) which have initiated, after a period of surprise and hesitation, serious debate in the West as to which extent proven policies of the past should be revised.

"From confrontation to cooperation" and "Beyond containment" are the new slogans which have evolved. But postwar history still is relevant. "To help or not to help Gorbi" remains a contended issue. It is in this context that a look back on forty years of controversy among Western nations is necessary.

East–West trade – what was it good for?

In the first years after World War II the general consensus on East–West economic relations and West–East technology transfer was easy. And it was more than justified in view of Stalinist expansionism. Later on, Western policy had to to deal with a dual strategy of Soviet foreign and security policy which proclaimed ideological struggle between social systems and an ambiguous design of peaceful coexistence for international relations. The Harmel Report of 1967, calling for credible deterrence against any military threat, but at the same time offering the East cooperation in fields of mutual benefit, defined an appropriate response of NATO countries – if only in very general terms.

Its principles even hold in the years of Perestroika and "New think-ing." But are past controversies over details of operational policy irrelevant today? In retrospect, issues like "selling the rope to the Russians," "energy dependency," "hemorrhage of militarily critical technology," or "punishing Soviet misbehaving" were just different variations in a kaleidoscope of "no trade with the enemy" which origin-ated in the old days of cold war. This problem remained much the same over the entire postwar period: How to assess the Soviet threat? How to weigh political opportunity in and commercial benefit from cooperation with the East against inherent security risks? How to operationalize the formula prescribed in the Harmel Report? Despite the considerable amount of theoretical and empirical research there was no clear answer for those who had to take political decisions.[1]

However, it would be inadequate to analyze differences in Western perceptions on East–West economic relations in terms of political weak-ness or lack of insight. Structural problems have to be considered, too, which complicate any move toward change or differentiation:

1 Economic relations between West and East have been essentially bilateral (due to the inconvertibility of Eastern currencies) contrary to the security relationship of military alliances on both sides, which is multilateral.
2 Contrary to the commonality of security interests, the economic inter-ests of individual Western countries are competitive in their search for new markets and diversification of imports.
3 Foreign trade regimes differ between planned economies with varying degrees of centralization. These differences have been growing with the lack of synchronization of economic reforms in the East.
4 Regulations for foreign economic activities also vary among Western countries. Contrary to traditions in Western Europe, the foreign economic activities of the United States are a privilege to be granted to private economic actors through governmental licensing rather than a right.

However, explicit and implicit security risks of incompatible political systems and the military confrontation between East and West deman-ded an integrated approach, combining the economic and political potential of the West in multilateral mechanisms of coordination. NATO, OECD, and COCOM have been offering some of the necessary organizational framework, reinforced in bilateral consultations. Yet, they worked better in facing up to periods of open confrontation by the Warsaw Pact than in the less strained intervals of *détente* when a more complex approach to the economic and political aspects of relations between East and West asked for skillful diplomacy.

Veritable crises in these relations with obvious security implications (the Berlin Wall of 1961–62, the intervention of Warsaw Pact troops in Czechoslovakia in 1968, the Soviet invasion of Afghanistan 1979–83, and the Polish crisis ending in the declaration of martial law 1981–87) forced the priorities to match in the agenda of Western countries. A common response in sanctions and denial of cooperation was in the logic of the prevailing military and political confrontation. On other issues like Soviet policy regarding Jewish emigration (1975–88) or repressive treatment of dissidents in the East (1978–87), however, the implications for economic relations between West and East met with less unanimity.

In fact, the policies of linkage and "economic diplomacy" were controversial over the entire postwar period. Practically every one of the cases mentioned above produced prolonged disputes about feasibility, range, and timing of Western reaction, and, as well, they were complicated by a lack of synchronization of the dominant arguments. An intricate mix of ideological and political premises (paradigms), political goals, empirical (though often selective) evidence, and *ex-post* rationalizations of "missed opportunities" or "unfeasible options" produced a recurrent pattern of misunderstandings and suspicion.[2]

As a rule, the axiomatic nature of political philosophies is taken for granted. This was particularly true for the economic relations between two antagonistic social systems and military blocs. In fact, it was hardly discussed at all in its central role for rationalizing practical policies. But there were differences:

1 regarding the ideological and political premises and assumptions about the substance of the East–West relationships (incurably antagonistic or potentially competitive);
2 about the nature of the Soviet political system (invariable in its totalitarian character or capable of change from within); and
3 with regard to the degree of confidence in Western societies' immunity and resistance to the political threat implicit in Soviet strategic geography and military power.[3]

The problem of empirical evidence regarding the distribution of benefit between East and West derived from economic and technological cooperation, i.e. the net effects of the transfer of resources (capital and equipment and technology), also caused controversy. Analyses of the contribution of Western civilian exports to the military potential of the Warsaw Pact[4] and the degree of economic integration and technological proliferation among Warsaw Pact countries mostly referred to inaccessible, extremely technical, or ambiguous information. Many of those who believed in systematic analysis turned into frustrated agnostics.

The same, unfortunately, is true with regard to the old controversy of change induced by *rapprochement* versus change forced by denial. Did economic cooperation strengthen the elements of change or was it to be held responsible for the prolonged coma of an unviable, repressive political system? The fate of the Jumbo-credits for Gierek implies a clear lesson as to what was not to be expected. But it is difficult to believe that a general denial of economic cooperation would have brought the CPSU to its knees. No wonder any general political conclusion about the extent of Western positive or negative economic leverage on Soviet domestic and/or foreign policy remained unconvincing for the opposing school of thought. In retrospect, the authors of empirical studies in the analytical community dealing with East–West economic relations and technology transfer will agree that the accumulated conventional wisdom of the West resulted, to a considerable extent, from educated guesswork rather than "measuring" in any sense of statistical analysis as it is available for the economic relations among Western industrialized countries.[5] Lack of reliable information, therefore, combined with a kind of "guru"-attitude ("if you knew what I know"), was bound to fuel controversies rather than clarify the issues.

An additional cause of controversy stemmed from the kind of sweeping definitions dealing with technology transfer.

1 The dimension of leads or lags in Soviet/East European technology levels *vis-à-vis* the industrial West, and the methodology of aggregating comparative performance by countries or even industries are far from secure – even among Western nations providing infinitely better statistical information.

2 Notions like "military relevance," "militarily critical," "dual use," or "strategic trade," and pledges of "No trade that would substantially contribute to the military or heavy industrial base of the USSR" were of little, if any, help in the complicated process of forging consensus on a common policy for restrictions on technology transfer.

3 Since the 1970s there has been no common denominator for defining the criteria of export control regimes among COCOM countries. The two operationally relevant lists for controlling US export of technology (the Commodity Control List managed by the DoC and the Militarily Critical Technology List, compiled by the US DoD) differ in their approach.

In retrospect, over the period since 1970, a "continental divergence" (i.e. US versus West European) on matters of East–West economic relations and tehnology transfer has been straining intra-Western relations. The controversy was shaped by differences in the scope of parliamentary debate and practice of publishing the results of hearings (most discussions on these issues have been reserved to specialists in administration, academia, and consulting). Even the formation process of national foreign and security policies differs. In the US, the situation has been characterized by a change of roles between White House and Congress in the argument over East–West economic relations and technology transfer: the Bush administration revised its line toward a more cooperative approach on trade and credit issues, while majorities in Congress have been uncertain with regard to the issue of how to retain leverage in relations with the allies. And for normalization of economic relations with the USSR the case of Lithuania turns out to be a reprise of the Jackson–Vanik amendment. In other Western capitals, however, there is no comparable "power game" between administration and legislator. At least, it has been less conspicuous.

The visibility of interdepartmental quarrels (primarily between ministries of foreign affairs and defense, but also between other main actors and institutions, i.e. offices of prime ministers, National Security Council, and functional ministries) varied in the respective countries, clearly reflecting differences in public interest and intensity of pressures for or against East–West economic relations, resulting from different traditions in the respective foreign relations and "political cultures." And last but not least, the role of the media as an instrument for mobilizing emotions of fear, frustration, and anger differs, too, in the way and means of professional processing of information and response to "directed leaks" from administrations and lobbies.[6]

The issue of technology transfers to the East may be well suited for sorting out elements of prejudice, conviction, and belief from "evidence." COCOM made sense in making life more difficult and more costly for the military–industrial complex of the USSR, thus safeguarding the West's lead in military technologies. Soviet designers of new weapons have been forced to reinvent one or the other wheel. On the other hand, COCOM did not put a brake on the Soviet military machine sufficiently strong to reduce its technological challenge to the level of a manageable threat. This can be seen in many ways. The most realistic interpretation is one of a combination of insufficient awareness and enforcement on the side of the West, on the other hand of close to equal levels of Soviet R&D, and of success of indigenous, independent efforts in the East.

It was relatively easy to call for "building high fences around narrow areas" of technology. But under the established mechanism and scope of coverage it is extremely difficult in view of rapid technological change even to administer a reduction of the list of proscribed products and technologies and to prevent bureaucratic overkill in enforcement. Quite logically, political pressure is building up to check this system in the light of past experience. But such efforts will not succeed in a workable compromise if the somewhat bashful discretion surrounding the aspect of commercial interest in discussions about "streamlining" is not abandoned (e.g. the bargaining in COCOM over a machine-tool for micro-computer swap in November 1989 and the line taken until today by the US Department of Defense, supported by alarmist public back-up).

Since the eighties, the comparative competitiveness of Western economies in the world economy is shaken by dramatic technological change and resulting structural adaptation. The declining performance in particular of the USA as an exporting and technological competitor increasingly compromises the weight of security arguments tabled in COCOM by its negotiators, even raising doubts with regard to the distribution of cost and benefit for Western countries stemming from export-controls among their economies. It may be instructive to analyze the bargaining of high-level meetings about "green-line" conditions for the USSR, about concessions on machine-tools versus micro-computers in November 1989, or the US veto against transfers of telecommunication equipment based on fibre-optic technology in June 1990.

In the experience of the past, the above-mentioned historical and structural factors boiled down to a problem of predictability for a common Western response to communist policies. Continuing uncertainty in the first years of the Gorbachev "era" about the nature of change in the USSR ("Whither the Soviet Union") was met with ambiguous signals of compromise among Western states: "The need of making economic relations with the East compatible with the security interests of the Western Alliance" (Toronto Summit, June 1988) and "Help for Gorbachev after careful assessment of progress on Soviet economic reform" (EC Summit, Dublin, June 1990) reflect mental reservations. Being relief actions rather than concrete design so far, they failed to produce final answers in a sense of integrating East–West economic relations into a comprehensive Western strategy. If, however, a veritable strategy is too academic a premise (or simply unfeasible), does not the West need minimal consensus in view of problems of stability in the East and of limited resources for dealing with even greater problems in Third World countries?

The continuation of Western controls makes sense, even today, as long as Soviet production of arms and military R&D keeps running in high gear. The benefit of efforts to perfect export controls and the bureaucratic monitoring of technological and scientific cooperation between East and West and among Western industrialized nations can be estimated, though not measured beyond doubt. Its effect has to be weighed against the costs: the slowing down of the transfer of technology among Western nations, the loss of markets, and the embarrassment of inconsistency with general pledges to normalize relations with communist countries which are reforming internally and cooperating in areas of foreign and security policy critical to Western interests.

The corrections of the list of proscribed technologies of June 1990, particularly for Eastern Europe and specifically for the GDR, were overdue. The USSR with all the unforeseeable consequences of internal decay and destabilization, however, is a different case which needs a more cautious approach. The practical problems of the past (conceptual, political, and organizational) remain very relevant.

The new environment and risk assessment

Change in the East, in particular moderation in Soviet policy, has boosted demands for a reassessment of Western policies for two reasons: (a) the perception of a Soviet threat which was valid in times of political and military confrontation is no longer plausible for a broader public in the West; and (b) dramatic political reforms in Eastern Europe have reached the stage of open demands to review Warsaw Pact membership of these countries. Since the coming down of the Berlin Wall on 9 November 1989, there is no clear divide anymore between formal Warsaw Pact membership and applications for association to the European Community. The opening of borders to the West and the unification of Germany with its economic implications changed the political geography of Europe. In a political and even in a security perspective, Eastern Europe already is part of a greater Europe. The inherited institutional arrangements still are important, but the political substance of this change is irreversible.

This bright view, however, is overshadowed by uncertainties surrounding the future of the Soviet Union. The USSR is no competitive economic great power – in fact it never was. The present state of its economy is dismal. The transition to a decentralized economic system and the dimensions of production, infrastructure, and services calling for new capital, technology, and organizational know-how will be deepening the critical situation for the next years rather than boosting the economic potential. Even the efforts to convert military into civilian production will, in the short run, add to, rather than erase, the political and economic strains.

For the time being, the USSR still is posing a military threat to the West, particularly to Western Europe. The issue of assessing change in Soviet policy, therefore, is one of weighing the risks of wishful versus

realistic response.[7] Decisions to be taken have become even more difficult since perestroika is a long-term process rather than a short-term
solution. The dimensions of economic aggregates to be moved, the
complexity of legislation and organizational structures to be designed
and implemented, sociopolitical traditions, and behavioral patterns to
be changed, are immense.

Possible Western responses to perestroika and New Thinking depend
on the scenarios considered and on the time horizon of such reasoning.
Conventional wisdom, among Soviet analysts also, assumes a transition
period of one or two generations necessary for the modernization of the
USSR. But while a very long technical lead-time of this modernization
can be taken for granted, there is no way to more than speculate about
the long-term ambitions of a future Soviet/Russian leadership.

It is, therefore, indispensable to consider realistic scenarios for a
medium-term perspective where obstacles to swift change and reform,
as described above, are slowing down the pace of modernization. A
USSR shrinking to a confederation or commonwealth of states around a
core "Republic of Russia" is more than likely. The "success" of
perestroika in this perspective is to be seen in keeping the process of
painful change on all fronts open. Drawbacks may be unavoidable, even
probable. After five years of fierce infighting over the pace and scope of
change, the following scenarios with regard to a recovery of Russian
great power potential seem to be relevant.

1 The scenario of "Stop-and-Go" policy in constant struggle with
social, regional, environmental, and national unrest; obviously, the
result is a slow-down of economic and technological progress in the
short term – with a chance, however, for long-term modernization.

2 The scenario of "Law and Order": repressive response to
simultaneous strikes, disruption of production, irredentist, separatist,
and violent activities (sabotage, terrorism, mass riots), maybe military
rule – but not a return to outright Stalinism. Economic recovery inevitably will be slowing down under such conditions, if happening at all.
Even in the long run, the modernization of the country, not to mention
competitiveness, would hardly have a chance.

3 The scenario of chaos, disorganization, decay of established structures, and the degeneration of perestroika to mere talk, and hopeless
and total grid-lock. Again: modernization or recovery to former
capabilities of power projection are bound to be choked in mismanage-
ment, and disillusionment.

In an analysis of implications for the outside world it must be kept in
mind that the starting point for perestroika had not been one of secure
great power status. Traditional insignia of great power (primarily mili-

tary potential and hegemonial control of an empire) have been wearing thin in the 1980s, degraded in the light of the Polish events and obvious defeat in Afghanistan. The present economic/political crisis in the USSR, the process of desertion of former allies and even union republics into the world of Western-type economic and political systems is beyond military control. Transition and systemic change with all its complexities will be taking many years. It is hard to see any hope for the Soviet Union/Russia to regain the kind of external influence it had over the last forty years, short of the argument of *de facto* economic interdependence in the region which had evolved in the past.

These developments are in line with change in the criteria of "great power" on a global scale: comparative international status can no longer be defined by standard quantitative economic indicators and military options alone. Qualitative aspects of structural adaptation and the "search capacity" of sociopolitical systems make the difference. In the world of today, innovation rather than expansion, openness and flexibility rather than rigidity and risk avoidance are the measures of successful performance. In these terms, there is no chance for a Soviet/Russian recovery to the status of a modern great power. But it must be kept in mind that this great power in decline still is a global military factor with a formidable potential of nuclear and conventional forces. Considerations of military security, i.e. thinking in categories of the worst case, therefore remain relevant.

In this perspective the scenario of "Law and Order" entails a risk of Soviet/Russian renewed adventurism based on whatever motivation (Marxist, nationalist, traditionalist, or some other): the atavistic reflex of invoking (or provoking) an external crisis for the sake of dampening internal failure cannot be discarded altogether. Military precautions, therefore, have to be maintained by the West, unilateral disarmament is not advisable as long as (a) the CFE negotiations in Vienna have not produced a balanced reduction of forces in Europe, and (b) a new regime for the nuclear balance has not evolved in talks between the USA and the USSR.

But what about the ongoing invitations, even calls of the Soviet leadership for cooperation (e.g. the application for observer status in GATT)? For them it makes sense to open the economy to the world outside. Shortage of hard currency caused by the persistent monostructure of Soviet export capacities precludes a strategy of large-scale imports both of capital and consumer goods. Since the terms-of-trade are not going to improve in the foreseeable future, and the neighbor countries formerly organized in CMEA are tied down in their own modernization dilemmas and in even tighter hard currency constraints, the industrial West remains the critical source of capital and technology.

East–West trade – what can it be good for?

All the concessions to reforming countries and programs for aid will not do away with the single most important problem for East–West economic relations: the lack of competitiveness of Soviet and East European economies and the inconvertibility of their currencies. Economic crisis and political collapse are a very real danger for these countries. This is why truly radical reforms in the countries of the East deserve consistent Western response by depoliticization, normalization, even aid. Western help, however big, is no safeguard. No Marshall Plan will be a safeguard against martial law in a critical situation.[8]

In view of the veritable crises that are building up in the USSR and in Eastern Europe, the following steps seem appropriate, even necessary:

1 Immediate relief programs, offering help by the transfer of food and of medical equipment for humanitarian reasons.

2 Commercial lending and the extension of credit guaranties to those who take the risk of investing in countries which go through the convulsions of perestroika. The residual risk of prolonged uncertainty differs from the situation in countries with basically market-type economic systems (e.g. Mexico). But the more complicated and unprecedented transition from a one-party rule, centrally planned economy system to pluralist structures definitely is in the Western interest, last but not least with regard to Western security.

3 Streamlining for the industrial list of COCOM. This should be possible with the intention of reducing bureaucratic red tape (computerized as it may be) which has been choking trade and cooperation among COCOM member countries and delaying business in areas with only a vague resemblance to militarily relevant technology or none at all. The willingness of East European countries to accept INF-type on-site inspection for equipment with dual-use capacity may help overcome traditional hesitations in the West. Hungary was the first country formally suggesting this way out of an old dilemma. Other countries of the Warsaw Pact, including the Soviet Union, have been signaling their willingness to accept such a regime, too. And streamlining makes sense as a way of making life easier for those who will have to ensure enforcement of indispensable controls around those "narrow areas" which will remain in economic relations with the USSR.

4 Unconditional cooperation with reforming countries. The Con-

ference on Economic Cooperation in Europe in Bonn of 1990 developed a workable framework for intensified efforts at cooperation.

5 Encouragement for the political elites and populations in opening talks, even negotiations on the terms and the time-horizon of association to the European Community. Even if concrete steps would be premature, this political signal will be important for generating trust in a new European solidarity.

The issue of East–West cooperation is one of political rather than of military risk assessment or of short-term cost–benefit analysis. The West has decided to respond in terms of gradual normalization. The overriding argument is not to miss a window of opportunity for promoting the process of demilitarization and secularization in East–West relations and not to frustrate expectations of those in the USSR who at long last have realized that economic reforms are worthless without political change.

This approach is even more plausible for economic relations with Eastern Europe. The allies of the USSR have been released into a new sovereignty, both politically and economically. There was no Soviet intervention into their sovereign approach toward reform. The responsibility for finding acceptance at home and reputation abroad, for probing their own route into the chilly waters of world-wide competition, rests with them. There is no more excuse for weak national leaders in waiting for or pointing to Moscow. This means that the former premise of NATO policy, i.e. considering these countries in terms of a sub-system of the Soviet threat, i.e. the "communist bloc," is no longer tenable. "Differentiation" – in former days a formula for awarding prizes to the most deviant foreign policy behavior of one or the other ally of the USSR – has to be redefined. Criteria for Western cooperation with the reforming countries in Eastern Europe now have to be adopted from the IMF in its dealing with indebted countries of the Third World ("help to self-help") rather than from continued ideological confrontation and military deterrence.

A Western attitude of wait and see would be anachronistic. Western policy has changed toward bilateral and multilateral financial arrangements such as credit lines extended by individual countries, by the World Bank, the IMF, the common effort of the 24, coordinated by the EC Commission, and the foundation of the European Bank for Reconstruction and Development of Eastern Europe. Practical steps began with the intention to help the first non-communist government in Poland restart the engine of its ailing economy. Later on, this approach was widened to the whole group of "reforming countries," which now even includes the Soviet Union. Military risk assessment continues, but it no longer dominates the overall balance of opportunities and risks. Political and economic chances for a consistent normalization in the East–West relationship have been gathering weight. The process of unification of the two German states and the future role of Germany in a CSCE framework can be seen as a safeguard against recidivism on both sides of the old divide.

The technical progress of today, above all in information technologies, has outgrown the traditional control philosophies in the context of the industrial list of COCOM. This constitutes an irreversible trend, beyond the grip of disparate bureaucracies and political appeals to stricter discipline. "The chips are all over," like termites, i.e. dual use is everywhere and growth of export potentials in the future is to be expected rather on the side of software than of hardware flows. For the foreseeable future, efforts to maintain secrecy and control over all kinds of exchange constitute an uphill struggle inevitably increasing the importance of political cooperation and confidence building. Economic and political competitiveness will be measured more and more by a country's performance in solving technical, economic, and social problems rather than by exports of commodities. The agenda of East–West relations will not be left untouched by this trend. The compass of restrictions policies is bound to follow the gravitation field of international tension which has moved from East–West ideological struggle to North–South conflict over the distribution of wealth and resources. A common control regime for the international transfer of militarily relevant technologies[9] has a chance to contain new imperialisms in the Third World only if implemented by all industrial countries, including those of the East.

Notes

1. As a rule, politicians show little interest in analysis which will not "verify" the preferred set of beliefs.
2. See, among others, G. C. Hufbauer and J. J. Scott, *Economic Sanctions in Support of Foreign Policy Goals*, Institute for International Economics, Policy Analyses in International Economics, no. 6, 1983; W. Root, "Trade controls that work," *Foreign Policy*, no. 56, D. Fall 1984; H. H. Höhmann and H. Vogel (eds.), *Osteuropas Wirtschaftsprobleme und die Ost–West-Beziehungen*, Nomos Verlag, Baden-Baden, 1984; R. Rode and H.-D. Jacobsen (eds.), *Economic Warfare or Detente*, Westview Press, Boulder, CO, 1985; P. Hanson, *Western Economic Statecraft in East–West Economic Relations*, Chatham House Papers 40, London, 1988; and R. Wagner, "*Die*

Politik des 'Economic Denial'," Europäische Hochschulschriften, ser. 31, vol. 118, Verlag Peter Lang, Frankfurt/Bern/New York/Paris, 1988.

3. For a systematic discussion, cf. H. Vogel, "Alternative westliche Strategien in den Wirtschaftsbeziehungen mit Osteuropa: die europäische Perspektive," *Osteuropas Wirtschaftsprobleme*... (see n. 1).

4. The kind of argument of "Hard currency not spent by the USSR on grain might have been diverted to imports of militarily relevant technology" used by the US DoD in 1983 or the denial of export licenses on national security grounds in 1988 for a management training scheme which was part of a US–Soviet joint venture.

5. Cf. J. Cooper, "West–Ost-Technologietransfer und sowjetische Verteidigungsindustrie," in C. Davies, H.-H. Höhmann, and H. H. Schröder (eds.), *Rüstung, Modernisierung, Reform – die sowjetische Verteidigungsindustrie in der Perestroika*, Bund Verlag, Cologne, 1990.

6. The notorious case of Toshiba/Kongsberg is only one of a number of incidents which reached front pages in the press with perfect timing.

7. Cf. H. Vogel, "The Gorbachev challenge: to help or not to help," in *The World Today*, vol. 45, nos. 8–9, August–September 1989.

8. Cf. H. Vogel, "Osteuropa braucht die Solidarität des Westens," *Handelsblatt*, 9 February 1990.

9. M. Lucas, "The abolition of COCOM and the establishment of a technology disarmament and transfer agency in the CSCE," *Bulletin of Peace Proposals*, vol. 21, no. 2, June 1990.

3 US interests in granting most favored nation status to the Soviet Union: economic versus political considerations

Joseph Pelzman

The unique contribution of the current reform process is its clear under-standing that Soviet reforms, to be successful, must have support from the industrialized West. This includes Western human capital transfers, the Westernization of Soviet goods and services, and the reduction of tariff and non-tariff barriers applied to Soviet goods in Western markets. The granting of most favored nation (MFN) status by the United States is a part of this Western participation and a crucial ele-ment in Gorbachev's "new thinking." The relative significance of improved US–Soviet economic relations is attested to by the com-mercial measures proposed by President Bush at the Malta Summit.[1]

From the Soviet point of view, liberalized East–West trade and investment serves two purposes. In the short run, it provides critically needed access to Western high-tech inputs, machinery and engineering equipment, and, more importantly, Western managerial skills – all cru-cial ingredients to its internal modernization program. In the long run, it is hoped that the introduction of Western hard currency investment will improve the quality of Soviet manufactured good exports. Gorbachev is determined to convert the Soviet Union from a "raw material appendage" to the West, (i.e. exporting its primary products for machinery that it cannot produce internally) to an exporter of high value and internationally competitive manufactured goods.[2] Liberalizing trade with the US, and in general with Western trading partners, facilitates Gorbachev's overall reform program.

From the US point of view, *the* important question, and the one addressed in this chapter, is what are the benefits and costs of normaliz-ing trade relations with the Soviet Union. Will granting most favored nation (MFN) status to the Soviet Union increase bilateral US–Soviet trade? What is the probability that increased bilateral US–Soviet trade will have a *net* positive impact on the US? Finally, are there any third country implications of granting MFN status to the Soviet Union?

The historical trade relationship between the US and the Soviet Union has not been characterized by a degree of "normalcy." Consequently, predictions of expanded future US–Soviet trade, under normal tariff conditions, is subject to considerable uncertainty. This chapter, therefore, presents estimates of expected "trade expansion" resulting from the US granting of MFN status to the USSR, based on a number of different methodologies. Each approach has its specific set of assumptions and caveats. Policy makers must therefore review the entire set of predictions and evaluate them in their entirety, rather than take any single approach.

An overview of the historical pattern of Soviet trade is presented in section 1. The various methodologies employed in assessing the probable impact of the US granting the Soviet Union MFN status is presented in section 2. Trade expansion estimates based on these approaches are presented in section 3. Concluding remarks are presented in section 4.

1   Review of Soviet international trade patterns

The distribution of Soviet international trade by major partners over the 1960–88 period is presented in Table 3.1. Over this period the partner country structure of Soviet trade has been, with the exception of oil trade, relatively fixed. Almost 49 percent of Soviet exports went to the European Council of Mutual Economic Assistance (CMEA) in 1988. Over the period 1960 to 1988, Soviet exports to European CMEA were above 40 percent of its total exports, fluctuating a bit in the first part of the 1980s when Soviet exports were partly diverted to market and less developed economies. Soviet exports to developed market economies in 1988 were 22 percent of total exports. This share was substantially lower than its 1980 high of 32 percent. This reduction in Soviet exports to the developed market economies is attributable to a single commodity, i.e. petroleum. In 1988, Soviet exports to market economy less developed countries (ME-LDC) represented 13.8 percent of total Soviet exports. The importance of ME-LDC to Soviet exporters has not increased substantially during the 1980s.

In 1988, Soviet imports from CMEA represented 54 percent of total imports and those from developed market economies 25 percent, and from ME-LDCs 8 percent. In 1988, the Soviet Union ran a deficit with both its CMEA and market economy trading partners, while it ran a surplus with its ME-LDC partners.

The commodity distribution of total Soviet imports and exports is presented in Table 3.2. These data include both hard and soft currency

Table 3.1. *Distribution of Soviet foreign trade (million dollars and percentage)*

Year	Item	Communist countries						Non-communist countries		
		Total trade ($)	Total (%)	East Europe (%)	China (%)	Other Asia (%)	Other (%)	Total (%)	Developed countries (%)	LDCs (%)
1960	Exports	5,558	75.7	55.3	14.7	1.2	4.6	24.3	18.4	5.9
	Imports	5,623	70.7	49.7	15.1	1.7	4.2	29.3	19.9	9.4
1965	Exports	8,166	68.0	55.7	2.4	2.0	7.9	32.0	18.4	13.5
	Imports	8,050	69.6	58.0	2.8	1.5	7.4	30.4	20.5	9.9
1970	Exports	12,787	65.4	52.8	0.2	3.2	9.1	34.6	19.2	15.5
	Imports	11,720	65.1	56.5	0.2	1.3	7.0	34.9	24.3	10.6
1975	Exports	33,406	60.7	49.4	0.4	1.4	9.5	39.3	25.7	13.7
	Imports	37,076	52.4	42.4	0.4	0.7	8.8	47.6	36.6	11.1
1980	Exports	76,437	54.2	42.1	0.3	1.6	10.1	45.8	32.6	13.2
	Imports	68,473	53.2	42.9	0.3	1.0	8.9	46.8	35.6	11.2
1983	Exports	91,652	55.7	42.9	0.4	1.9	10.4	44.3	29.1	15.2
	Imports	80,445	56.5	46.2	0.4	0.9	9.0	43.5	31.5	11.9
1984	Exports	91,495	56.7	43.6	0.6	2.0	10.5	43.3	28.9	14.4
	Imports	80,409	58.5	46.7	0.8	1.0	10.1	41.5	30.1	11.3
1985	Exports	87,196	61.3	46.8	1.1	2.8	10.7	38.7	25.8	12.9
	Imports	83,315	61.2	47.6	1.2	1.0	11.4	38.8	28.0	10.8
1986	Exports	97,053	67.0	52.6	1.3	3.3	9.8	33.0	19.4	13.6
	Imports	88,874	66.9	53.2	1.5	1.2	11.0	33.1	25.5	7.7
1987	Exports	107,664	65.0	50.4	1.1	3.6	9.9	35.0	21.1	13.9
	Imports	95,970	69.4	56.5	1.2	1.3	10.4	30.6	23.0	7.6
1988p	Exports	110,740	64.1	48.9	1.5	3.9	9.8	35.9	22.2	13.8
	Imports	107,316	66.7	54.1	1.3	1.5	9.8	33.3	25.4	7.9

Note: Other Asia communist countries = Cambodia, Laos, North Korea and Vietnam; Other communist countries = Cuba, Mongolia, and Yugoslavia. Imports and exports are fob values; p = preliminary.

Source: Central Intelligence Agency, Directorate of Intelligence, Handbook of Economic Statistics, 1989, Table 136. Official Soviet statistics are converted using the official $US/ruble exchange rate.

Table 3.2. *Commodity composition of total Soviet world trade ($US billion)*

	1970	1975	1980	1983	1984	1985	1986	1987
Exports:								
Machinery and equipment	2.8	6.2	12.0	11.4	11.4	12.1	14.5	16.7
Fuels and related materials	2.0	10.5	35.9	49.2	49.7	45.9	45.9	50.0
Of which:								
Petroleum	1.5	8.2	27.9	38.1	38.0	33.8	32.0	36.0
Ores and concentrates	0.4	0.9	1.0	1.0	1.0	1.0	1.2	1.3
Base metals and manufactures	2.0	3.8					4.4	4.8
Chemicals	0.3	1.0	2.0	2.3	2.7	2.8	2.8	3.0
Wood and wood products	0.8	1.9	3.1	2.6	2.6	2.6	3.3	3.5
Textile raw materials and semimanufactures	0.4	1.0	1.4	1.3	1.1	1.2	1.3	1.6
Of which:								
Cotton fiber	0.4	0.9	1.4	1.1	1.0	1.0	1.1	1.4
Agricultural products	1.5	2.4	2.7	2.3	2.2	2.2	2.4	2.9
Industrial consumer goods	0.3	0.8	1.3	1.3	1.2	1.3	1.7	2.1
Other	2.3	4.9	16.9	20.2	19.5	18.1	19.4	21.8
Total	12.8	33.4	76.4	91.7	91.5	87.2	97.0	107.6
Imports:								
Machinery and equipment	4.2	12.6	23.2	30.7	29.5	31.0	36.1	39.7
Of which:								
Transportation equipment	1.2	3.3	4.7	6.7	6.5	7.6	8.2	8.3

Fuels and related materials	0.2	1.5	1.1	3.0	3.4	3.0	2.5	3.6
Of which:								
Petroleum	0.1	0.7	0.9	2.7	3.1	2.7	2.2	2.6
Ores and concentrates	0.3	0.6	0.9	0.9	1.0	1.0	1.2	1.4
Base metals and manufactures	0.7	3.6	4.7	4.9	4.7	4.9	5.3	5.5
Of which:								
Ferrous metals	0.6	3.3	4.6	4.9	4.6	4.9	5.3	5.5
Chemicals	0.5	1.5	3.3	3.2	3.3	3.7	4.0	4.5
Wood and wood products	0.2	0.8	1.4	1.0	1.0	1.0	1.0	1.0
Textile raw materials and semimanufactures	0.5	0.9	1.5	1.7	1.3	1.4	1.2	1.4
Of which:								
Wool fiber	0.1	0.3	0.5	0.6	0.4	0.5	0.5	0.6
Agricultural products	2.3	9.1	17.4	17.7	18.7	17.5	14.8	15.3
Industrial consumer goods	2.1	4.8	8.2	9.2	9.2	10.3	11.7	12.2
Other	0.4	1.5	6.4	7.7	8.1	9.1	10.8	10.8
Total	11.7	37.1	68.5	80.4	80.4	83.3	88.9	95.9

Source: Central Intelligence Agency, Directorate of Intelligence, Handbook of Economic Statistics, 1989, pp. 160–61. Official Soviet statistics are converted using the official $US/ruble exchange rate.

transactions, as reported by the Soviet Union. The primary Soviet exports in 1987 were petroleum (accounting for 33 percent of total Soviet exports) and machinery and equipment (15 percent of total exports); exports of other commodities were less significant. In terms of Soviet imports, 70 percent of Soviet imports in 1987 were accounted for by: machinery and equipment (41 percent), transportation equipment (8.6 percent), agricultural products (16 percent), and industrial consumer goods (13 percent).

Hard currency transactions account for a substantial portion of total Soviet exports and imports of several items. In 1987, Soviet hard currency exports of the following commodities accounted for a substantial portion of total Soviet exports of those items: 28 percent of petroleum exports, 27 percent of natural gas exports, 34 percent of wood and wood product exports, and 28 percent of chemical product exports. On the import side, Soviet hard currency imports of the following commodities accounted for a substantial portion of total Soviet imports of those items: 80 percent of grain imports, 69 percent of rolled ferrous metals imports, and 63 percent of chemical imports. By way of comparison, Soviet hard currency imports of consumer goods accounted for only 7 percent of total Soviet imports of those items.

During the period 1970–87, several important changes have taken place in the structure of Soviet trade. There has been a sharp increase in the importance of petroleum exports, matched by an equally sharp decline in importance of agricultural, raw material, and manufactured good exports. Exports of chemical products have maintained a fairly constant, though small, share of total exports over the period. In large part, these changes reflect dramatic changes in world primary commodity prices and the Soviet acumen to exploit these short-term advantages.

Prior to the first world oil shock in 1973, Soviet exports of oil and natural gas accounted for less than 25 percent of all Soviet exports. By 1974, after world prices had risen four-fold, the share of these products in total Soviet exports had risen above 30 percent and, by the first half of the 1980s, it had peaked at 70 percent. Over this same period, the importance of exports of basic manufactures and machinery declined from over 30 percent of total exports to less than 20 percent.

In terms of Soviet imports, two broad commodity groups – agricultural products and manufactured goods, including machinery – have accounted for most of Soviet imports. Over the 1970–88 period, the importance of agricultural and raw materials imports have declined while that of chemicals has increased. Imports of manufactured goods, including machinery and consumer goods, have remained fairly stable over this period, accounting for about 60 percent of all Soviet imports.

The overall pattern of Soviet–East European trade is characterized by the Soviet Union serving as supplier of fuels and other minerals in exchange for East European machinery. With the current reforms in both the Soviet Union and in Eastern Europe, the Soviet Union may no longer be able to subsidize its exports of raw materials to Eastern Europe. Similarly, East European exports to the USSR of convertible commodities may also halt. Despite the talk about reforms, it is unlikely that drastic revisions in intra-CMEA trade patterns will occur in the next five to ten years. Earlier work on the determinants of Soviet trade with Eastern Europe demonstrate that Soviet exports of chemicals, raw materials, and fuels were determined by East European demand. Likewise, the export of machinery from Eastern Europe was determined by the supply availability in Eastern Europe. As long as East European equipment is based on the Soviet standard, there will not be, in the next ten years, a deterioration in East European demand for raw materials and fuel.[3] Furthermore, the economic cost of restructuring the respective East European economies may necessitate using the Soviet market as a buyer of last resort, where non-competitive manufactured goods can be disposed of, with the minimum loss in earnings.[4]

The other major Soviet trade partners are the ME-LDCs and NATO. Unlike the earlier Soviet trade pattern with Eastern Europe, Soviet imports from its ME-LDC trading partners are predominately composed of food, crude materials, and basic manufactures. These three categories represent 70 to 80 percent of total Soviet imports from the ME-LDCs. Until the mid-1980s, the primary Soviet exports to ME-LDCs were basic manufactures and machinery. During the Andropov/ Chernenko period, Soviet exports shifted toward mineral fuels, which peaked at 65 percent of total Soviet exports, in 1983. During the first two years of Gorbachev's term, Soviet exports to the ME-LDCs declined, primarily due to a drop in oil sales.

Soviet imports from NATO have been concentrated in food, chemicals, basic manufactures, and machinery. Soviet exports to NATO have increasingly been composed of a single product – oil. In fact, as Soviet exports of basic manufactures declined from 20 percent to less than 10 percent, exports of oil became the predominant item in Soviet–NATO in trade.

Historically, Soviet–US trade has been very small and dominated by Soviet grain purchases from the United States. In terms of Soviet imports, the importance of food has been maintained since the mid-1960s. Imports of chemicals and machinery and transport equipment have also been important elements. On the export side, there has been a shift in the composition of Soviet exports from crude materials and basic manufactures to the exports of mineral fuels, chemicals, and basic manufactures.

Table 3.3 presents the leading US imports from the Soviet Union over the 1983–89 period, distributed by the three-digit US Standard Industrial Classification (SIC). Of the 1989 total imports of $690 million, the largest import commodity was petroleum which equalled $227 million. Other leading items included industrial chemicals and metals.

The leading US exports to the Soviet Union are presented in Table 3.4. Of the 1989 total of $4.2 billion, over 50 percent ($3.0 billion) were grain exports. Other fats, oils, and agricultural chemicals added an additional $600 million. The remaining products were composed of industrial machinery, parts, and assorted industrial inputs. While substantially larger than US imports, US exports to the Soviet Union are subject to a great deal of fluctuation, primarily due to Soviet grain purchases. Despite the Soviet desire to be self-sufficient in agricultural products, the US is expected to continue as its major supplier of grain and other food products. In the long run, depending on the nature of and success of Soviet joint ventures, the United States may become an exporter of non-food related exports such as construction, farm machinery and equipment, and scientific and professional instruments.

Before addressing the estimation of the probable expansion of Soviet trade due to reduced US tariffs, we confront the issue of Soviet export competitiveness. In what follows we present a decomposition of the Soviet Union's export growth, over the 1962–87 period, using the econometric framework referred to as the Constant Market Share (CMS) model.[5] Although changes in export shares, as measured by the CMS model, are not entirely determined by changes in competitiveness, they nevertheless have become an accepted measure of changes in a country's competitiveness.

The CMS model decomposes actual growth of a country's exports into four components: those related to the growth in world trade, change in commodity composition, change in country-partner market distribution, and (residual) competitiveness. Formally, the CMS identity for a change in a country's exports can be written as:

$$X^{00} - X^0 = r X^0 + \sum_i (r_i - r) X_i^0 + \sum_i \sum_j (r_{ij} - r_i) X_{ij}^0$$

$$+ \sum_i \sum_j (X_{ij}^{00} - X_{ij}^0 - r_{ij} X_{ij}^0) \quad (1)$$

where X is total Soviet exports, X_{ij} is the Soviet exports of commodity i

Table 3.3. *Leading US imports from the Soviet Union by 3-digit SIC Group (Customs value, $US thousand)*

SIC	Description	1983	1984	1985	1986	1987	1988	1989
291	Petroleum refinery products	55,968	194,413	104,010	68,767	97,451	185,087	227,505
335	Rolled, drawn and extruded nonferrous	8,475	18,794	5,522	21,288	17,201	20,451	93,628
281	Industrial inorganic chemicals	98,627	141,928	118,671	84,049	62,285	76,450	82,859
333	Smelter and refined nonferrous	71,886	75,506	47,114	220,986	87,803	95,069	71,339
131	Crude petroleum and natural gas	0	0	0	5,622	1,509	10,237	54,188
208	Beverages and flavoring extracts	11,403	8,885	10,744	13,275	17,606	20,284	19,040
920	Used or second-hand merchandise	5,611	3,028	2,192	1,873	5,291	7,150	16,336
331	Blast furnace, steel works	2,897	3,323	4,556	3,854	9,137	17,904	15,265
286	Industrial organic chemicals	1,930	9,124	16,116	16,932	15,096	11,331	15,185
27	Animal specialties	8,306	10,192	7,909	14,649	19,977	17,066	14,375
910	Scrap and waste	294	5,750	6,694	19,059	24,501	29,249	11,063
353	Construction, mining and oil machinery	805	729	1,075	3,367	5,068	9,230	10,778
287	Agricultural chemicals, napf	43,047	53,690	57,145	59,695	10,887	24,183	9,027
221	Cotton broad woven fabrics	0	0	10	128	6,893	2,898	7,618
209	Miscellaneous food preparation	4,616	5,256	3,327	1,382	2,664	5,185	5,136
326	Ceramic sanitary and industrial	99	114	66	87	180	1,340	3,536
990	Miscellaneous commodities, nap	406	545	787	975	993	680	3,283
349	Fabricated metal products, nap	84	100	161	71	101	371	3,269
13	Field crops, except cash grain	350	162	132	533	52	128	2,847
91	Fish, fresh, chilled, or frozen	12,737	11,719	8,697	858	64	2,887	2,621
249	Miscellaneous wood products	2,396	3,069	3,353	3,931	4,783	4,382	2,122
243	Millwork, plywood, and veneer	3,013	2,677	1,518	2,432	2,884	1,125	1,739
329	Abrasive, asbestos, and miscellaneous	132	138	135	17	483	1,421	1,714
980	United states goods returned	311	182	1,056	1,500	1,489	1,671	1,504
21	Livestock, except dairy, poultry	0	0	0	0	0	161	1,450
352	Farm and garden machinery	479	149	198	360	698	852	1,354
387	Watches, clocks, clockwork	0	0	0	9	0	1	1,099
367	Electronic components and accessories	667	850	1,302	385	478	2,786	1,078
	Total, Leading imports	334,539	550,323	402,490	546,084	395,574	549,579	680,958
	Total, All imports	341,059	556,114	406,899	554,898	408,187	563,862	690,893

Source: US Department of Commerce.

Table 3.4. *Leading US exports to the Soviet Union by 3-digit SIC Group ($US thousand)*

SIC	Description	1983	1984	1985	1986	1987	1988	1989
11	Cash grains	1,348,661	2,574,454	1,660,862	593,571	813,313	1,809,658	2,989,157
207	Fats and oils	21,509	38,951	61,158	20,704	80,933	277,481	414,593
287	Agricultural chemicals	221,442	188,118	232,439	203,979	182,375	174,787	237,075
331	Blast furnace, steel works	408	132	1,886	2,765	2,630	27,197	106,763
353	Construction, mining & materials handling	42,815	35,074	38,773	92,629	22,766	34,609	69,530
355	Specific industrial machines & equipment	4,383	7,134	5,757	3,175	4,948	8,641	48,677
308	Miscellaneous plastics products	476	1,163	2,170	3,606	6,572	5,079	36,564
382	Instruments for measuring, detecting	15,714	8,364	6,653	9,155	49,963	26,476	36,523
354	Metalworking machine & equipment	9,437	3,702	5,186	5,761	8,751	5,945	23,732
261	Pulp mill products	4,154	6,263	1,448	7,938	12,976	20,169	20,968
291	Petroleum refinery products	18,339	21,277	31,559	41,848	39,655	42,508	19,637
206	Sugar and confectionery products	2,953	24,501	67,663	37,613	27,360	46,848	19,509
356	General industrial machinery & equipmertt	12,856	7,694	12,085	5,511	12,482	15,353	18,538
282	Plastic material & synthetic resins	22,253	25,543	26,284	7,563	1,530	4,528	18,190
357	Office, computing, accounting machines	320	1,762	381	1,160	1,949	2,423	16,367
281	Industrial inorganic chemicals	7,731	5,442	7,758	13,085	20,446	27,442	15,360
286	Industrial organic chemicals	3,289	5,836	5,286	12,980	7,564	14,323	12,502
283	Drugs	1,039	1,542	1,109	942	964	1,647	12,499
201	Meat products and meat packing products	12,494	10,864	9,738	2,787	2,458	2,238	11,611
351	Engines & turbines, parts & accessories	19,124	13,015	6,268	1,858	6,428	3,915	10,982
371	Motor vehicles & motor vehicle equipment	3,380	3,068	2,912	4,748	4,454	4,907	9,739
299	Petroleum and coal products, napf	3,125	8,178	21,694	13,898	13,637	9,676	8,327
384	Surgical, medical & dental instruments	5,042	3,147	4,930	8,740	2,560	7,490	8,198
335	Rolled, drawn, and extruded nonferrous	2,753	1,097	126	696	250	292	7,992

Code	Commodity						
365	Radio/TV sets, phonograph, receivers	120	52	135	1,439	74	2,235	6,297
306	Fabricated rubber products, napf	2,902	76	1,130	2,067	4,725	4,204	5,896
358	Refrigeration machines, parts	408	298	1,028	246	217	734	5,780
381	Aircraft flight, navigational	492	903	1,275	464	2,884	2,785	5,392
359	Flexible tubing & piping of base metals	1,753	1,607	622	820	1,604	1,161	4,831
369	Electrical machinery, apparatus	913	541	641	846	2,742	2,995	4,783
362	Electrical industrial apparatus	2,039	1,878	7,761	9,531	8,633	12,153	4,779
284	Soaps, detergents & cleaning preparations	2	6	6	47	1	19	4,439
91	Fish, frozen or chilled	0	0	0	0	4	425	4,249
352	Farm & garden machinery & equipment	32,335	25,462	23,273	17,730	4,873	13,780	4,026
990	Special classification provisions	2,639	657	285	797	423	3,594	3,902
374	Railroad equipment	109	531	0	0	0	0	3,169
386	Photographic equipment and supplies	869	880	307	297	888	2,188	2,562
367	Electronic components and accessories	348	307	576	634	402	1,496	2,421
3	Manufactured commodities, other	376	1,578	1,701	1,197	1,028	1,155	2,167
329	Abrasive, asbestos	3,831	1,633	1,438	1,531	2,098	962	2,166
27	Animal specialties	0	0	0	0	1,163	574	1,796
349	Fabricated metal products, napf	374	889	439	783	145	3,136	1,400
275	Commercial printed matter	68	176	22	135	219	396	1,399
342	Cutlery, hand tools, and hardware	852	528	302	116	510	397	1,360
289	Miscellaneous chemicals	1,507	1,639	1,266	1,200	2,103	773	1,000
	Total, Leading exports	1,835,634	3,035,962	2,256,332	1,136,592	1,361,700	2,629,541	4,246,847
	Total, All exports	2,001,951	3,282,652	2,421,948	1,246,831	1,477,399	2,762,754	4,262,336

Source: US Department of Commerce.

to market j, X_i is total Soviet exports of commodity i, r is the rate of growth of total world exports, r_i is the rate of growth of total world exports of commodity i, r_{ij} is the rate of growth of world exports of commodity i to market j, o is the initial period, and oo is the second period.

The first term on the right-hand side of equation (1) is the world trade component and measures what Soviet exports would have been had they grown at the same rate as total world exports. The second term (commodity composition effect) measures whether the specific Soviet export composition was skewed toward commodities whose rate of growth either exceeded or fell short of total world export growth. The third term (market distribution effect) measures whether Soviet exports were concentrated in markets where demand was growing either faster or slower than total world export demand in those markets. The fourth term (residual competitiveness) measures the difference between the actual increase in Soviet exports and the increase that would have occurred had the Soviet Union maintained its export share in each market with respect to each commodity. In theory, an increase (decrease) in competitiveness is indicated by a positive (negative) value of the residual.

In applying the CMS procedure to Soviet trade flows over the 1962–88 period, it was decided to break up the entire period by five-year planning cycles. Each period chosen reflects a five-year plan with a distinctive trade reform agenda. They are – Khrushchev Period: 1962–65; Brezhnev/Kosygin Period I: 1966–70; Breszhnev/Kosygin Period II: 1971–75; Brezhnev/Kosygin Period III: 1976–80; transition to Perestroika – The Andropov/Chernenko Period: 1981–85; and Gorbachev Period: 1986–88. The results of this investigation are presented in Table 3.5. Market shares were calculated at the one-digit level of the SITC nomenclature. Soviet exports are compared to the exports of EFTA, US, and Canada to the world,[6] exports of the EFTA countries to the Canadian and Latin American market, and the exports of the US and Canada to the European market.

Evaluating Soviet export growth relative to the exports of EFTA, US, and Canada to the world, the results indicate that Soviet export growth appears to have been retarded by a decline in its competitiveness. In the latest two five-year periods, Soviet export growth was negative. The major factor causing this decline in both periods was a decline in competitiveness. The greatest enhancement of Soviet export growth in these periods was its market distribution. In the Gorbachev period, even the growth of world trade could not reverse the decline in Soviet exports. Given that our market, as defined, also includes purchases of Soviet petroleum products, the reduction in oil prices may be dramatizing the reduction in Soviet export competitiveness in this latter period.

Comparing Soviet export growth with that of EFTA countries to the Canadian and Latin American market, the results point to a general negative competitiveness effect. On the other hand, the positive effect of the world trade expansion is also widespread across all periods. Apart from the large residual effects, this sub-competitive comparison points to the strong impact of the market distribution effect on Soviet export growth.

The final comparison is with US and Canadian exports to the European market. With the exception of the Gorbachev period, Soviet export growth was retarded by the competitiveness effect. Soviet export growth was enhanced by both the growth in world exports and by the market distribution of Soviet exports. Overall, the results indicate that over the entire period, the major positive source of Soviet export growth was a general increase in world exports (under all definitions), whereas the major factor retarding Soviet export growth was reduced competitiveness.

2   Estimating the effects of normalized US–USSR trade

The predominant economic policy question concerning the reduction of US tariffs to MFN levels for the Soviet Union involves the determination of the change in Soviet exports to the United States in terms of volume and composition. Past attempts to provide empirical answers[7] to this question have been beset with methodological and data problems as well as with uncertainties associated with Soviet behavior. This section briefly discusses how this question might be addressed, reviews the major difficulties involved in analyzing MFN tariff reductions, and presents the collection of approaches employed in this chapter.

The economic implication of granting MFN status to the Soviet Union is treated as a reduction in duties from column 2 to column 1 rates.[8] This reduction in US import duties on Soviet products is assumed, *ceteris paribus*, to result in an increase in US imports from the Soviet Union as domestic buyers substitute the now lower-priced Soviet goods for both domestic goods as well as imports from other countries. Formally, the customs union literature treats "gross trade creation" or total trade expansion as the total increase in Soviet exports brought about by a tariff reduction, regardless of whether it replaces US domestic production or other US imports from countries whose tariffs have not been reduced. "Net trade creation" refers to newly created trade that occurs at the expense of domestic production, while "trade diversion" refers to

Table 3.5. *Constant market share estimates of Soviet exports to the world, Canada and Latin America, and Europe*[a] *($million and percentage of actual growth of exports)*

	Actual trade changes ($)	World trade effect (%)	Commodity composition effect (%)	Market distribution effect (%)	Competitiveness (residual) effect (%)
Soviet exports compared to EFTA, US and Canadian exports to the world[a]					
Khrushchev Period	1,257	62.0	−11.3	635.2	−585.9
Brezhnev/Kosygin Period I	1,195	166.4	12.1	4305.5	−4384.0
Brezhnev/Kosygin Period II	12,288	64.0	12.3	751.0	−727.3
Brezhnev/Kosygin Period III	22,794	77.0	42.2	1572.9	−1592.1
Transition to perestroika					
Andropov/Chernenko Period	(10,503)	29.1	−24.2	−657.5	752.6
Gorbachev Period	(8,147)	−92.4	43.9	−510.0	658.5
Soviet exports compared to EFTA exports to Canada and Latin America					
Khrushchev Period	42	116.1	−14.3	544.5	−546.3

Brezhnev/Kosygin Period I	120	236.5	-63.8	2019.0	-2091.6
Brezhnev/Kosygin Period II	895	120.6	-4.1	550.9	-567.4
Brezhnev/Kosygin Period III	(1,943)	-65.6	-12.2	-358.0	535.9
Transition to perestroika					
Andropov/Chernenko Period	357	-5.1	1.5	33.2	70.4
Gorbachev Period	74	46.9	96.9	368.8	-412.6
Soviet exports compared					
to US and Canadian exports					
to Europe[c]					
Khrushchev Period	334	128.7	-26.5	55.7	-57.8
Brezhnev/Kosygin Period I	332	267.8	-10.7	685.3	-842.3
Brezhnev/Kosygin Period II	5,095	44.3	19.1	282.8	-246.3
Brezhnev/Kosygin Period III	12,962	69.1	12.7	330.9	-312.7
Transition to perestroika					
Andropov/Chernenko Period	(872)	386.7	177.7	1052.2	-1516.6
Gorbachev Period	1,734	148.3	-265.4	-367.2	584.3

[a] Calculated at the 1-digit SITC level for the 1962–63, 1966–70, 1971–75, 1976–80, 1981–85, and 1986–87.

[b] The total world market includes Canada, Japan, Africa, OPEC, Latin America, EEC, Command Economies, New Zealand, South Africa, Other Europe, Asia, and South Pacific.

[c] Europe includes EC and EFTA.

the substitution of imports from the Soviet Union for those from other countries not affected by the shift from column 2 to 1 rates. Given the structure of Soviet trade, as noted above, as well as the current Soviet industrial supply bottlenecks, the granting of MFN by the United States should not lead to any immediate or substantial trade diversion. In the short run, and apart from US imports of petroleum products, the total expansion of US imports from the Soviet Union would be primarily from trade creation and not trade diversion effects. In the long run, if the export-based joint ventures are successful there may be a possibility of some trade diversion.

The decomposition of the total trade expansion effects of a tariff reduction into trade creation and trade diversion has important analytical and policy implications. Trade creation, the fraction of total trade expansion which substitutes for displaced domestic production, is the relevant number if our interest is on the impact of the tariff reduction on domestic US output and employment. On the other hand, if we are interested in total Soviet earnings then the appropriate measure is total expansion. Since our concern lies in determining changes in total US imports from the Soviet Union, and we believe that trade diversion is a minimal phenomenon, our measure of total trade expansion will closely approximate trade creation.

In what follows we present the various estimating procedures used to estimate this expected Soviet trade expansion.

Elasticity approach

The elasticity approach requires the use of US import demand and Soviet export supply elasticities to determine the responsiveness of US buyers and Soviet sellers to a reduction in US import duties. In addition to the appropriate elasticities, it is necessary to make assumptions or inferences about the potential price response by Soviet producers to a change in US import duties. Subject to supply constraints, Soviet producers may pass through all, some, or none of the duty reduction to US buyers by maintaining export prices unchanged, raising them by a fraction of the tariff reduction, or raising them by the full amount of the tariff change. The magnitude of the pass-through, given current Soviet production possibilities, depends on the degree of monopoly power and Soviet preference structure. If US import demand were very unresponsive to price changes, Soviet authorities might simply raise export prices by the amount of the tariff reduction in order to maximize short-run dollar earnings.[9] On the other hand, if Soviet foreign trade planners were interested in increasing their share of the US market, they might pass through the entire tariff reduction to US consumers. In sum, the total trade expansion will depend on the US import demand elasticity, the export supply elasticity, the pricing strategy of Soviet exporters, the magnitude of the change in US tariffs, and the current volume of US imports from the USSR.

The above approach reduces to the estimation of a single equation reflecting the change in Soviet exports as US consumers alter their purchasing patterns to consume the now cheaper Soviet products. Formally this relationship was:

$$\hat{M}_{ik} = [\eta_{ik} / (1 - \eta_{ik} / \varepsilon_{jk})] \cdot \hat{t}_{ik} \tag{2}$$

where M is the volume of US imports from the Soviet Union, η is the relative price elasticity of import demand, ε is the export supply elasticity, t_{ik} is the ad-valorem equivalent tariff [differential between column 1 and 2] rate applicable to US imports from the Soviet Union, and ^ denotes percentage changes.[10]

The partial equilibrium approach just outlined is conceptually straightforward. Nevertheless, attempts to implement it to "non-market" economies are clouded by a number of methodological and data problems. The most severe constraint arises from the fact that, with the exception of Soviet purchases of US grain, there is no long-term pattern of trade between the United States and the Soviet Union. Thus, the historical pattern of US–Soviet trade does not reflect the "normal" flows that would exist if the Soviet Union were a market economy and both trading partners were fully aware of their respective market conditions and trading opportunities.

The partial equilibrium approach can, therefore, measure only one facet of the normalization process – that part due to the reduction in US tariffs to MFN levels. It cannot measure the change in trade volume and composition that may arise from the current Soviet reforms and joint venture opportunities. In large part, the usefulness of granting the Soviet Union MFN status will come about only if the required supply side measures are implemented successfully in the Soviet Union.

Despite these limitations, the partial equilibrium approach may be a useful *first step* in trying to answer the question – by how much can the Soviets expand their exports to the United States as US duties are reduced under different assumed Soviet supply elasticities? To answer this question we estimate equation (2) under various supply scenarios, with the assumption that Soviet export prices do not rise as a result of US tariff preferences (i.e. complete pass-through of the tariff reductions is assumed).

Shift–share and constant-share projection models

As an alternative to the elasticity approach, estimates of the impact of granting the Soviet Union MFN status can be derived based on shift–share and constant-share projection models.[11] As a first step, projections of future Soviet exports to the United States can be made on the assumption that these exports will grow at some constant rate. This simple constant-share model is written as:

$$\hat{X}_{jk,\,t+n} = a_{jk,\,(t-m,\,t)}\, X_{jk,\,t} \tag{3}$$

where X is Soviet exports and a is the constant-share term based on a historical period $(t-m, t)$. Given the lack of information on "normal" Soviet trade growth in convertible currency, we use a number of alternative constant-share terms. First, the average growth rate of Soviet exports to the NATO countries; second, Soviet exports to its less developed country aid recipients; and finally, the average growth rate of Soviet exports to the world.

Despite the fact that such constant-share models track well, these models are very simplistic. In order to provide an additional measure and to deal with the simplistic nature of the constant-share model, Soviet exports to the United States are projected using a regional model which allows for changes in the constant-share term. This model, known in the literature as the shift–share model is specified as:

$$\hat{X}_{jk,\,t+n} = [r_{hk,\,(t,\,t+n)} + b\,(R_{jk,\,(t-m,\,t)} - r_{hk,\,(t-m,\,t)})]\, X_{jk,\,t} \tag{4}$$

where r is the average export growth rate for the defined world "norm" (either NATO, the World, or LDC, designated as h) and R is the growth rate of Soviet exports to the United States. The scaler b adjusts for differences in the length of the historical period $(t-m, t)$ and the projection period $(t, t+n)$. The other terms have been defined earlier.

Based on these two projection models, Soviet exports to the United States are projected for 1989. These projections as well as the growth rates are based on 1962–88 data deflated by the 1984 implicit US GNP deflator. Departures from actual trade are attributed to the impact of granting the Soviet Union MFN status.

3   Empirical results

This section presents estimates of the expansion in US imports from the Soviet Union resulting from a reduction of US tariffs to MFN levels using the various approaches presented above.[12]

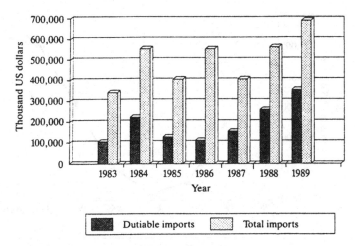

Figure 3.1 Total and dutiable US imports from the USSR

In order to determine the probable impact of granting MFN to the Soviet Union, via the elasticity approach, we need to establish the size of Soviet trade subject to duty and the differential rates between the non-MFN duty (column 2) and the MFN duty (column 1). A comparison between total and dutiable imports from the Soviet Union are presented in Figure 3.1. Of the 1989 total of $690 million US imports from the Soviet Union, $356 million or 52 percent were subject to US duties.

While the total size of dutiable imports is as limited as is total imports, the size of the duty differential is not trivial. In addition to the expected high differential rates for textile and apparel products (where the duty differentials are over 40 percentage points), a large tariff differential also exists for such products as wood products (over 40 percentage points), watches and clocks (40 percentage points), headgear (26 percentage points), and glass products (22.5 percentage points). Overall, the arithmetic average tariff differential for non-MFN countries is about 29 percentage points. If this trade differential were trade weighted, the constrained trade would provide a trade-weighted average differential of only 5.5 percentage points.[13] Given the magnitude of these rates, one would expect that granting MFN status to the Soviet Union would have the potential of inducing an expansion of Soviet exports to the United States. The limiting factor, however, is the ability of the Soviet Union to supply tradeable products.

Figure 3.2 presents the projected 1989 US imports from the Soviet Union using the elasticity approach. In order to take into account the

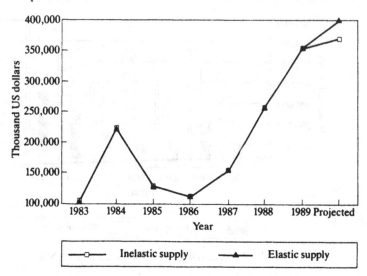

Figure 3.2 Projected US dutiable imports from the USSR based on elasticity model

Soviet supply constraints, our projections are based on the two extreme supply conditions – perfectly elastic and perfectly inelastic Soviet export supply. Furthermore, given that we do not have a "normal" base year for US–Soviet trade, it was decided to take the highest dutiable value of Soviet exports over the 1983–89 period as our base level of trade. The tariff differential is based on actual 1989 tariffs. If the Soviet supply elasticity were perfectly elastic, then one should expect a trade expansion of $43 million in dutiable US imports. If the Soviet supply elasticity were perfectly inelastic, then the trade expansion would equal $14 million. Relative to total US dutiable imports from the Soviet Union these trade expansion figures represent an increase in trade of 3.9 to 12.1 percent (or 2.0 to 6.2 percent of total US imports from the Soviet Union).

In the case of a perfectly elastic Soviet export supply response, 69 percent of the total trade expansion would result from an increase in sales of the following products – industrial inorganic chemicals, beverages, plywood, electrical components, smelter and refined non-ferrous metals, refined petroleum products, wood products, steel, scrap and waste, sanitary and industrial ceramic ware, glass products, and furniture. If the Soviet export supply were completely inelastic, then the trade expansion would occur as a result of increased sales of beverages, smelter and refined non-ferrous metals, and refined petroleum products.

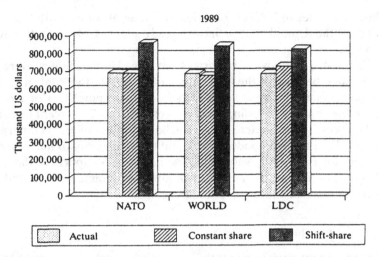

Figure 3.3 Projected US imports from the USSR based on constant-share and shift–share models

The trade expansion figures presented thus far are based on an expansion in US imports from the Soviet Union that are subject to US import duties. However, since a substantial portion of current US imports from the USSR is not subject to US import duties, and the fact that granting MFN status to the USSR is likely to have repercussions beyond the mere lowering of tariffs, total US imports are projected based on a number of different projection models with different presumed rates of growth.

Estimates of total Soviet trade expansion based on the constant-share model and the shift–share model are presented in Figure 3.3. These projections use the average rate of growth of Soviet exports to the world, NATO countries, and ME–LDCs, applying them to deflated base period values of US imports from the Soviet Union by one-digit SITC category.

The projected expansion in Soviet exports to the US, based on the constant-share model, equals $43 million or 6 percent of current US imports from the Soviet Union. Using a shift–share projection model, Soviet exports to the US are predicted to expand on average from $140 million to $170 million, or 20 to 25 percent of 1989 US imports from the Soviet Union, depending on whether Soviet exports emulate world, NATO, or ME–LDC export patterns.

Both projection methods indicate that moderate to more substantial trade expansion might be possible if, as the result of the US granting the Soviet Union MFN status, Soviet exports were to approximate their

2

Joseph Pelzman

historical rates to NATO countries – most all of whom, with the exception of the United States, have already granted MFN to the Soviet Union.

Estimates of Soviet imports from the United States were not generated because of the high degree of administrative control of those imports. A major obstacle to increased Soviet purchases of US merchandise other than grain, which represents over 70 percent of current US exports to the Soviet Union, will be the ability of Soviet enterprises to purchase foreign goods directly and the availability of hard currency to pay for them. Any substantial increase in US exports to the Soviet Union will depend on the extent of Soviet economic reforms and on a general increase in Soviet national income.

4   Conclusion

In the current environment, the uncertainty revolving around both the continuation of Gorbachev's reforms as well as its effectiveness, constrain the estimates presented in this chapter. The various models employed should not be interpreted as our presentation of all possible estimates. Rather it should be viewed as presenting a range of possible outcomes in a very unstable environment.

At the lower end of our estimates, one should expect that Soviet dutiable exports to the US would expand in the range of $14 to $43 million in the short run. A mid-range estimate of total Soviet export expansion based on a constant-share projection model would predict a trade expansion of $43 million. At the upper bound, the shift–share model would place the expansion in the range of $140 to $170 million. Overall, the short-run trade expansion from the Soviet Union will be modest, both in terms of Soviet exports and Soviet imports to and from the United States. This result is due more to the limited basket of Soviet exports to and imports from the United States and the resulting shortages of hard currency than to existing US trade barriers.

Notes

I am grateful to Greg Schoepfle for invaluable comments on earlier drafts. Financial support from the Office of International Economic Affairs, Division of Foreign Economic Research, the Bureau of International Labor Affairs, US Department of Labor is gratefully acknowledged. The views expressed here are solely those of the author and do not necessarily reflect the positions or opinions of the US Department of Labor.

1. See *Presidential Documents*, 3 December 1989, p. 1886.
2. *Moskovskie Novosti*, 1987.
3. See J. Pelzman, "Economic determinants of Soviet foreign trade with Eastern Europe," *European Economic Review*, vol. 14 (July 1980), pp. 45–59.
4. This assumes that the hard currency equivalent price for poorly manufactured East European products will be lower than comparable products (with equal or marginally higher quality) from the West, and therefore acceptable to budget conscious Soviet purchasers.
5. For a review of this literature, see H. P. Bowen and J. Pelzman, "U.S. Export Competitiveness: 1962–1977," *Applied Economics*, vol. 16 (June 1984), pp. 461–73.
6. The total world market includes all major trading countries except Taiwan (Canada, Japan, Africa, OPEC, Latin America, EEC, New Zealand, South Africa, Asia, and the South Pacific).
7. Earlier studies of the impact of granting the Soviet Union MFN status include: T. Wolf, "The quantitative impact of liberalization of United States unilateral restrictions on trade with the Socialist countries of Eastern Europe," US Department of State, External Research Study, 1972; and USITC, *Probable Impact on U.S. Trade of Granting Most-Favored-Nation Treatment to the U.S.S.R.*, Publication no. 812, 1977.
8. It is understood that the granting of MFN status to the Soviet Union may, in the long run, create structural changes whose impact cannot be measured via the approaches implemented here.
9. If export prices rise by the amount of the tariff reduction there will be no substitution of Soviet imports for either domestic goods or imports from other sources because the relative prices of these goods to US buyers will be unchanged.
10. The derivation of equation (2) is presented in J. Pelzman and G. K. Schoepfle, "The impact of the Caribbean Basin Economic Recovery Act on Caribbean nations' exports and development," *Economic Development and Cultural Change*, vol. 36, no. 4, 1988, pp. 753–96.
11. See J. Pelzman, "Forecasting waterborne exports with alternative regional economic models: a statistical analysis based on the Charleston Port," *The Review of Regional Studies*, vol. 8, no. 1, 1978, pp. 97–106.
12. The projected trade flows at the disaggregated commodity detail are available from the author. The commodity sector detail varies by methodology. In the case of the elasticity approach the level of detail is the three-digit Standard Industrial Classification (SIC) level, while in the case of the projection models, the level of detail is the one-digit SITC level.
13. Since the trade-weighted average differential is biased by the high tariffs, it is not used in the calculation of expected trade creation.

4 New developments in economic relations between Japan and CMEA countries

Wojciech Bienkowski and Masumi Hakogi

For the countries of Eastern Europe and the Soviet Union, Japan is an extremely attractive economic partner. Her huge market, roughly half of the USA and about half of the EEC, and her technological achievements have attracted the attention of East European and Soviet businessmen and consumers for decades. One could hardly find in the region an engineer or manager not attracted by Japanese achievements in modern engineering, electronics, or sophisticated managerial technics. The general public, i.e. consumers, in turn has been hungry for Japanese home electronics and cars. It now seems customary for most travelers from this region to Japan to bring back such consumer durables in quantity. Soviet imports of VTR and color TV from Japan have increased nearly seven and five times respectively during 1989. Its imports of passenger cars also greatly increased and imports of used cars are popular among Soviet sailors visiting Japanese ports. One may mention that economic ties with Japan are an important political variable as well which some governments in Eastern Europe and the Soviet Union add to an equation when they plan their foreign economic policy undertakings. In short, there are plenty of reasons why one has to pay a great deal of attention to the developments of this region's economic relations with Japan.

Eastern Europe and the Soviet Union in turn seem to be equally attractive partners. The countries of the region represent roughly 400 million consumers and deliver one-fifth of the world's material goods. In addition, these countries are endowed with vast and numerous natural resources, some of which lie still untapped or badly utilized. In short, Eastern Europe and the Soviet Union represent a huge market for Japanese products and technology and an attractive opportunity for Japan, whose economy is hungry for energy and poorly endowed with natural resources.

The arguments presented above and numerous others show us that both sides are mutually great potential markets for their respective products. And yet, when one looks at the statistical data reflecting the development in trade relations between Japan and Eastern Europe and the Soviet Union over the past two decades, one can hardly find any real upsurge in turnover which would exceed that of world trade trends or even match the world growth rate in trade.

Looking at the data in Table 4.1, one may start to wonder *why* economic relations between Japan and the CMEA countries are stagnating or even declining during certain periods. In other words, the question is what makes these natural partners reluctant or unable to develop any valuable and strong relationships which could match or even exceed in intensity other segments of East–West relations.

As students and observers of East–West economic relations for decades, we have come to the conclusion that the main reason for such a weak and unsatisfactory development in this relationship is the failure of the Soviet Union and the East European economic systems so far to utilize the potential for a mutually advantageous set of economic relations. This inability stems from the very nature of the centrally planned economic system which has been unable to produce quality products, to generate new technology and/or to diffuse acquired foreign technology quickly enough so as to catch up with ever-changing Western and Japanese technological developments.[1]

As the result of this generic quality of the centrally planned economies, neither the Soviet Union nor any country of Eastern Europe have been able to deliver any substantial number of quality and technologically attractive products to Western countries for decades. Detailed analysis of many East–West trade observations proved that neither Soviet exports nor East European exports have been able to increase or even to maintain their market shares in the West, especially when value added or technologically advanced goods are concerned.[2] We do not believe that this tendency has been reversed in recent years.

One may only hope that the recent developments in the Soviet Union and the countries of Eastern Europe would lead to a dramatic change in their economic systems and, as a result, would help to reverse the anti-quality ingredients in their systems by creating, as a consequence, a better and more competitive structure for their exports. This systemic transformation is indispensable so as to make these economies attractive again for any economic partner outside as well as inside the region.

At present, the systemic transformation seems to be most advanced in Poland because both the change in the country's political system and the reform of its economic system make the whole undertaking logically coherent. One should remember that many attempts at economic reforms, whether in Poland, the Soviet Union, China, or any other country in the so-called socialist world, have always been limited to

Table 4.1a. Japanese trade with East European countries and the Soviet Union ($US million)

	Bulgaria			CSSR			GDR			Hungary			Poland			Romania		
	X	M	B/T	X	M	B/T	X	M	B/T	X	M	B/T	X	M	B/T	X	M	B/T
1970	21	9	12	10	15	-5	15	39	-24	12	4	8	22	40	-18	26	4	22
1975	54	14	40	45	26	19	49	29	20	33	11	22	257	80	177	136	46	90
1977	51	17	34	35	46	-11	43	18	25	49	12	37	300	73	227	259	40	219
1978	55	18	37	30	49	-19	58	20	38	54	17	37	266	63	203	232	63	169
1979	45	24	21	39	60	-21	268	28	240	49	23	26	221	73	148	181	115	66
1980	65	22	43	63	49	14	139	40	99	107	17	90	228	62	166	203	66	137
1981	111	18	93	110	46	64	148	45	103	97	25	72	99	36	63	187	58	129
1982	87	20	67	69	45	24	193	37	156	73	22	51	61	39	22	91	34	57
1983	141	20	121	61	51	10	326	31	295	66	34	33	78	58	20	69	97	-28
1984	84	66	18	63	63	0	154	42	112	51	48	3	63	72	-9	74	130	-56
1985	123	22	102	57	53	4	137	44	93	83	52	31	73	67	6	90	65	25
1986	161	18	143	62	57	5	119	52	67	82	61	21	146	56	90	111	95	16
1987	117	25	92	63	81	18	201	59	142	92	98	-6	167	76	91	76	133	-57
1988	161	50	111	48	117	65	155	93	62	101	165	-63	258	116	142	53	142	-89
1989	164	45	119	56	130	74	95	83	12	108	148	-40	200	130	70	50	202	-152

Notes: X = Exports, M = Imports, B/T = Balance of Trade.
Source: SOTOBO, Chosageppo, February 1983, February 1990.

Table 4.2b. *Japanese trade with East European countries and the Soviet Union ($US million)*

	Eastern Europe's total					Soviet Union				
	Total trade	r.g.	X	M	B/T	Total trade	r.g.	X	M	B/T
1970	217		106	111	−5	822		341	481	140
1975	780		574	206	368	2,796		1,626	1,170	456
1977	943		737	206	531	3,356		1,939	1,422	517
1978	925	−1.9	695	230	465	3,944	17.5	2,502	1,442	1,060
1979	1,126	21.7	803	323	480	4,372	10.9	2,461	1,911	550
1980	1,061	−5.6	805	256	549	4,638	6.1	2,778	1,860	918
1981	980	−7.6	752	228	524	5,280	13.8	3,259	2,021	1,238
1982	771	−21.3	574	197	377	5,581	5.7	3,898	1,682	2,216
1983	1,032	34.0	741	291	450	4,277	−23.4	2,821	1,456	1,365
1984	910	−11.8	489	421	68	3,912	−8.5	2,518	1,394	1,124
1985	866	−4.8	563	303	260	4,180	6.9	2,751	1,429	1,322
1986	1,020	17.8	681	339	342	5,122	22.5	3,150	1,972	1,178
1987	1,188	16.5	716	472	244	4,908	−4.2	2,563	2,345	218
1988	1,458	22.7	776	682	94	5,896	20.1	3,130	2,766	364
1989	1,411	−3.2	673	738	−65	6,085	3.2	3,081	3,004	77

Notes: X = Exports, M = Imports, B/T = Balance of Trade, r.g. = rate of growth.
Source: SOTOBO, *Chosageppo*, February 1983, February 1990.

economic matters alone. Few of these attempts only referred to the necessity to reform the political system itself and none dared to undermine such ideological systemic dogmas as full employment, egalitarian principles, state ownership, or a political system based on a one-party monopoly. These self- or Soviet-imposed limitations on previous attempts at reforms in Eastern Europe made reform efforts fruitless from the start, for one cannot build any feasible market-oriented economic mechanism without freeing oneself from such constraints as full employment dogma, and the principle of dominant state ownership. A common understanding was that there was no necessity to have political parties to represent the diversified economic interests of independent economic units. In other words, until recently there has been no understanding of the fact that the feasibility of an efficient economic system rests upon and/or is directly related to a multiparty political system which would be able to reinforce an economic reform process through a check and balance mechanism and a real platform to work out a valuable and creative consensus between the various actors of the development process.

A new model, that of working out an efficient economic system paralleled and reinforced by a multiparty parliamentary political system, has been introduced for the first time, and only recently, in Poland. The new political environment has been gradually implemented in Poland since June 1989. The systemic transformation in economics has been undertaken by the Polish government from 1 January 1990. It aims at bringing stabilization and adjustment in the economy and, eventually, a recovery. In the longer term, it will create an ability to compete. The Polish economy has recently stabilized. In March 1990, inflation on a monthly basis came down to 5 percent as compared to 76 percent in January 1990. The budget has been balanced; subsidies have been reduced by half and prices have been almost completely freed to reflect new market conditions. Convertibility and a stable rate of exchange have been introduced as well, and government foreign trade monopoly has been abandoned.[3]

In short, stabilization has been achieved at the expense of growing unemployment and a sharp decline in industrial production. In the months to come, an adjustment and recovery program is to be implemented as well. This is to be achieved by the creation and implementation of such institutional and systemic changes as the creation of capital and labor markets, building a new banking system, the reprivatization of state property so as to reach proportions typical of Western economies, and also through a policy of deregulation and demonopolization in order to create a flexible and competitive internal economy, able to adjust itself quickly to constantly changing patterns of world demand, and able to feed back market information to its production enterprises so as to make them produce goods adjusted in accordance with such information. This would presuppose quicker decision making on the part of these enterprises. Only such an economic mechanism, freed from the rusted cloth of the old central planning system and ideological dogma may have a chance to cope with an ever-changing and more internationalized and therefore more competitive world economy.

Poland hopes to achieve that ability to compete in this decade. The first part of its economic program has been completed already and a kind of stability has been reached. An adjustment and recovery program may take two to three years before the consumers feel the effects in their daily lives. It may be as late as 1994–95 when a full-scale recovery and a large expansion catches the attention of many businessmen including very cautious businessmen from Japan. Japanese businesses are now paying much closer attention to the investment environment in East European countries such as Poland, Hungary, and

Czechoslovakia. Though on a small scale, joint ventures are actually being set up and affiliated offices of Japanese enterprises are being increasingly opened up in these countries. Pol-Nippon, management consulting joint venture in Poland, Auto-Korsen, Suzuki Motor's passenger car joint venture in Hungary, Daiwa Securities' joint venture with Hungarian Banks in Budapest, SSP Anty, Japan–Czech shopping center joint venture, are several examples.[4]

Poland has entered uncharted water, untapped by any other country in the world and not described by any academic textbook, because up to 1990 there was no successful and yet relatively peaceful attempt at moving from socialism back into capitalism. Hungary and Czechoslovakia are following suit.

The Soviet Union itself cannot escape the economic reform and systemic transformation similar to that Poland is undertaking now, if it wants to build a solid economic relationship with any Western partner. Japan, which was cautious and wise so many times in recent decades when building any economic relationship with other countries and regions, will most probably not engage in any shaky business. In other words, only if and when political stability and a systemic tranformation program in Eastern Europe and the Soviet Union are well structured and carried out, and when, under these conditions, economic stabilization and adjustment programs are completed, will a solid foundation for further expansion of Japanese economic relations with Eastern Europe and the Soviet Union be seriously contemplated, and the present stagnation and/or decline in these relations could be reversed.

Notes

The authors have benefited from discussions with Franz-Lothar Altmann, Marie Lavigne, Gabor Bakos, and others.
1. See Wojciech Bienkowski, "CMEA trade with the West. Present problems and future prospects," Shogaku-Ronshu, October 1986.
2. Wojciech Bienkowski, "CMEA countries' competitiveness in Western markets," in J. S. Berliner et al. (eds.), Economics of the Socialist Countries, Fukushima International Symposium Organizing Committee, 1989.
3. For an extended and detailed evaluation of recent changes in Poland's foreign trade organization and Joint-venture Law, please look at the chapters in this book by K. Szymkiewicz and J. Misala respectively.
4. SOTOBO (Japan Association for Trade with Soviet Union & Socialist Countries of Europe), Chosageppo (Monthly Bulletin on Trade with USSR and East Europe), recent issues in 1990 (in Japanese).

5 Perestroika and its implications for Soviet foreign aid

W. Donald Bowles

A recent World Bank report (World Bank, 1990) suggests that the central effort in less developed countries (LDCs) must be to stimulate economic development through *structural adjustment* and *policy reform*, with increasing attention paid to direct alleviation of poverty ("adjustment with a human face") as government spending is reduced and there is increasing privatization, exchange rate devaluation, "getting the prices right," and the like. More generally, long-term, self-sustaining economic development must be based on a triad – market orientation, a strong but defined role played by an effective government, and grassroots development leading to some form of representative democracy to provide checks and balances. Interestingly, the policy conditions now attached to grants and loans by major international donors bear a striking resemblance to the kind of changes currently suggested by the Soviet leadership for the Soviet economy itself.

Current Soviet economic, political, and ethnic disarray make it difficult to define the role that might be played by Soviet foreign aid in Third World development. Self-examination of principles underlying Soviet aid has been underway since the mid-1980s.[1] The new approaches include Soviet willingness to participate in the alleviation of world poverty, and repudiation of the concept of class struggle in international relations. Emphasis is now on a sharply reduced role for the state, priority of agriculture over industry, and recognition of the limits of planning and import substitution. There is growing acceptance of the concept of structural adjustment.

By Soviet accounts, the aid program had become stagnant by the mid-1980s, reflecting the state of the economy. Today, the hallmark of perestroika is "intensification" of the economy, higher levels of technology, and factor productivity. For foreign aid, this suggests an emphasis on more manufactured goods (especially machines), which in turn will permit LDCs to export more manufactured goods to the USSR. Also, because agriculture is again stressed in development theory, more Soviet assistance is intended for this sector.

The amount of Soviet aid

The quantitative record of Soviet aid is much disputed. This issue is important in two respects. It affects our understanding of the Soviet contribution to Third World development and the Soviet sacrifice made internally to sustain such foreign assistance.

OECD data shown in Table 5.1 suggest that in 1988, by conventional Western definition, Soviet disbursements of economic assistance were about $4.6 billion gross, and net of repayments were about $4.2 billion.[2] This figure was about 90 percent of CMEA aid in that year, and represents a considerable increase over levels in the mid-1980s, but a decline from 1987. Two-thirds of gross disbursements went to three countries: Cuba, Mongolia, and Vietnam, with the bulk of the remainder going to Afghanistan, Kampuchea, North Korea, and Laos. For comparison, in 1987, the net flow of resources from DAC to developing countries and multilateral agencies totalled $65.7 billion.

If one takes into account direct economic aid on a net basis, and the indirect effect of price subsidies (plus and minus) on Soviet imports from and exports to communist LDCs, the Soviet figure is much higher. On this basis, as shown in Table 5.2, total net disbursed USSR aid to communist LDCs was about $6.3 billion in 1989, down substantially from the peak of $7.8 billion reached in 1987. Aid to six Marxist governments increased sharply in 1989 to $1.4 billion (mainly to Afghanistan). Aid to other LDCs declined, falling from $1.8 billion in 1985 to $1.5 billion in 1989. A country breakdown of aid actually disbursed to this group is not available, but in terms of assistance extended or committed (not disbursed), the figures were highest for Mozambique in Africa, Nicaragua in Latin America, and India.[3]

Soviet figures on aid exceed those provided by the CIA. A recent study by Soviet scholars at the Institute of World Economy and International Relations of the USSR Academy of Sciences in Moscow suggests that during the period 1976–80, Soviet aid minus debt payments totalled about R30 billion, and for the period 1981–86 the figure was R63 billion.[4] The yearly ruble average for the earlier period was R6 billion rubles, and for the latter period was almost R11 billion. Soviet aid in the 1980s is said to represent about 1.3 to 1.4 percent of GNP, far exceeding the aid contribution in relative terms of all other countries.[5] About one-fifth or one-sixth of Soviet "aid," excluding military shipments, is purely concessional (see below p. 71).

The Soviets provide four explanations of these higher estimates. First, Soviet figures include the following items which are not usually included in calculations of Western assistance: subsidies provided for partial pay-

Table 5.1. *Estimated USSR aid disbursements ($US million)*

	1970	1975	1980	1983	1984	1985	1986	1987	1988p
1. CMEA LCDs									
Cuba	141	535	542	619	708	655	532	656	663
Mongolia	104	150	552	624	568	550	706	804	715
Vietnam	320	500	458	901	914	1,056	1,457	1,811	1,658
Total	565	1,185	1,552	2,144	2,190	2,261	2,695	3,271	3,036
2. Countries having special links									
Afghanistan	28	34	337	373	220	219	283	200	201
Kampuchea	–	–	134	86	87	98	150	161	172
Korea Democratic Republic	145	60	75	26	46	96	123	62	63
Laos	–	–	57	99	77	99	81	110	104
Total	173	94	603	584	430	512	637	533	540
3. Other developing countries	351	389	571	703	651	644	1,101	904	809
4. Scholarships	25	45	130	185	180	190	200	220	220
5. Multilateral contributions	4	5	7	4	4	4	5	7	7
Total, gross	1,118	1,718	2,863	3,620	3,456	3,611	4,638	4,935	4,612
6. Repayments	320	454	550	574	565	547	520	450	400
Of which:									
CMEA LDCs and Korea Democratic Republic	100	110	140	140	140	140	145	150	150
Other LDCs	220	344	410	434	425	407	375	300	250
Total net	798	1,264	2,313	3,046	2,891	3,064	4,118	4,485	4,212

Source: OECD, *Development Cooperation, 1989 Report* (Paris: OECD, 1989), p. 262.

Table 5.2. *USSR net economic aid disbursed to LDCs, 1985–1989 ($US million)*

	1985	1986	1987	1988	1989
Communist LDCs	7,669	6,821	7,772	6,882	6,344
Cuba	5,300	4,383	5,011	4,345	4,159
Vietnam	1,160	1,325	1,575	1,366	1,162
Mongolia	918	905	991	987	800
Cambodia	98	128	134	139	159
Laos	100	74	94	86	80
North Korea	93	6	−33	−41	−16
Marxist clients	700	660	765	740	1,430
Afghanistan	225	205	225	180	820
Nicaragua	235	240	340	340	415
Angola	25	40	20	35	40
Ethiopia	85	55	70	65	60
Mozambique	55	35	65	50	45
South Yemen	75	85	45	70	70
Other	1,765	1,720	1,675	1,725	1,450
Total	10,134	9,201	10,212	9,347	9,224

Source: Unpublished CIA data. There is no military component in these figures.

ment of Soviet specialists working in LDCs; provision on a concessional or grant basis of scientific–technical documentation together with shipments of equipment, other goods, and services; and, trade subsidies realized as the differential between world price and the price charged for Soviet exports or paid for by Soviet imports of goods and services. Second, there is "double counting" in keeping national accounts, which was said to represent almost 40 percent of GNP in 1985. Third, many Soviet organizations did not always make a clear distinction between commercial operations and aid; in effect, trade credits were often counted as aid. Finally, use of the official exchange rate to cite Soviet aid in dollars inflates the value of aid.

What is the opportunity cost to the Soviet economy of foreign aid? In December 1989, Andrei Kortunov set off a debate in a liberal weekly by alleging that the R12 billion budgeted for aid in 1989 represents a substantial drain on Soviet resources.[6] Although he considers this figure grossly inflated (see above), he suggests that it is useful for comparative purposes. Thus, the aid budget exceeded by one-third the appropriations for science or for law enforcement bodies. It was over three times the expenses on education, vocational training, culture, arts, and mass media taken together. It was twenty-one times the outlays on public health and physical education. In brief, Kortunov states that this sum nearly equals all the outlays on activities aimed at raising the people's living standard in 1990 (R13.4 billion).

While these figures may be correct in a nominal sense, they are of somewhat ambiguous economic meaning. For example, Soviet oil sold abroad can be converted to a dollar value at any given ruble–dollar exchange rate, and compared, say, with the value of gold sold abroad at the same rate. Comparison of these two figures provides a common, if flawed, measure of value. However, to compare the value of Soviet oil sold abroad with the value of social expenditures which are heavily subsidized is to compare two variables with two different yardsticks – the ruble means one thing internationally and many other things domestically, depending on the pricing principle applied to particular domestic products or services. In effect, Kortunov calls attention to the sacrifice made by Soviet citizens to finance foreign aid, but is unable to state clearly the extent of that sacrifice.

What is to be the size of future Soviet foreign aid? The approved budget for 1989 contained R12.5 billion for "state credits and non-repayable aid to foreign states," which was 2.5 percent of the total state budget. The comparable figures for 1990 were R9.7 billion and 2.0 percent.[7] In a last minute amendment to the general outlines of the reform package proposed by President Gorbachev in June 1990, it was stipulated that there would be drastic cuts in foreign aid (along with cuts in military expenditures and large development projects) by 1 September.[8] Such cuts were included in the "500-day plan" announced in September. Originally set to begin on 1 October it calls for a 75 percent cut in non-economic foreign aid.[9] One can speculate that plans which replace this will also reduce aid.

Until the Soviet Union adopts a standard methodology and provides more comprehensive data, and until the ruble emerges as a better measure of economic worth, estimates of the Soviet aid program will remain difficult to interpret.

Because most Soviet "aid" is really credit, and much of this has not been repaid, the accumulated sum is now of concern to policy makers. In March 1990 the Ministry of Finance revealed that sixty-one countries owe the USSR R85.8 billion, with Cuba topping the list at R15.5 billion; about one-quarter of the total was hard currency debt.[10] Of the total, R545 million were written off (including interest) as of 1 November 1989, and R17.4 billion (including interest) were rescheduled over the period 1986–89. The repayment schedule is as follows: R7.2 billion in

1990, R39.4 billion in the 13th five-year plan, and R34.5 billion after that.

Soviet specialists and government officials have suggested that LDCs need debt forgiveness. Some Soviet debts have been written off, but perhaps not nearly as much as will eventually be the case. A considerable portion of the existing debt is associated with previous arms deliveries for which payment is expected (this is not strictly aid, therefore). Alexander Konovalov, citing Western sources, notes that 75 percent of all arms sales were bought by the five countries.[11] The debt and the deferred portion thereof are shown below (in billions of rubles):

	Debt	Deferred		Debt	Deferred
Angola	2.0	0.768	Libya	1.7	0.360
India	8.9	–	Syria	6.7	1.7
Iraq	3.8	1.4			

These relationships led Konovalov to suggest that "it is extremely doubtful that such trade could be a serious source of hard currency." These figures also led Andrei Kozyrev, chief of the International Organizations Directorate of the USSR Foreign Ministry, to suggest that since these countries "are not in a position to repay their debts on the original terms ... it is quite probable that not only our arms trade does not bring in those famous multi-billion profits, but that is is even unprofitable."[12] In another context, Elena Arefieva, an important critic of the present aid program, revealed that "outright aid accounts for one-fifth to one-sixth of all [aid] expenditures, not counting the vast military assistance we provide." She suggests that, "the problem is one of ensuring that our remaining outlays are not outright gifts as well."[13]

This question is important, of course. Senior and well-placed Soviet officials such as Admiral Yuri Grishin, Deputy Minister of Foreign Economic Relations of the USSR, continue to maintain that military shipments remain profitable, and largely because they are "high-tech" goods rather than oil or timber.[14] Grishin goes further and suggests caution on conversion of military to civilian consumption, because the Soviet "scientific and engineering elite is concentrated in these industries." He adds, "I don't think it would be feasible to convert the manufacturing capacities that generate profit." Whether military shipments in the future will result in unplanned credit extension remains to be seen. A reduction of such shipments would suggest that this source of debt will fall.

The important point here is that military shipments are usually made on credit. When default occurs it clouds the question of how much economic assistance is provided or should be provided by the USSR. Finally, it is unclear what kind of Soviet pressure can be exerted on LDCs to speed repayment in light of reduced cold war tensions.

Soviet critique of Soviet foreign aid

Very little is known about how the Soviet foreign aid mix is coordinated at the policy level, how decisions are made on allocations to each type of aid and to each recipient, and how judgments are made on aid effectiveness. The future of aid administration is under active consideration at the highest levels. Lacking direct evidence, for the moment it is only possible to speculate on anticipated changes to be made by looking at criticism of the present setup by Kortunov.[15]

Here are the highlights of existing problems at the policy level. There is no inventory of Soviet obligations to other countries, their legal basis, their political significance for the USSR, or their costs. Part of the reason for this is that commercial relations are mixed in the data with economic assistance. The Supreme Soviet ratifies a "package" of expenditures without discussion of specific programs and projects. In this matter it is suggested that the Supreme Soviet could shift part of the economic and humanitarian aid programs to non-governmental organizations, and voluntary funds and societies. There is little correlation of aid with Soviet internal conditions. There is little aid cooperation with the West, and with multilateral organizations.

Here are the highlights of existing problems at the administrative level, presented as steps which need to be taken from the Soviet perspective. There should be an independent organization to implement aid programs (remove it from the Ministry of Foreign Economic Affairs, which is more concerned with trade). This new organization should not become an uncontrollable bureaucracy, with departmental interests and secrecy. Resources for such an agency could come from state budget appropriations and from the budgets of the union republics, from the dues of public organizations (for example, the Committee for the Defense of Peace, the various committees of solidarity, and friendship societies), and, from individual contributions. Finally, state enterprises and cooperatives that have trade–production ties with developing countries could contribute their share. Additional resources for foreign aid should also be derived from new taxes.

There should be annual reports on the aid program, public hearings, and the like. The personnel system needs to be strengthened. Because

Soviet personnel in Africa fare less well than their counterparts at home, there must be a shake-up in compensation and perquisites. "Bureaucrats" who prefer a "quiet life" must be replaced. The Soviet Union needs not the "tens" of Africanists now working in this field, but "hundreds of thousands" of people who have a real professional interest and enthusiasm for Africa, or the Arab countries.

Soviet people must be informed about the importance of foreign aid for the poorest of the world. The new aid organization needs an effective consulting-information service about the economic and political situation in the aid-recipient countries, and about their ability to utilize what has been provided them. There is too much waste as equipment delivered as aid often simply rusts in ports, collects dust in warehouses, or is resold to other countries.

Cuba is of interest in both the West and the Soviet Union because it represents a special set of geopolitical and economic problems. Soviet public discussions of aid to Cuba tell us a great deal about the broader debate beginning to occur over Soviet foreign aid in general.

In the absence of systematic Soviet figures, we present CIA data on Cuban aid in Tables 5.3 and 5.4. In 1989 total USSR aid (the net transfer of economic resources from the Soviet Union to Cuba) was slightly over $4 billion (R1=$US1.59), with two-thirds of this in the form of trade subsidies. The subsidy was positive for sugar[16] but negative for petroleum. The price charged to Cuba for oil was based on a five-year moving average of the world price. In the early 1980s, this average was lower than the world price, so there was a net positive benefit to Cuba. By the mid-1980s this ratio was reversed, and the net benefit became negative. Unclassified data released by the CIA in November 1991 suggest a substantial downward revision of Soviet aid to Cuba, (see note to Table 5.3).

There is growing controversy over the effects of Cuban aid on the economy of the USSR. Here are some arguments *favoring Cuban aid* based on economics and political philosophy:

1 To produce 4 million tons of beet sugar (the amount supplied by Cuba) 1 million hectares of cultivated land would need to be cleared and about R8 billion would need to be invested.[17]

2 Cuba makes it unnecessary for the USSR to depend on the "limited free market of sugar." If the Soviet Union were to begin buying in the world market, prices would certainly increase to four or five times the present $211 per ton (most sugar is sold according to fixed quotas and at preferential prices, i.e. above world prices). And payment would have to be made in dollars, just as would be the case for nickel, which is also purchased in Cuba.[18]

Table 5.3. USSR net economic aid disbursed to communist LDCs, 1980–1989 ($US millions)

Dollar/Ruble Exchange Rate	1.54	1.39	1.38	1.35	1.23	1.20	1.42	1.58	1.65	1.59
	1980	1981	1982	1983	1984	1985	1986	1987	1988	1989
Total economic assistance	5,330	6,478	7,042	7,145	7,197	7,671	6,821	7,775	6,879	6,388
Economic Aid	2,388	3,230	3,099	3,842	3,315	3,468	4,719	5,038	4,905	4,234
Development Aid	1,358	1,181	1,422	1,440	1,361	1,519	1,825	2,176	1,949	1,848
Other Trade Credits	760	1,758	1,387	2,112	1,664	1,659	2,554	2,522	2,617	2,104
Technical Services	219	240	240	240	240	240	290	291	290	277
Grants	50	50	50	50	50	50	50	50	50	24
Price subsidies	2,943	3,248	3,943	3,303	3,882	4,202	2,102	2,737	1,973	2,154
Cuba										
Total	3,243	4,253	4,871	4,994	5,152	5,300	4,384	5,012	4,344	4,159
Economic Aid	906	1,371	1,058	1,725	1,280	1,057	1,737	1,605	1,576	1,447
Development Aid	542	453	446	521	490	473	531	649	663	636
Other Trade Credits	214	767	462	1,054	641	434	1,005	755	713	620
Technical Services	149	150	150	150	150	150	200	201	200	191
Trade Subsidies	2,338	2,883	3,813	3,268	3,872	4,243	2,647	3,406	2,769	2,713
Sugar	1,167	1,389	2,632	2,696	3,565	4,259	4,425	4,941	4,929	4,484
Oil	1,161	1,366	1,039	436	210	-138	-1,930	-1,640	-2,160	-1,771
Nickel	9	128	142	136	97	122	152	106	0	0
Vietnam										
Total	939	1,120	1,000	1,040	1,040	1,160	1,325	1,575	1,366	1,109
Economic Aid	580	900	950	1,025	1,040	1,180	1,581	1,920	1,782	1,480
Development Aid	178	142	188	227	228	311	422	611	447	390
Other Trade Credits	282	633	637	673	687	744	1,034	1,183	1,209	995
Technical Services	70	75	75	75	75	75	75	75	75	72
Grants	50	50	50	50	50	50	50	50	50	24
Oil Subsidies	355	220	50	15	0	-20	-256	-344	-416	-371

Mongolia

Total	835	830	885	885	785	918	905	991	987	886
Economic Aid	770	765	865	880	785	929	1,048	1,183	1,210	981
Development Aid	552	503	662	635	568	600	704	796	716	708
Other Trade Credits	218	247	188	240	202	314	329	371	479	259
Technical Services	0	15	15	15	15	15	15	15	15	14
Oil Services	65	65	20	5	0	−11	−143	−191	−223	−95

North Korea

Total	260	145	130	40	55	93	6	−33	−41	−0
Economic Aid	75	65	70	25	45	103	124	62	63	48
Development Aid	75	65	70	25	45	103	124	62	63	65
Oil Subsidies	185	80	60	15	10	−10	−118	−95	−104	−48

Cambodia

Total	0	81	70	86	87	98	128	134	137	159
Economic Aid	0	81	70	86	87	98	149	160	170	186
Development Aid	0	0	26	12	12	11	21	28	38	40
Other Trade Credits	0	81	44	74	75	88	128	131	132	146
Oil Subsidies	0	na	na	na	na	na	−21	−25	−33	−27

Laos

Total	57	49	86	100	77	101	74	95	86	75
Economic Aid	57	49	86	100	77	101	81	109	106	92
Development Aid	11	18	30	30	18	22	23	28	21	10
Other Trade Credits	46	31	55	70	59	79	58	81	84	83
Oil Subsidies	na	na	na	na	na	na	−7	−14	−20	−17

Note: New preliminary unclassified data available in November 1991 suggest that Soviet aid to Cuba was considerably less than that indicated by previously available figures, and that aid in 1991 declined precipitously. These lower revised Cuban aid figures since 1986 are as follows, in millions of US$: 1986 − 3,380; 1987 − 3,645; 1988 − 3,200; 1989 − 3,590; 1990 − 3,980; 1991 − 1,000. Figure for 1991 is based on fragmentary information.

Table 5.4. *USSR trade and aid relationships with Cuba, 1984–1988*

	(Transaction prices (million rubles))				
	1984	1985	1986	1987	1988
Soviet exports	4,383	4,897	4,883	4,716	4,820
oil	1,955	2,279	2,298	2,162	2,148
wheat	155	159	100	73	103
machinery and equipment	1,030	1,058	1,105	1,113	1,190
unspecified	410	480	464	471	485
other	833	921	916	897	894
Soviet imports	3,464	4,140	3,800	3,827	3,900
sugar	3,226	3,867	3,531	3,554	3,540
nickel	166	190	185	192	209
other	72	83	84	81	151
Dollar/Ruble exchange rate	1.23	1.2	1.42	1.58	1.65
	(Transaction prices ($US million) calculated)				
Soviet exports	5,391	5,876	6,934	7,451	7,953
oil	2,405	2,735	3,263	3,416	3,544
wheat	191	191	142	115	170
machinery and equipment	1,267	1,270	1,569	1,759	1,964
unspecified	504	576	659	744	800
other	1,025	1,105	1,301	1,417	1,475
Soviet imports	4,261	4,968	5,396	6,047	6,435
sugar	3,968	4,640	5,014	5,615	5,841
nickel	204	228	263	303	345
other	89	100	119	128	249
	(World prices ($US million))				
Soviet exports	5,601	5,738	5,004	5,811	5,793
Hard goods	2,805	2,788	1,475	1,891	1,554
oil	2,615	2,597	1,333	1,776	1,384
wheat	191	191	142	115	170
Soft goods	2,796	2,951	3,529	3,920	4,239
machinery and equipment	1,267	1,270	1,569	1,759	1,964
unspecified	504	576	659	744	800
other	1,025	1,105	1,301	1,417	1,475
Soviet imports	599	588	819	999	1,507
Hard goods	510	488	700	871	1,258
sugar	403	382	589	674	913
nickel	107	106	111	197	345
Soft goods	89	100	119	128	249
Total assistance	5,152	5,300	4,383	5,011	4,345

Source: Unpublished CIA data. There is no military component in these figures. The CIA
definition of Soviet economic assistance to Cuba is: *sum* of Soviet exports to Cuba
at world prices *less sum* of Soviet imports from Cuba at world prices *plus* grants and
technical assistance.

3 Sergei Tarasenko, head of the Assessment and Planning Department of the USSR Ministry of Foreign Affairs, wrote in December of 1989 that it is true that the USSR pays Cuba four times the world price for sugar, but he asks: can Kortunov (see below) name a country where 4 million tons of sugar (a third of USSR needs) can be bought at the going world price for Soviet rubles? He adds sarcastically that if the purchase is made in Moscow, one must first obtain a sugar ration card.[19]

4 Tarasenko notes that citrus fruits can also be bought on the free market, but there they could not be exchanged for the "notoriously poor quality Soviet engineering products." Cuba provides 40 percent of Soviet citrus fruits.

5 Cuba provides a sixth of Soviet requirements for nickel and cobalt concentrate, according to Tarasenko. Among other things, he suggests that this makes it unnecessary "to build a new factory above the arctic circle where this concentrate would cost its weight in gold."

6 Soviet merchant ships are serviced in Cuban ports. In 1988 this saved 318 million rubles worth of hard currency, according to Tarasenko. Four million rubles are saved in repairing fishing vessels. Aeroflot saves R12 million a year using Cuban airports.

7 Tarasenko suggests that the frequent Cuban gifts to the USSR (disposable syringes, medical equipment, wheelchairs, school computers, sports gear, paintings, and libraries), show that the Soviet Union appreciates receiving things from abroad, so the USSR should give aid as well. Sergo Mikoyan, the editor-in-chief of *Latin America* (in Russian), asks whether it is the "Afghan syndrome" which is leading the USSR to question foreign aid.[20] Moreover, the USSR should never betray its friends.

Here are some of the arguments *opposing Cuban aid* suggested by Andrei Kortunov.[21]

1 While it is true that the USSR does not pay for sugar in hard currency the high price (four times world level) could be better used at home. For example, according to Kortunov many Soviet agrarian economists suggest that if this price were paid to Soviet producers, they would have eliminated the domestic sugar deficit in just a few years.

2 The so-called "currency saving" on Cuban sugar is misleading. It has to be balanced against the cost of the fuel, grain, and raw materials sent to Cuba rather than being sold for hard currency on the world market.

3 The idea of profitable economic relations with Cuba has to be questioned in light of Cuba's debt to the USSR estimated at $10–12 billion.

4 A staff correspondent noted in *Izvestia* on 14 July 1990 that Soviet

imports of Cuban sugar had grown so high that Cuba buys sugar from a French company on credit to meet the demand. In turn the USSR guarantees its debt, which exposes it to the double risk of paying for the sugar twice – with oil to Cuba and hard currency to the French. He notes that "this is utterly absurd," although he adds, apparently tongue in cheek, that he could be mistaken since L. I. Abalkin, a prominent economist, considers such operations to be "standard practice." Abalkin, who is Vice-Chairman of the USSR Council of Ministers, recently negotiated an agreement to extend Soviet aid for another five years with the starting date to be in early 1991.[22]

5 The argument that aid serves Soviet foreign and military policy is questionable in light, for example, of Cuba's recent vitriolic criticism of perestroika.

6 Alexei Izyumov, an economist, sides with Kortunov, suggesting that the main criticisms are that aid often is not very effective, it is often granted to countries which need it less, and the military component is too large. In addition, aid is allocated behind the scenes, "without the participation of the Supreme Soviet – to say nothing of the people."[23]

While this debate is not what might be called high economics, it is a useful window onto the increasing struggle to introduce economic rationality into Soviet international relations.

In the absence of direct evidence of changes in the administration of foreign aid, it is tempting to speculate on whether the reorganization of the foreign trade apparatus tells us anything about the possible reorganization of Soviet foreign aid. At the moment, the prospects do not look promising.

An economist, Vladimir Kuznetsov, in late 1989 summarized what might be termed the "liberal critique" of trade administration.[24] He noted that even after three years of reform raw materials have grown as a percentage of total exports. The foreign debt is reaching what he called "ominous proportions," and he suggests that if this trend continues Soviet debt payments may exceed both export and non-commercial revenues.

Basically, he contends that the remaining administrative system of foreign trade "suffocates any attempts at a market system." For example, when there are shortages of everything, enterprises typically shun the ruble preferring to earn hard currency by selling their product at give-away prices. To prevent this, and to keep the domestic market from collapsing, the state is introducing licensing of most exports, excluding some industrial machinery and technology. (Soviet exports of these items are payable in hard currency and account for less than 3 percent of total exports.) However, the obvious need for licensing goods needed on the domestic market is being used to sharply increase the monopoly of specialized foreign trade organizations run by the ministries. Having been granted multiple licenses, these organizations thrust their go-between services on enterprises which have been denied licenses by the ministries. This monopoly was finally sealed, in Kuznetsov's view, when state-run, cooperative, and joint ventures were told they could not act as go-betweens in foreign trade deals, and independent trade enterprises were forced to "coordinate" their export prices with specialized foreign trade amalgamations.

Another illustration of the failure to introduce market elements in the administrative system is the decision to evaluate the results of export operations on the basis of foreign trade prices calculated in rubles using differentiated hard currency indices. The attempt to "import" market prices (even if they have been "corrected" by the indices) has clashed with the administrative system of pricing based on expenditures of individual Soviet producers. Enterprises which export their product on the basis of commands from above naturally demand compensation for the manufacture of the product. As a result, the manufacturer of export items today, as in the past, is reimbursed for expenses plus a specified share of the income. If export revenues exceed established norms, the money goes to the state budget. In other words, a paying concern gives away part of its profit to pay for the losses of unprofitable enterprises. Kuznetsov concluded that the absurdity of this approach is obvious. In effect, the domestic economy remains essentially closed.

In August of 1989 the Minister of Foreign Economic Relations (Katushev) noted that while Soviet enterprises and cooperatives now have the right to operate directly in world markets that "does not mean that the Soviet Ministry of Foreign Economic Relations is no longer necessary."[25] "For example," he states, "someone has to draw up plans of foreign economic relations, to regulate the export of goods of national importance, which account for 52 percent of our exports, as well as imports financed from centralized funds."

This view from the center seems reminiscent of the conditions which prompted Nikoli Bukharin in the 1920s to label the Ministry of Foreign Trade "Glavzapor" – Main Administration for Constipation. Interestingly, the policy and execution of foreign aid would seem to be a "natural" for considerable centralization. For example, there is no single, unified foreign aid program in education. Instead, one program is under the Ministry of Foreign Affairs, another is under the Ministry of Education, and yet a third is under the "Fund for Foreign Students in the USSR." As a result, among other things, there is no single set of data which expresses the total Soviet financial commitment to Third

World education. As an aside, much of the data available are in terms of aid in kind – schools built, teachers trained, etc. Consolidated financial accounts need to be established so that the economic costs of these programs can be understood. This will also be important externally as the USSR seeks membership in international organizations which will request this kind of information.

Possibly the kind of reorganization suggested by Kortunov (above) is being delayed by the same forces of administrative inertia that impede in general full implementation of the law on enterprises promulgated in 1987. It remains to be seen whether the 500-day plan, or its successors, will change any of this.

Speculation on a revised Soviet foreign aid program

What changes might be made in Soviet foreign aid, and how will those changes affect the usefulness of Soviet aid in the Third World? Here are a few permissible speculations in light of what is required for LDCs and what the Soviet Union is capable of supplying.

Current Third World strategy emphasizes agricultural development, efficient industry (particularly small-scale industry) to provide high-quality, low-cost agricultural inputs and consumer goods, and assistance for breaking into world export markets. The Soviet Union has limited positive experience in any of this, and is therefore not well placed to provide assistance for these purposes.

Because Soviet capital requirements will drive policy for decades to come, concessional lending and grants will be under great pressure. It is already clear that Soviet direct contributions to Third World development are to be reduced.

The decades-old Soviet dream of industrializing its export balance continues to be elusive, and Soviet manufactured goods as aid have not yet begun to make possible increased Third World manufactured exports to the Soviet Union in significant quantities. In the most needy part of the world – Sub-Saharan Africa – the USSR has been a minor trader and aider, so to speak. Soviet exports were about 1 percent of African imports and Soviet imports were about 2 percent of African exports. With the exception of one country (Mozambique), the Soviet economy as it stands today is somewhat irrelevant to African problems.

Despite some changes, Soviet imports and exports remain administered flows, with the domestic economy essentially isolated from the world economy. The central issue can be described at the "agency problem." No changes have yet been made which significantly free actual importers and exporters to make their own decisions, and yet the techniques by which the bureaucratic center attempts to influence the operating officers in trade organizations remain clumsy and economically dysfunctional. The practical importance of this for Soviet foreign aid is that under perestroika such aid will be carried out by cost accounting enterprises. If such enterprises remain constrained administratively, they will act bureaucratically in both trade and aid decisions. The problem remains of encouraging an enterprise which can earn foreign exchange by exporting to become interested in participating in a foreign aid program. In effect, it is unclear whether under existing circumstances the administration of Soviet aid can in fact be "reformed" as suggested by Soviet critics.

The growing Soviet participation in multilateral and bilateral aid reflects not only the "de-ideologization" of Soviet foreign policy. It may also reflect the fact that as resource constraints increase, the small remaining amounts of Soviet aid can be used as a lever to greater political as well as economic effect in concert with others rather than bilaterally. Further, it also means that as Soviet scholars become more aligned with Western analyses of Third World problems the pool of economists able to assist the Third World will be enlarged.

In a curious way, one aspect of earlier Soviet foreign aid thinking may be retained. Japan is the largest country donor, and there is the suggestion (in a report to the Finance Ministry by an advisory group in June 1990, headed by former Finance Vice-Minister Tomomitsu Ohba) that LDCs would be well advised to follow the Japanese model of development in which a strong government takes the lead in partnership with private business to advance selected industrial sectors. The importance of this approach for Soviet policy is that it gives credence to those remaining Soviet scholars who continue to insist that the government play a leading role in development despite the now common understanding that government's role should be reduced.

Conclusion

Foreign aid represents a decision to use resources abroad rather than domestically. In this sense, all foreign aid is political – it involves trade-offs in a political process between groups with different agendas. At the same time, every country has two political constituencies – domestic and international. For this reason, even though the Soviet economy is in acute difficulty, one can expect a continued if reduced Soviet foreign aid program. Economic difficulties, however, will force this aid away from grants and increasingly into credit flows which have a payoff for the Soviet economy itself. Unfortunately, it may be that such flows will be of little help to the poorest LDCs because those countries are not in a position to generate the kinds of payback exports to the Soviet Union required for the furtherance of perestroika – namely, manufactured goods.

There is a further anomaly here. While Soviet economists now seem to agree with Western prescriptions for LDCs, many reject conditionality as an infringement on the sovereignty of those countries. If this means that Soviet aid will flow only to those countries with *existing* good economic policies, then the very poorest may be excluded because these very countries in many cases suffer from the least effective economic leadership.

In one of many poignant moments at the IV World Congress of Soviet and East European Studies in Harrogate, England, in the summer of 1990, a senior and well-known Soviet economist (Georgi Mirsky) revealed in a sentence the turmoil among Soviet students of the Third World. "Nobody gives a damn about socialist orientation any more," he said. Further, the concept was invented by Soviet scholars in an attempt to catch up with policy already in place, and to provide *ex post* a rationale for Soviet policy. In a word, reorientation of the Soviet aid program will be as difficult as reorientation of the Soviet economy because the previous philosophic and ideological underpinnings of each have disappeared.

Soviet perspectives on foreign aid and development have changed significantly over the last five years. The question is, has this new approach made any difference in Soviet foreign aid practice? The answer for the time being is no, not much. Soviet specialists suggest that fundamental change will need to wait on fuller implementation of perestroika (they also say this about Soviet foreign trade in general). The design problem faced in all Soviet aid is illustrated by what a Soviet correspondent speaking of Cuba called "the fundamental contradiction between the political goals and the economic interests of [Soviet] ties."[26]

In sum, over the near term (3–5 years) the effects of perestroika will be to reduce aid flows, and the associated military shipments almost certainly will be cut sharply. Although it is too early to say, reduced East–West tensions may permit the Soviets to concentrate more on economic assistance to needy countries, with less attention paid to cold war allies (this may mirror a similar opportunity for Western powers). Accounting and economic evaluation of Soviet trade and aid will improve, and there will be more cooperation with other donors, especially in the scientific and environmental fields.[27]

*   *   *

In the wake of the summer coup collapse, the future of the Soviet Union remains unpredictable, and along with it the future of Soviet foreign aid. President Yeltsin has said that his republic (RSFSR) does not intend to provide aid abroad, and the leadership attitude in the other republics may be similar. Yet, when the crisis over, and these same republics enter the world political mainstream, they will be under pressure once again to respond to the needs of the impoverished, especially in places such as Sub-Saharan Africa, and possibly in those countries in which the USSR along with the US played a role in peace settlements. When economic stability returns, most Soviet republics will be seen as fairly prosperous and in some cases very well endowed with natural resources. Pleading their relative poverty in the face of absolute poverty in less-developed countries will weaken any leadership role the republics might seek to play on the world stage. Moreover, the Eastern European market for Soviet machinery and equipment has dried up, and maintenance of the Third World market for these products may require some kind of preferential trade credits. Also, in Cuba and elsewhere, Soviet republics may be in a position to supply manpower as assistance to some countries, although such aid to Cuba might be excluded in the face of US opposition.

Total aid to non-Communist developing countries in 1991 may only be $1–1.5 billion, perhaps half the level of 1990. Future assistance from the former USSR, as it is now called, may be determined by the individual nations now emerging in that region.

Notes

1. Except as noted otherwise, this account of changing perspectives and practices of Soviet aid draws on Richard Feinberg and Rachik M. Avokov (eds.), (*U.S. and Soviet Aid to Developing Countries: From Confrontation to Cooperation?*, Washington: Overseas Development Council, 1991) and the writer's three meetings, one in Washington in 1987 and one each in Moscow in 1988 and 1989, with Soviet scholars from the Institute for World Economy and International Relations of the USSR Academy of Sciences, and The American University. Several summaries of Soviet thinking on the Third World are available from Western scholars: Stephen Clarkson, *The Soviet Theory of Development*, Toronto, University of Toronto Press, 1978; Elizabeth Kridl Valkenier, *The Soviet Union and the Third World: an Economic Bind*, New York, Praeger, 1983; Jerry F. Hough, *The Struggle for the Third World: Soviet Debates and American Options*, Washington, The Brookings Institution, 1986; Francis Fukuyama, *Moscow's Post-Brezhnev*

84   *W. Donald Bowles*

.

OK

.

Reassessment of the Third World, Santa Monica, The Rand Corporation, 1986; David E. Albright, *Soviet Policy Toward Africa Revisited*, Washington, The Center for Strategic and International Studies, 1987; Giovanni Graziani, *Economic Strategy in the Third World*, New York, Praeger, 1990 published for the Center for Strategic and International Studies in Washington.

2. OECD, *Development Cooperation, 1989 Report*, Paris, OECD, 1989. US Congress, Report of the Task Force on Foreign Assistance to the Committee on Foreign Affairs, *U.S. House of Representatives*, Washington, Government Printing Office, February 1989.
3. Central Intelligence Agency, *Handbook of Economic Statistics 1989*, Washington, CIA, 1989.
4. Richard Feinberg and Rachik M. Avakov (eds.), *U.S. and Soviet Aid to Developing Countries: From Confrontation to Cooperation?*, Washington, Overseas Development Council, 1991.
5. It is difficult to reconcile this figure with Western estimates of the Soviet GNP, although this need not detain us here. Suffice it to say that this very high estimate requires clarification.
6. *Moscow News*, no. 49, 1989.
7. *Izvestia*, 27 September 1989.
8. *The New York Times*, 14 June 1990.
9. *The New York Times*, 4 September 1990.
10. *Izvestia*, 16 August 1989.
11. Konovalov, "Soviet Arms Trade," *USSR* July–August 1990, (London, 1980), p. 62.
12. Cited in Konovalov.
13. *Izvestia*, 24 July 1990.
14. Interview in *Business in the USSR*, July–August 1990, pp. 60–61.
15. *Trud*, 15 February 1990.
16. The calculation for sugar can involve more than is considered in the CIA calculation (A. Zimbalist, *The Cuban Economy: Measurement and Analysis of Socialist Performance*, Baltimore, Maryland: The Johns Hopkins Press, 1989, ch. 7). A relatively small proportion of world sugar is actually sold at free world market prices (less than a fifth). In effect, preferential prices for most sugar cause world supply to be greater and world demand to be lower than would be the case under free market conditions. In effect, the world price is lower than the scarcity price, which means that the CIA figures on the sugar subsidy could be adjusted downward.
17. *Moscow News*, no. 7, 1990.
18. Ibid.
19. *Moscow News*, no. 52, 1989.
20. *Moscow News*, no. 7, 1990.
21. *Moscow News*, no. 49, 1989.
22. *Izvestia*, 14 July 1990.
23. *Moscow News*, no.7, 1990.
24. *Moscow News*, no. 51, 1989.
25. Tass Radio, 25 July 1989, cited in *FBIS-SOV-89-157*, 16 August 1989, pp. 85–86.

26. *Izvestia*, 14 July 1990.
27. The possibilities for cooperative action look promising, as discussed in W. Donald Bowles and Elena Arefieva, *Tripartite Projects: Proposals for Joint U.S.-U.S.S.R. Cooperation with Developing Countries*, Washington, Overseas Development Council, 1990; and Anatoly A. Gromyko and C. S. Whitaker (eds.), *Agenda for Action: African-Soviet-U.S. Cooperation*, Boulder, Colorado, Lynne Reiner Publishers, 1990.

6 Features and trends of East Germany's aid and trade with the Third World

Siegfried Schultz

East Germany used to target its development aid very specifically; this applied to individual countries as well as to sectors.[1] The main emphasis of both the aid program and trade relations focused on socialist countries. A constant feature was the sometimes substantial fluctuation in the volume of trade flows. Since East Germany failed to publish any comprehensive figures on aid and the trade data were truncated, the West had to rely on estimates.

Depictions of the development policy of the German Democratic Republic (GDR) and its foreign trade relations with the Third World have always been burdened with great uncertainties. With respect to aid, the GDR had problems with unbiased statistical coverage of its aid program. After entry to the UN, and because of the pressure for disclosure and justification this entailed, the GDR orientated itself toward the categories of the UN system.

There was as good as no exchange of information between the various ministries and no clear mutual understanding. Development cooperation did not have its own budget allocations, it was for the most part financed from other budgets. For this reason a complete yearly balance for development aid was not drawn up. There was just as little evaluation and little by way of a more comprehensive annual report, although this was increasingly felt to be a deficiency. The lack of information also had a negative effect on research which was based extensively on speculative data.

Concerning the GDR's foreign trade, the state monopoly was a regulatory feature of the economic system. The monopoly served to guarantee the coordination and planning of foreign trade by the state. Basically, only special state enterprises, authorized by the then Ministry for Foreign Trade, had the right to handle foreign trade transactions on their own. However, the state trade monopoly and the strict bilaterally arranged foreign trade activity, in the interest of tight planning and control, continued to hinder the foreign trade sector.

The role of foreign trade as an instrument for growth was only discovered late. Until then it had had purely compensatory functions: imports were supposed to serve to procure any resources missing and to bridge gaps in the assortment (deficiency-compensating function). Exports were viewed as a necessary evil for the financing of desired imports. Also, the preeminence of politics influenced foreign trade. Basically, precedence was given to trade with other socialist countries. A comprehensive analysis of foreign trade relations has been impossible because detailed figures were only published for around a dozen selected countries.

As regards the GDR's development aid, there was plenty of scope for speculative comment on its volume and quality. This also applied to the transitional period until the establishment of a single German development policy. With respect to trade, the picture one may draw on the basis of published data must necessarily be incomplete. One of the main reasons for hiding part of the tansactions is assumed to have been the provision of military equipment.

Development aid

East Germany first submitted figures to the United Nations on its development aid in 1982.[2] According to these, East German aid amounted to 1.5 billion marks in 1981 and, following yearly increases of 5 to 10 percent, contributed somewhat over 2.2 billion marks in 1988. (For a compilation of the East German data published on aid and trade, see Table 6.1.) In 1986 the government of the GDR charged the former State Plan Commission with the development of a concept which would regulate the integrated coordination and accounting of the GDR's aid contributions to developing countries (by means of the state budget, the Solidarity Committee of the GDR,[3] and social organizations), and which would set down the corresponding responsibilities. Following on from the experiences gathered in this coordination and accounting, rules were decided upon at the end of 1988 by the cabinet of ministers for the coordination and accounting of aid contributions.

The State Plan Commission then undertook the coordination and accounting of all the activities of state and social organizations (more than sixty in number) involved in the GDR's aid programs. For this purpose, the aid contributions to developing countries were categorized as shown in Table 6.3.

Preferential prices for certain manufactures and products, which were paid on the basis of corresponding agreements, as well as credit on concessional terms were made available to countries such as Cuba, Vietnam, Cambodia, Laos, Mongolia, and Nicaragua.

Table 6.1. *The GDR's aid contributions to developing countries and national liberation movements; foreign trade*

	Unit	1981	1982	1983	1984	1985	1986	1987	1988	1989
I. Financial support[a]	Mill.M	1,530	1,588	1,662	1,820	2,001	2,243	2,323	2,207	
(of which to LLDC[b])	Mill.M		259	243		283				
Change over previous year	%		(3.8)	5.0	9.5	9.9	12.1	(3.6)	(−5.0)	
Share of NMP	%	0.78	0.79	0.79	0.82	0.86	0.89	0.89	0.64	
Share of GNP	%							0.70		
(LLDC share of NMP)	%		0.13	0.12		0.12				
A. Disaster aid[c]	Mill.M				90	100				
B. Personnel aid										
Foreign worker agreements	persons						11,904	47,000	78,000	86,650
Professional training[d]	persons	12,827	4,222	6,522	7,558	10,973	7,897	6,548	6,889	4,927
(of which from LLDC)	persons									
Started	persons							2,892	2,958	
Completed	persons	5,088			10,465	8,993		3,046	3,883	
(of which from LLDC)	persons	807	805	838		898	637	1,040	1,115	1,073
Trained since 1970[e]	persons	50,000	54,000	60,500	71,000	80,000	88,000	91,000		
Attending at year's end	persons	26,488	29,249	29,157	26,247	27,647	29,474	3,645	2,643	
Graduate & postgraduate training (including technical schools[f])	persons								9,407	6,802
(of which from LLDC)	persons	31%								2,528
Started	persons	2,062	1,435	1,562	2,352	2,615	2,821	1,971	2,901	
Completed	persons	1,519			1,753	2,126	2,039	1,979	1,927	
(of which from LLDC)	persons		450	518		743	648	604	1,815	
Graduates since 1970[g]	persons	13,000	14,500	16,050	17,800	19,900	21,900	23,900		
Attending at year's end	persons	5,709	5,951	6,573	7,388	7,500	8,073	7,382	7,575	
UN courses for DCs' experts partic.	persons					330	200	250		

GDR experts and advisers[h]	persons							
(of which to LLDC)	persons	32%	32%	32%		33%		
Total since 1970	persons	20,000	20,800	21,600	22,600	23,000		25,100
Sent during the year	persons	954	814	793	788	1,031	990	832
Number at year's end	persons	1,156	970	996	881	1,538	1,503	1,160
Medical care for DCs' citizens[i]	patients	889	740	1,244	1,033	1,046	1,174	1,059
(of which from LLDC)	patients				306	317	348	237
Total since 1970	patients	2,850	3,500	4,400	5,140	6,400	7,400	8,400
II. Foreign trade with developing countries								
Turnover	Mill. VM[j]				14,945	14,127	12,956	12,495
(of which with LLDC)	Mill. VM[j]							297
Change over previous year	%	4.7	1.4		7.8		(−8.3)	(−3.6)
Share of total turnover	%	9.2	8.6			7.8	7.3	7.0
Finished and semi-finished goods' imports: share of total imports from developing countries	%	40.0	35.8		41.5	43.3		34.4
Change over previous year	%					6.3	1.8	
Installations: under construction	number	67	79	72		75	59	66
agreed	number		72	68	33	28	19	30
handed over	number		16	25	12	32	26	
Licence contracts concluded	number	65	80	78	66	66		50

Notes: [a] Bi- and multilateral. [b] 1970–80 more than 285 mill.M in material aid. [c] Ethiopia. [d] 1988 47,394 man-months. [e] Until 1979: 40,000. [f] 1988 85,553 man-months. [g] Until 1979: 10,000. [h] 1988 11,469 man-months. [i] 1988 2,063 man-months. [j] 1981–89 one Valuta-Mark equalled US$ 0.2971, 0.2947, 0.2881, 0.2625, 0.2555, 0.3041, 0.3382, 0.3473, 0.3397. These data on turnover are not directly comparable with the data published in the Statistical Yearbook. The above data are adjusted for CMEA members and 'socialist' countries.

Sources: 'Außenpolitische Korrespondenz' (Ministry for Foreign Affairs), various issues; UN General Assembly or UNCTAD conference documents, respectively; results of GDR Round Table talks, modified using West German estimates.

Table 6.2. *Contributions of the Solidarity committee, by type (in thousand Marks)*

	1988	percent	1989	percent
1 Education	112,561.4	52.6	81,057.6	38.9
2 Material deliveries[a]	86,861.0	40.7	114,033.7	54.7
3 Transportation	6,500.0	3.0	5,982.3	2.9
4 Information, advertising and administration costs	1,817.9	0.9	1,777.0	0.9
5 Therapeutic treatment and care of children	3,050.0	1.4	2,818.8	1.3
6 Other areas	3,071.1	1.4	2,654.5	1.3
Total expenditure	213,861.4	100	208,323.9	100

Note: [a] Including emergency aid (given in the form of goods deliveries, means of transport and medical care.)
Source: "Inter-Aktion." Documentation of the GDR Round Table on Development Policy. Evangelische Akademie Berlin–Brandenburg, March 1990.

Table 6.3. *Categories of aid contributions*

	1989, preliminary (in mill. GDR Mark)
1 Contributions free of charge	383.1
Material deliveries and contributions (Ministry for Material Economics; Solidarity Committee)	87.8
Professional training and further education (State Secretariat for Professional Training)	72.6
Training at Universities and technical schools (Ministry for Higher Education and Technical Schools, Ministry for Foreign Affairs)	101.9
Dispatch of experts on the basis of scientific and technical cooperation (Ministry for Foreign Trade) and cultural and scientific cooperation (Ministry for Foreign Affairs)	65.8
Medical care (Ministry for Health)	9.9
Governmental donations	39.7
Voluntary UN contributions	5.4
2 Deliveries at preferential prices (concessional element)	712.1
3 Governmental and special credit (concessional element)	813.9

Of the GDR's *free* aid contributions between the years 1986 and 1989 50 percent are supposed to have been financed from state budget, 45 percent from the Solidarity Committee's fund, and 5 percent from the fund of the "social" organizations. The hard currency necessary in the context of transportation was made available to all aid-contributing organizations exclusively from the state budget.

Of the *total* expenditure on aid contributions in the same period, around 89 percent is said to have been financed by means of the state budget and 11 percent by means of the Solidarity Committee's and other "social" organizations' funds.

These statements are noteworthy in that East Germany had previously been extremely reticent in naming any figures with the result that, for a long time, its aid could not be quantitatively compared at all with that of other states. It could not, however, be ascertained from the official data for the volume of aid, what exactly these totals consisted of and whether they just reflected commitments or actual disbursements. All that was explained was that East German aid was used to support independent states and liberation movements in the Third World. Quite apart from the problem of choosing a suitable exchange rate,[4] a direct comparison with the West's performance in the field of development aid was not possible for the following reasons:

> in the West aid payments are usually calculated by subtracting repayments from gross expenditure (net payments);
>
> "development aid" in OECD country reports includes credit concessions and gifts, but not trade credit and financial credit under market conditions;
>
> military support does not count as development aid.[5]

In view of the all too scarce information from East German sources it seems reasonable to use Western estimates for cross-checking. According to the data in the OECD Chairman's Report of the Development Assistance Committee (DAC) on the world-wide provision of development aid, East German aid had developed as follows (in millions of $US):

1970–71	1975–76	1980–81	1987–88
(156)	135	245	184

Official East German sources contained few concrete facts about the conditions attached to this aid. What they did reveal amounted to little more than the claim that the conditions were to the recipients' advantage. According to Western literature, long-term reconstruction loans offered by East Germany and the other CMEA members ran for approximately eight to fifteen years and at an interest rate of 2.5 percent to 3 percent. The conditions attached to commercial loans were stricter in comparison (4–5 percent interest). The grace period usually was one year, i.e. the obligation to repay generally came into effect a year after the completion of the project. It was to the developing countries' benefit if they were able to make agreements whereby repayments were made in the goods manufactured with the equipment received on a credit basis, or with other (even traditional) goods produced by the recipient country. There is little information available about regulations according to which a part of the repayment had to be made in convertible currency. Alternatively, the settling of financial relations between trading partners could be achieved by using a currency agreed upon for accounting purposes (bilateral clearing). As a rule, repayments were strictly tied to procurement from the donor country. This occurred more or less automatically when the aid was provided in kind; when payments were made in money the lack of convertibility led to the same outcome.

The personnel sector as a focus for aid

The strengthening and support of state planning in developing countries was a prime objective in the East German aid program. Professional training and further on-the-job training formed a traditionally strong branch of East German activities. Quite often, such training constituted part of the setting up of industrial production plants.[6] But adult education and the building up of mass media were also supported. This kind of assistance comprised both longer-term professional training and short-term measures (specific instruction courses, summer courses, seminars, courses of practical work, etc.). The forms that such support took ranged from the further education of student trainees and the retraining or ongoing education of future "cadres" from developing countries, the provision of student places in East German technical colleges and universities, to sending out their own experts. The main professional groups were doctors and other medical personnel, lecturers, teachers, engineers, technicians, and agricultural experts. Also there were training programs implemented by the party and other mass organizations such as trade unions, the FDJ, and consumer cooperatives that provided training in their institutions or sent advisers abroad. In this context, the FDJ Youth Brigades which worked under difficult circumstances and with a high degree of personal motivation in up to eleven countries should also be mentioned. Another section of the advisory activities of East German experts was devoted to the area of security, i.e. the police and the military – an area fairly unknown as regards the number of people involved and the ultimate effect of the effort.

As with all CMEA countries, the larger part of East German aid went to socialist or socialist-orientated developing countries. Relations to

developing countries within CMEA were, for political reasons, different
in nature to relations with Third World countries. East Germany also
used to maintain special relations with those countries which were following a "socialist path of development" (a category that had been
suspended in the recent past). Since the material support of the
economically backward CMEA members (Cuba, Mongolia, and
Vietnam) took political priority – according to OECD estimates, four-
fifths of total CMEA aid went to these countries – there was little room
for maneuver with what remained. The focal points in East German aid
to non-CMEA developing countries partly corresponded to the activities of the other CMEA states,[7] and were partly evidence of a certain
division of labor within that political group. Thus a concentration of
East German attention was to be observed on African countries (in
particular Angola, Ethiopia, and Mozambique) as well as the Middle
East or Arab countries. Of course, Afghanistan, Nicaragua, Yemen
(PR), the PLO, SWAPO, and the ANC should also be mentioned. To a
more limited extent there was some provision of aid to Congo, Zambia,
Mali, Madagascar, and Benin. (For estimates on the basis of partner
country statistics, see Table 6.4.)

As a relatively new means of repayment for received loans a few,
particularly poor, recipient countries (e.g. Vietnam) sent – mostly
unskilled – workers to the GDR under foreign worker agreements,
usually on a five-year basis.

A change of attitude toward the UN target

It had already been decided for the second UN development decade
(1971–80) that each developed country should transfer 1 percent of its
gross national product (GNP) annually to developing countries; a further target was that aid on concessional terms from the government
sector should be at least 0.7 percent of GNP. For many years East
Germany – as well as the other CMEA members – had ignored this
target and basically rejected the idea of a "development tax."[8] If one
follows UN reports, there had been an evident shift toward a more open
stance on this matter in the recent past. The same UN documents that
stated the totals of the alleged annual East German contributions also
showed percentages relating to national income, the most significant
figure in the East's national accounting system: at the beginning of the
1980s just under 0.8 percent; 1986/87 reportedly 0.89 percent.[9] These
figures cannot be compared with values measured in terms of GNP
because they do not give adequate consideration to services in particular.[10] Expressed as a proportion of GNP, the aid that East Germany

Table 6.4. *Gross disbursements of East Germany's development assistance ($US million; estimates)*

	1985	1986	1987	1988
Afghanistan	2.1	2.0	2.0	3.0
Cuba	(50.0)	(50.0)	(50.0)	(50.0)
Egypt	25.7	–	–	–
Ethiopia	12.1	1.9	6.0	n.a.
Kampuchea	5.0	8.3	10.0	(5.0)
Laos	2.8	9.5	(9.0)	18.0
Mongolia	(3.0)	(3.0)	(3.0)	(3.0)
Mozambique	0.5	15.4	28.9	18.5
Nicaragua	8.0	9.9	23.8	2.5
Syria	3.2	3.5	2.6	0.8
Vietnam	(51.0)	(55.0)	(55.0)	(55.0)
Yemen (DR)	7.9	9.1	8.9	4.9
Other recipients[a]	2.0	5.5	0.8	–
Unspecified[b]	(26.0)	(29.0)	(29.0)	(29.0)
Total	199.3	202.1	229.0	189.7

Notes: [a] Total of a group of countries each having received less than 3 mill. $ per annum in the reporting period. [b] Scholarships, etc.
　　　Figures in parenthesis: estimates.
　　　n.a. not available.
Source: The above figures are rough estimates on the basis of the World Bank Debtor Reporting System, UNDP country reports as well as other sources. The basic data are subject to frequent revisions.

claimed to have provided must necessarily have been less than the released ratios. More recently, there were data published on the GNP ratio which was allegedly 0.7 in 1987 and slipped to 0.64 in 1988.

Since no details were being provided on the methodology of obtaining these figures one had to fall back on DAC figures. Estimates of this kind are naturally dependent on the method used. By and large the known figures for aid payments, including aid to the poorer countries within the CMEA group, were converted into net disbursement according to figures from past experience and were adjusted for factors which, according to the OECD procedure, were not actually elements of development aid proper. The most significant of such factors was the *de facto* subsidization of pricing in foreign trade. This occurred in particular when CMEA countries obtained sugar and (until 1979) nickel from Cuba at prices above the world market level. Conversely, crude oil supplies to Cuba were cheaper than they would have been on the world market. The thus adjusted payment figure was then applied to the Western estimated value for the Eastern GNP.[11] The figures arrived at in this way for East Germany lay between 0.15 and 0.17 percent p.a. at the start of the eighties. Even when the values are adjusted upward slightly – as was the general trend of revision in 1984 when the OECD recalculated its figures for CMEA aid[12] – the level of aid was said to little exceed 0.2 percent. This would mean East Germany lay, together with other CMEA countries, at the lower end of the scale of values for OECD countries. In the recent past the DAC Secretariat became very cautious and felt unable to indicate the share of aid in relation to GNP due to the lack of comparable and reasonably reliable GNP data for CMEA countries. For this reason the publication of such ratios has been discontinued since 1988. It is impossible to tell where the figure stood exactly; however, it may be safe to assume that East Germany had not reached the target set by the UN. From what can be gathered from informal discussion, there may be some recalculation of the overall figure since the training component in the GDR's aid effort seems to be somewhat underestimated.

Little trade integration with a high degree of regional concentration

Besides education and training East Germany saw foreign trade as an important contribution toward the economic and social development of the Third World.[13] But although the *turnover*[14] of foreign trade with developing countries (defined according to political criteria) had shown nominal increases in individual years of up to 30 percent, these new levels have not always been sustainable. In the past, trade with developing countries, expressed as a proportion of the total volume of foreign trade, has – showing no clear trend – fluctuated between approximately 5 and 6 percent.[15] Seen over a longer time span it appears that fluctuations could be considerable from one year to the next without necessarily having indicated new trends; phases of rapid increase could give way to several years of stagnation or sometimes even a total relapse.

The UNCTAD Secretariat, as well as other UN statistics, classifies developing countries according to a country's stage of development. From these UNCTAD figures – which give exports and imports separately – it becomes evident that East Germany, compared with the other CMEA member countries, used to be at the bottom end of the scale for foreign trade with developing countries. As was also the case in most other CMEA countries (with the exception of Romania), the value

Table 6.5. *East Germany's 15 most important foreign trade partners[a] among non-European developing countries[b]*

1970	1980	1985	1986	1987	1988
Cuba[c]	Iraq	Cuba[c]	Cuba[c]	Cuba[c]	Cuba[c]
Egypt	Cuba[c]	Iran	Brazil	China(PR)[d]	China(PR)[d]
China(PR)[d]	China(PR)[d]	Iraq	China(PR)[c]	Brazil	Brazil
India	Brazil	Angola[d]	Iraq	Iraq	India
Brazil	Iran	Brazil	India	India	Iran
Vietnam[c]	Algeria	China(PR)[d]	Egypt	Iran	Vietnam[c]
Korea(DPR)[d]	Libyan Arab Jamah.	Algeria	Iran	Egypt	Iraq
Mongolia[c]	India	Egypt	Vietnam[c]	Vietnam[c]	Egypt
Syrian Arab Republic	Syrian Arab Republic	India	Angola[d]	Syrian Arab Republic	Korea(DPR)[d]
Colombia	Vietnam[c]	Vietnam[c]	Colombia	Ghana	Nicaragua
Peru	Egypt	Nicaragua	Nicaragua	Nicaragua	Syrian Arab Republic
Iraq	Angola[d]	Syrian Arab Republic	Algeria	Algeria	Algeria
Lebanon	Mozambique[d]	Korea(DPR)[d]	Syrian Arab Republic	Korea(DPR)[d]	Mongolia[c]
Iran	Colombia	Ghana	Ghana	Angola[d]	Colombia
Sudan	Argentina	Mongolia[c]	Korea(DPR)[d]	Mongolia[c]	Angola[d]
A: 71.6%	60.7%	68.3%	68.6%	64.0%	61.9%
B: 6.1%	6.8%	5.9%	5.8%	5.1%	4.8%

Notes: A (B) indicates the share of the countries listed in the GDR's trade with the developing countries (the world).
[a] Arranged by diminishing trade turnover; [b] Including CMEA and "socialist"; [d] countries.
Source: Statistical Yearbook 1989 of the German Democratic Republic, Berlin 1989; DIW calculations.

placed on trade with developing countries had been greater for exports than for imports. This is an expression of the East European trade surpluses with respect to the group of developing countries.

East Germany's economic relations with developing countries were concentrated on just a few partner countries. The exchange of goods with the CMEA countries Cuba, Vietnam, and Mongolia, used to account for approximately a quarter of East Germany's trade with developing countries (Table 6.5). For the remaining developing countries there were clear regional focuses of attention. These have, however, shifted since the seventies: Egypt and India had lost their leading position to the oil producing countries of the Middle East. Here Iraq was at the forefront for some years but had more recently fallen behind Iran. Brazil followed in next place. It can thus be seen that – apart from CMEA members – the three countries having enjoyed the largest exchange of goods with East Germany accounted for just under half of East Germany's extra-"bloc" trade with developing countries.

Traditional pattern for the exchange of goods

East German reports maintained that the economic cooperation with developing countries, in conjunction with other CMEA countries, was fundamentally different – in terms of the kinds of goods traded – from the economic cooperation of capitalist countries. The "special nature of the international division of labor" was essentially politically defined (respect for sovereignty, non-intervention in internal affairs, equality) but also had economic dimensions (mutual advantage, more importing of semi-finished and finished goods).

Overall, the following pattern can be discerned:[16] East Germany's exports to developing countries were principally capital goods such as machinery, factory equipment, and other industrial finished products.[17] Prominent sectors of the economy were those concerned with the infrastructure (in particular transport and telecommunications) and the textile, construction, and printing industries. The import side was dominated by industrial raw materials (including mineral oil) and tropical foodstuffs as well as semi-finished products. On the whole, leaving aside the fact that trading partners were chosen on political grounds, East Germany's foreign trade with developing countries displayed definite characteristics of a complementarily structured exchange of goods and thus adhered to the traditional model.

In this framework of economic relations, basically bilateral in character, suitable partners for East Germany were both those countries already enjoying a certain degree of industrial development – and thus within the framework of industrial cooperation using the investment supplied to them to produce products which were taken up by East Germany – and also those countries which were significant suppliers of raw materials and whose products were in demand as inputs for industrial production. For raw materials in particular it was impossible to draw a complete picture of purchases from developing countries because of the great gaps in the available information.[18] Certainly, even after the supply shortages of 1982/83 East Germany bought most of its fuel, such as oil and natural gas, from the USSR. In meeting the rest of East Germany's requirements for oil (about a quarter), the supplies from Iraq and Iran, despite the reduction in supply as a result of the Gulf war, together with Libya – be it directly, by means of a third state or on the spot market – played an important role without this being evident in the published figures. In 1985 Iran and the Soviet Union agreed to resume the deliveries of natural gas which were discontinued after the overthrow of the Shah in 1979. Naturally a share of these supplies was to be re-exported to East European countries.

Conclusion

East Germany's Third World policy in the area of aid and trade was, like that of other (even Western) countries, determined by its own interests. Above humanitarian and charitable motives, which explain the donations and contributions made by the company groups of the trade union (Freier Deutscher Gewerkschaftsbund), the so-called Solidarity Committee and the Red Cross, (foreign) policy considerations remained at the fore. However, economic interests were also an important factor in the comparatively close association between aid and trade in East Germany's relations with the Third World.

For a number of years East Germany tried to avoid a separate discussion of its development aid performance but rather pressed for the inclusion of trade relations ("aid by trade"). This position somehow strained relations with developing countries demanding, *inter alia*, an increased and more multilateral allocation of resources. Despite its considerably increased political engagement within the framework of the UN, the GDR's multilaterally assigned share continued to be practically meaningless. Amongst the United Nations' various development funds and programs the GDR was concentrating on the child welfare organization UNICEF and on the Industrial Development Fund.

In the field of foreign trade, both a diversification in the supply sources for raw materials required by industry and a greater degree of cooperation in production with partners in developing countries could have stimulated an expansion of the exchange of goods with the Third World. It must, however, be noted that, despite the allegedly "mutually advantageous economic relations" which have been set up in the framework of long-term umbrella agreements on a permanent basis, considerable yearly fluctuations in the trade flow in both directions were a permanent feature. Here a more steady flow of goods and services would have been to the benefit of either side. As a matter of fact, permanent imbalances did characterize bilateral trade relations with quite a number of partner countries. As a rule, developing countries ranked highly in the list of those countries *vis-à-vis* which East Germany maintained a creditor position. In particular, this applied to Cuba, Nicaragua, Mozambique, Syria, Ethiopia, and Iraq.

The GDR's development cooperation was a part of its socialist-orientated foreign policy. It served to promote socialist states and social structures. With the new political orientation in the GDR practically all aid projects of the GDR were being reviewed. However, the last GDR government holding office before German unification had promised at the very beginning to maintain the support for a number of projects in Angola, Nicaragua, Tanzania, South Yemen, and Zimbabwe.

During the ultimate period of a separate GDR government the following elements of a change in policy were noticeable.

> The governmental declaration by the first non-communist GDR Prime Minister, de Maizière, showed that the end of the East–West conflict was not interpreted in such a way that the North–South conflict will automatically receive more attention. Rather, this was seen as a political obligation.

> The previous attachment of blame to the former colonial powers for the problems of underdevelopment was being given up. Readiness to take on a share of the responsibility for a solution to the development problems of the Third World was apparent.

> A government which was going over to a free market economy in its own country will recommend a course open to the world market for the future of most developing countries.

> The socialist orientation of developing countries was no longer offered as the only way out of their situation. Rather, the schematic transfer of social models from the Second World was rejected and self-determination in developing countries in choosing their own socioeconomic course of development was supported.

In this context the Federal government saw its most important task during the transition period as beginning a broad-based dialogue on development policy with the new government and affording the GDR's government its desired advice on the restructuring and new construction of the GDR's development cooperation.

Future unified German development cooperation most likely will take place primarily according to the following objectives.

The ecological orientation of development policy will be a focal point.

Germany will do justice to its responsibility toward the developing countries also in the face of German unity. The volume of German development cooperation in total should therefore be maintained at least at the previous level.

A single German development policy might benefit from the GDR's good relations with states with which the Federal Republic had few or only bad relations and *vice versa*.

Future single German development cooperation is tied to the aim of efficiency which means that an essential criterion for allocation of budgetary means will be the readiness of partner governments to create suitable political, economic, and social conditions for their national development and international development cooperation.

Notes

1. It seems reasonable to classify the group of developing countries according to their level of development using the criteria of the United Nations or the World Bank or the OECD. On the other hand, it must be remembered that relations with the developing countries within the Council for Mutual Economic Assistance (CMEA), Cuba, Mongolia, Vietnam, have a different character for political reasons. Apart from this, the GDR used to have special relations with those countries who followed a "socialist path of development."
2. H. Ott, UN General Assembly, 37 session, A/C.2/37.5 (21 October 1982); H. Sölle, UN Conference on Trade and Development, 6 session, Belgrade, TD/304 (14 June 1983).
3. For the sectoral distribution of the Solidarity Fund, see Table 6.2.
4. The GDR's mark was a purely internal currency and its purchasing power parity *vis-à-vis* Western currencies was not published.
5. Informal communication with officials in East Berlin gave some indication that (1) figures were calculated on the basis of net disbursements, and (2) military assistance had been included if it was provided within the framework of an official credit line.
6. In some cases the training component was not necessarily provided free of charge.

7. See H. Machowski and S. Schultz, "RGW-Staaten und Dritte Welt – Wirtschaftsbeziehungen und Entwicklungshilfe," Forschungsinstitut der deutschen Gesellschaft für Auswärtige Politik, 5, Arbeitspapiere zur Internationalen Politik, Bonn, vol. 18, 1981.
8. According to Eastern philosophy, aid is a resource transfer of a political–moral nature to which solely the Western industrialized countries are being obliged on the basis of their historic responsibility for colonial exploitation and the present underdevelopment of the former colonies.
9. UN document A/C.2/37/5 (21 October 1982); UNCTAD, TD/304 (14 June 1983). For 1983 and subsequent years, see various issues of *Aussenpolitische Korrespondenz* or, respectively, English language versions submitted as UN documents to the General Assembly and UNCTAD conferences.
10. The Eastern concept of national income excludes the vast majority of the so-called "non-producing" sectors – for example, the contribution of the state sector, finance, and insurance as well as other services. On the other hand, Eastern national income is stated net of depreciation while the Western GNP includes this item.
11. Here the OECD used World Bank estimates of the level of GNP in CMEA countries.
12. Since then the CMEA aid to Mongolia had also been included in the figures. Price concessions in foreign trade with developing countries and the arrangement for cheap freight rates have continued to be omitted from OECD aid statistics.
13. Using political criteria, the GDR statistics for foreign trade used to differentiate three groups of countries: socialist countries (CMEA members plus China, Laos, North Korea, and Yugoslavia), capitalist countries, and, as a residual, developing countries. Albania, Cuba, Mongolia, and Vietnam belong to the CMEA. Albania's membership is suspended, however. Since 1980 there has been no detailed listing of countries or groups of countries in the methodical sections in the GDR's statistical yearbook. According to statements by government officials in early 1990 a revision of foreign trade data was planned to take place from 1985 onward.
14. A separate analysis of exports and imports was not possible in the past with the available official figures, because, apart from a few chosen partners, only the size of turnover was given. This is supposed to be changed too.
15. GDR, *Statistical Yearbook 1985*, various issues.
16. German Institute for Economic Research, *Handbuch der DDR-Wirtschaft*, various issues, as well as selected data on the commodity structure of trade with twelve single named countries (Algeria, Angola, Brazil, Colombia, Cuba, Egypt, Ethiopia, India, Iran, Iraq, Mozambique, Syria) listed in the GDR's *Statistical Yearbook*.
17. For the aspect of asymmetry of the commodity structure of East European exports *vis-à-vis* the pattern of import demand of developed and developing countries, cf. I. I. Dioumoulen, "Principal factors and prospects in inter-systems trade, East–South trade in particular," UNCTAD/ITP/TSC/7 (24 November 1989), pp. 27f.
18. There are some indications, however, that the foreign trade figures for the past will be revised beginning with those for 1985.

Part II

Growth: technology transfers and joint ventures

7 East–West technology transfer and Soviet regional development: continuity and change

Michael J. Bradshaw and Denis J. B. Shaw

This chapter reports on the results of a two-year research project which has examined the relationship between East–West technology transfer and Soviet regional development.[1] The project united two sets of literature and academic research: one dealing with the role of East–West trade and technology transfer in Soviet economic performance; the other the process of regional development in the Soviet Union. The first part of this chapter introduces the spatial dimensions of technology transfer. The second part reviews the regional aspects of Soviet industrial policy. Having provided the "geographical" context, the rest of the chapter reviews the findings of our research, examining the dynamics and structure of technology transfer and its spatial distribution with the Soviet Union. The final section considers the interrelationship between economic reform, technology transfer, and regional development.[2]

Spatial dimensions of technology transfer

It is a well-known fact that the Soviet economy is planned by sector rather than by region. Although a structure of regional plans does exist,[3] they have been of relatively minor significance in actual economic decision making. It would therefore be naive to imagine that the import of Western technology takes place in response to a carefully considered strategy of spatial planning. Nevertheless, given the facts that regional economies vary in structure and that different sectors have benefited from Western technology to differing degrees, it seems reasonable to suggest that technology transfer has influenced the process of regional development in the Soviet Union. The traditional approach adopted by Western economists has been to examine the impact of technology transfer upon key sectors in the Soviet economy, such as the chemical and automotive industries.[4] An equally important question to be addressed is the impact of technology transfer upon the development of various regions in the Soviet Union. Is it the case, for example, that the import of Western technologies has helped in the solution of specific regional problems, such as labor shortages or environmental difficulties? Have such technologies been vital in overcoming the friction of space? Or have they been significant in the development of key industries which in turn have acted as multipliers in regional economies? Such questions are difficult to answer, given the notorious reticence of Soviet statistics when it comes to regional data. But they must be considered if the full story of the importance of technology transfer to the Soviet economy is to be told.

When considering the regional impacts of technology transfer, it is important to understand such impacts within the context of the broader regional issues facing the Soviet Union at the present time. Miller has identified four categories of economic problems currently constraining economic growth in the Soviet Union: resource problems, labor problems, financial problems, and structural–organizational problems.[5] Space is central to the first two. As regards natural resources, for example, the Soviet Union is an energy-intensive economy requiring substantial increases in energy consumption to sustain industrial growth. As the fuel–energy complex shifted during the postwar period from a dependence on coal toward oil and then natural gas, so the energy base moved eastward into Siberia and latterly northward toward the high Arctic, greatly increasing the costs of energy production. Similar trends are evident in other sectors, such as mining and forestry, placing excessive strains on the transport system. It is therefore hardly surprising that resource conservation is a key component of economic restructuring. Labor problems are likewise a question of distribution rather than of absolute supply. In the European USSR heavy industrialization and urbanization have greatly reduced the rate of population growth in an economy that has long been lavish in its use of labor. In Siberia and the Far East the new resource developments have been taking place in regions with a slender population base and whose relatively harsh environment acts as a hindrance to immigration. Finally, in Central Asia, a predominantly rural population and traditional Islamic culture foster high demographic growth rates. The consequent labor surplus has been exacerbated by a failure to locate sufficient labor-intensive economic activities within the region.[6]

At the heart of the economic problems that have plagued the Soviet economy since the 1960s, then, is a spatial mismatch in the factors of production: resources, capital, and labor. Before considering the spatial significance of technology transfer in this context, however, it is necessary to say something about Soviet industrial policy and how that has influenced the regional picture.

Regional aspects of Soviet industrial policy

Since the 1960s Soviet economic policy has been characterized by two significant features. First, there has been the effort to increase the supply of inputs which the growing economy needs. This policy has been most successful in terms of the supply of material resources. Since the European USSR produces about 80 percent of the industrial output, it is this territory which first felt the impact of this policy. However, as local resources have dwindled or become ever more expensive, so the peripheral territories have grown in importance. The second significant policy has been the attempt to switch the economy from what Soviet economists term the "extensive" pattern of development, depending for its growth on commensurate increases in all kinds of inputs, to an "intensive" pattern emphasizing greater productivity. The aim of the 1965 economic reforms was to achieve just such a transformation, but these reforms failed to move the economy from its traditional Stalinist orientation. Ever growing costs of inputs and other problems gradually put a brake on Soviet economic performance. The accumulating difficulties were to some extent finally recognized in the 10th five-year plan (1976–80) which aimed for an "intensive" mode of development by accenting labor productivity rather than new capital investment. However, the necessary measures to achieve these goals were not taken. The consequence has been a continuing deceleration in growth rates which Gorbachev's perestroika has been attempting to address.

The two policies referred to above have affected different parts of Soviet territory in different ways. The easy accessibility of coalfields in European USSR, vested interests of the coal ministry, the rigid planning machinery, and problems of transportation all helped to sustain a dependence on coal and other local fuels (oil shales, peat, firewood) until long after the Western world had moved toward dependence on petroleum. The switch to oil and gas, associated with a new emphasis on cost accounting and a growing capability in building pipelines, was ordered by the 21st Party Congress in 1959. By this stage, the conveniently located Volga–Urals oilfield was already surpassing in production the Baku field which had been operating since before the revolution. By the mid-1960s, 70 percent of the USSR's oil came from the Volga–Urals. The accent on oil and gas, and on cheap energy generally, encouraged investment in energy sources both in the European USSR (Donbass and other coalfields, Dashava, Shebelinka, the North Caucasus, and Orenburg for natural gas) and also, as European sources proved expensive or limited, in remoter regions (Kuzbass, Karaganda, Pechora and ultimately Kansk-Achinsk, Ekibastuz, and South Iakutia for coal, Mangyshlak and West Siberia for oil, Central Asia, Ukhta, and ultimately West Siberia for natural gas). By 1980 West Siberia was producing over half the USSR's oil and almost a third of its natural gas; these proportions continued to grow thereafter. Developments in Siberia, however, proved expensive, and the 10th five-year plan (1976–80) emphasized the need for cheap energy to support the European industrial base: hydroelectric power (already well developed in that region), atomic power, open cast mining, and long-distance, high-voltage power transmission.

The rapid development of a network of oil and gas pipelines from the 1950s enabled the relatively cheap energy from peripheral territories, including Siberia, to be moved to industrial centers in the European USSR. The pipeline network gave new flexibility to industrial location which was enhanced by the development of integrated electric power grids. No longer was heavy industry to be tied to coalfield locations. Along the Volga and toward the Urals, for example, there arose new chemical and petrochemical industries to supply the nation's growing need for fertilizers, plastics, and other materials. The new industries were initially supplied by local oil and gas and powered by locally generated hydro and thermal electricity. Soon, however, oil and gas were being piped from Siberia to supply these and other industrial centers, adding to supplies already drawn from the North Caucasus, Central Asia, and elsewhere. Large industrial agglomerations such as Moscow and Leningrad thus continued to attract industrial development in what might otherwise have been fuel-deficient areas. The new locational flexibility also permitted the development of chemical, engineering, and other industries in territories of the European USSR (such as Belorussia and the Transcaucasus) and to some degree in suitable small towns to take advantage of local labor surpluses.

A further important development from the 1960s was the attempted modernization and diversification of the metallurgical industries to raise the quality of production and to produce new metals needed by electronic, aerospace, nuclear, and other industries. Rather like the case of chemicals and petrochemicals, this development was very demanding of energy. European USSR is well endowed with ferrous metals but diminishing ore quality has meant additional investment in enrichment capabilities. The most important development in European USSR was that of the Kursk Magnetic Anomaly and associated metallurgical and supporting industries, but other ore suppliers (such as Krivoy Rog) and iron and steel centers were expanded and modernized to meet the needs of metal-hungry industrial consumers such as the oil and gas industries. The modernization program, despite the rationalization and intensification of traditional production patterns, proved insufficient to cope with demand, especially for high-quality products.

The widely dispersed and diversified machine-building industry has long been a high priority sector attracting above-average investment and characterized by higher than average growth rates. There is a fairly close association between heavy machine-building and metal-demanding branches of the sector, and traditional centers of heavy industry such as the Urals and Donets–Dneiper. However, many less metal-intensive branches are attracted to areas with some labor surpluses, while skilled labor has been the decisive factor in instrument making with associated electronics, computers, telecommunications, and other high technology industries, hence the importance of Moscow, Leningrad, the capitals of the Baltic states, and other centers. The recent policy changes associated with Gorbachev place particular emphasis upon the development of high technology sectors, the retooling of the machine-building sector, and other measures to improve productivity. Given the present distribution of industrial activity, these measures tend to favor the developed regions of the European USSR.

From at least the 1960s, if not before, arguments raged over the respective merits of industrial development in the resource-rich east and the resource-poor west.[7] One compromise has been in policies to promote energy-intensive industries in the east and labor-intensive ones, including textiles, food, and similar industries catering to the consumer, in the west. Siberia has experienced rapid industrial development over the period, particularly in such sectors as non-ferrous metallurgy, chemicals, and petrochemicals, partly in association with resource-oriented territorial–production complexes. However, environmental difficulties and labor shortages have raised the costs of Siberian production thus encouraging the continued growth of energy-intensive industries in such western regions as the Volga. The western part of the country retains many advantages for industrial development despite such problems as the energy deficit, water shortages, and serious pollution difficulties especially toward the south. Developing economic relationships with CMEA and Western partners have spurred economic growth, particularly close to the western frontier and along the Baltic and Black Sea coasts.

The structure and dynamics of East–West technology transfer

Prior to considering the temporal, sectoral, and spatial dimensions of technology transfer it is necessary to discuss the data problems encountered when examining Soviet foreign trade. The single greatest problem has been a complete lack of data on regional patterns of foreign trade participation in the Soviet Union. At the same time aggregate trade statistics, especially those published in the Soviet Union, seldom provide a comprehensive and consistent break-down of trade activities. Data on the geographical distribution of technology imports have been analyzed by the construction of a computer data base of major contracts between the Soviet Union and the industrialized West. Information on trade contracts has been obtained from the Western business press, especially those publications concerned with East–West trade such as: *Business Eastern Europe*, *East–West Markets*, *East European Markets*, and *Soviet Business and Trade*. At present the data base contains information on 2,500 contracts, covering the period from the early 1970s to the end of 1989. The use of a PC-based relational data base makes it possible to sort information on contracts by sector, region, year, Western partner, and so on.

From the early 1970s through to the mid-1980s both OECD and Soviet foreign trade statistics report a significant increase in the value of Soviet–West trade. The rapid growth in East–West trade during the 1970s was financed by windfall profits generated by OPEC-inspired increases in resource prices. However, during the late 1980s over-dependence on resource exports proved a major weakness as the dramatic decline of energy prices seriously eroded the Soviet Union's foreign currency purchasing power. The recent rejuvenation of East–West trade is being financed by increased volumes of mineral resource exports (particularly the sale of precious metals), but also by increased borrowing which is reflected in the escalating deficit in trade with the West. The rise in oil prices in the wake of the 1990 Gulf Crisis may bring some short-term relief, but the Soviet Union is still experiencing payment problems at the present time.

The commodity structure of East–West trade reveals an export profile dominated by exports of mineral fuels and energy, while imports are predominantly food, manufactured goods, and machinery and equipment. Over the past two decades the share of food imports has increased relative to that of manufactured goods, machinery, and equipment. Trade with the West reflects how the Soviet Union is using exports of energy to purchase food and technology to compensate for the failings of the domestic economy. In the case of food imports, trade compensates not only for the uncertainties of the domestic harvest, but also for the failure of the food processing industries fully to utilize domestic production. In the case of technology transfer, imports compensate for the failings of the domestic innovation process and the inability of Soviet industry to produce sufficient quantities of high-quality products for key industrial sectors.

In any one year imported technology represents a very small proportion of total industrial investment in the Soviet Union. However, because those imports have tended to be concentrated in particular sectors (and we argue regions) its impact is amplified. The sectors that have been the major recipients of Western technology include the automotive, chemical, oil and gas, and forest industries.[8] This pattern of sectoral specialization is also revealed by our analysis of contracts: the chemical industry accounts for 20.6 percent of contracts, the automotive industry 14.4 percent, the oil and gas industry 12.9 percent, and the forest industry 8.0 percent.

The most important Western trading partners, as revealed by Soviet statistics, are West Germany, Finland, Italy, Japan, the United States, and France. A similar pattern has been found in our analysis of contracts; however, there is considerable variation between industrial sectors in the pattern of trading partners. In the case of the chemical sector, West Germany, Japan, France, and Italy have been the most important suppliers of equipment. In the forest industry, Finland and Japan are the dominant suppliers. As we shall see, the different patterns of supply are also reflected in the spatial distribution of Western technology within the Soviet Union. The fact that the sectoral distribution revealed by our analysis of contract data is similar to that of the aggregate trade statistics suggests that the information in the data base is representative of Soviet–Western trade relations.

While aggregate statistics reveal a sustained increase in the value of Western imports to the Soviet Union through to 1984, the disaggregated data on Western machinery imports reveal a different dynamic. The share of the West in total Soviet machinery imports experienced rapid growth between 1972 and 1976, but subsequently went into decline.[9] The absolute value of machinery imports continued to increase through the late 1970s and early 1980s, partly due to the impact of inflation, but during the mid-1980s the absolute value of machinery imports also showed significant decline. This pattern of heightened activity during the mid-1970s followed by a decline is also found in the dynamics of contract activity. As one would expect, the peak in contract activity is somewhat earlier, but the decline is equally dramatic. The very low levels of contract activity in the early 1970s reflect a lack of information as much as a lack of trading activity.[10] In recent years the advent of joint ventures has led to a rapid expansion of contract activity, but as yet this has not been translated into imports of manufactured goods, machinery, and equipment.[11]

The decline in the share of Western machinery imports since the late 1970s cannot initially be explained by balance of payments problems and is more likely the result of a complexity of internal and external factors. Internal factors included a backlash against large-scale imports of Western equipment which were not providing the expected productivity increases. At the same time the increasing cost of grain imports limited the funds available to import Western technology. External factors included the increased politicization of East–West trade due to events in Afghanistan and Poland, and the scandal over Toshiba's sale of machine-tools to the Leningrad shipyards. More recently the fall in energy prices has undoubtedly led to a reduction in imports of Western technology.

Whatever the reasons for the decline, it is clear that during the early 1970s a combination of internal and external factors provided an opportunity to increase imports of Western technology to bolster a faltering domestic economy. East–West trade was seen as a means of avoiding radical domestic economic reform. In retrospect, it is also clear that the ills of the Soviet economy could not be cured by an injection of Western technology (perhaps there is a lesson here for those who advocate massive Western aid for perestroika). The question remains: what is the relationship between this infusion of Western technology and the patterns of regional development discussed earlier in this chapter.

Spatial dimensions of East–West technology transfer

Because there are no published data available on the geographical distribution of Western technology in the Soviet Union, the following analysis is based upon the contract information we have collected from the Western press. Of the 2,500 contracts for which we have information, we have locational data for approximately 1,800, over 70 percent.[12] In the following analysis the distribution of technology is organized by the current set of economic regions.

Figure 7.1 shows the spatial distribution of all the contracts for which we have information. From these graphics and the information in Table 7.1, it is clear that the Volga and Central economic regions have been the major recipients of Western technology. This is, perhaps, to be expected as the Central region contains Moscow, and the Volga region has been a focus of industrial development since the 1960s. Other

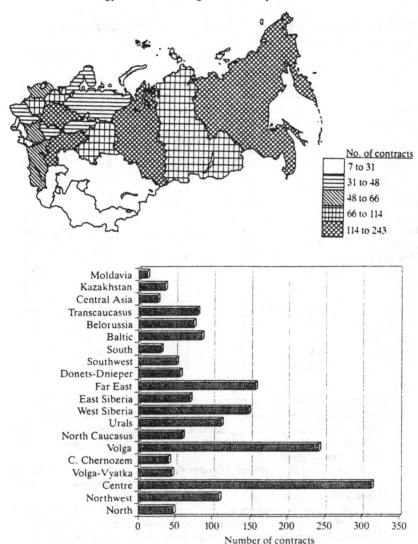

Figure 7.1 Regional distribution of technology transfer, by economic region

important regions include Siberia and the Soviet Far East. Just as note-worthy are the regions that have not been the beneficiaries of Western technology such as the older industrial regions of the European USSR and Central Asia. In short, the aggregate distribution of technology transfer reflects the geography of major growth industries of the past

Table 7.1. *Regional distribution of industrial employment, turnkey contracts, and joint ventures*

Economic region	Industrial employment[a]	LQ1	Turnkey contracts	J.V.s	LQ 2
North	2.6	1.1	2.9	1.4	0.5
Northwest	3.6	1.5	5.4	8.7	1.4
Centre	13.6	0.8	10.6	46.1	2.7
Volga-Vyatka	4.2	0.7	3.0	0.6	0.2
C. Chernozem	2.9	0.9	2.7	0.9	0.4
Volga	7.1	2.2	15.9	3.2	0.2
North Caucasus	4.9	0.7	3.6	2.0	0.6
Urals	9.5	0.7	7.4	1.2	0.2
West Siberia	5.6	1.7	9.7	1.7	0.2
East Siberia	3.2	1.4	4.4	1.7	0.4
Far East	2.7	3.6	9.8	4.1	0.5
Donets-Dneiper	10.4	0.3	3.6	1.2	0.4
Southwest	7.2	0.4	3.0	2.3	0.8
South	2.2	0.8	1.8	1.4	0.8
Baltic	3.4	1.0	3.5	10.1	2.1
Belorussia	4.0	1.2	4.7	2.0	0.5
Transcaucasus	3.7	1.1	4.2	5.5	1.2
Central Asia	4.2	0.4	1.6	1.2	0.8
Kazakhstan	3.8	0.5	1.8	3.2	1.6
Moldavia	1.0	0.5	0.5	1.4	2.2
Total	100.0		100.0	100.0	

Notes: LQ 1 is a simple location quotient: percent of turnkey contracts divided by the share of industrial employment. A LQ greater than 1 indicates a region where the share of technology transfer for the period 1970–89 is greater than the regions' share of industrial employment in 1985.
LQ 2 is percent of joint ventures divided by the share of turnkey contracts. An LQ greater than 1 indicates the region has a greater share of joint ventures than other types of technology transfer.
Source: Data on industrial employment are from M. J. Sagers, 1990, "Regional industrialization trends in 1985 and recent trends in industrialization in the USSR," Center for International Research, US Bureau of the Census, Washington, D.C., unpublished paper.

two decades, particularly the chemical, oil and gas, and automotive industries. The relationship between the sectoral distribution of imports and their impact upon regional development is made more apparent by the use of case studies.

The sectors and regions chosen for closer examination are the chemical and forest industries and the Central and Volga regions of the European USSR as well as the aggregate pattern for Siberia and the

Table 7.2. *Sectoral distribution of technology transfer by key region (percent of total)*

Sector	USSR	Centre	Volga	SIBFE
Oil and Gas	12.9	0.6	5.8	33.5
Other energy	2.5	1.0	0.0	8.2
Forest	8.0	2.2	0.8	14.9
Chemical	20.6	13.1	26.7	12.0
Metals	5.5	1.3	1.6	6.1
Machines	3.2	4.8	1.2	0.8
Automotive	14.4	14.6	57.2	0.3
Transport	4.7	1.0	0.0	14.6
Food	6.4	7.0	0.8	5.9
Textiles	7.3	9.2	2.5	1.1
Light industry	7.0	15.9	2.1	1.3
Other[a]	7.5	29.3	1.2	1.3
Total	100.0	100.0	100.0	100.0

Note: [a] Other: includes producer and consumer services.
Source: Project data base.

Soviet Far East (Table 7.2). The regional distribution of chemical equipment imports (Figure 7.2) reflects the continued dominance of the European USSR, the most important regions being the Volga, Central, Urals, and Belorussia economic regions. As discussed earlier, in the postwar period the chemicalization of the economy has been a significant component of Soviet industrial policy. In the Volga region local feedstocks and the construction of pipelines in combination with a developed infrastructure have led to the development of chemical centers at places such as Kazan, Kuybyshev, Nizhnekamsk, Saratov, Togliatti, and others. The Urals region has also benefited from local mineral deposits as well as a location between the resource-producing regions of Siberia and major markets in the European regions. In the case of Belorussia it is the expansion of the market in Eastern Europe that has promoted the development of petrochemical complexes at places such as Grodno, Mogilev, and Novopolotsk. In the absence of regional data on industrial performance it is difficult to be precise. Nonetheless, it would seem the case that Western technology has played a role in the formation of many of the major industrial centers of the European USSR, while imports of pipe and equipment have enabled the majority of growth to be concentrated in market-oriented locations rather than in the more remote resource-producing regions.[13]

The regional distribution of imports to the forest industry shows a

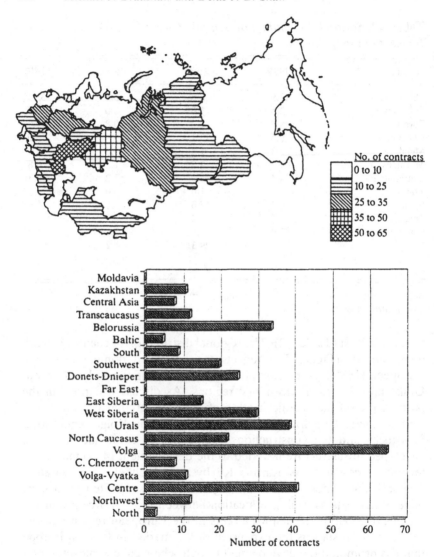

Figure 7.2 Regional distribution of chemical imports, by economic region

very different geography (Figure 7.3). Three regions dominate: the Northwest, East Siberia, and the Far East. Closer examination reveals that Japanese companies have been the major partners in the Far East, whereas Scandinavian companies have dominated in the Northwest; in East Siberia there is a mix of Western partners. The trade relations in

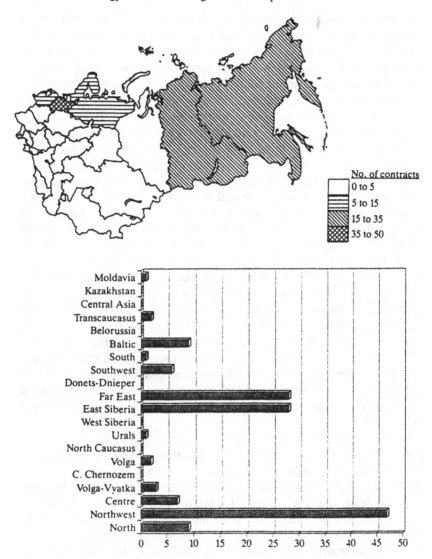

Figure 7.3 Regional distribution of forestry imports, by economic region

the Far East and the Northwest illustrate contrasting roles for technology transfer in regional development. In the Far East a series of large-scale, long-term forestry agreements between Japan and the Soviet Union have provided forestry equipment in return for exports of timber. Here imports have been used to extend the harvesting of the local timber resources and have compensated for the failure of the local machine-building industry to provide the necessary equipment. In the Northwest, Scandinavian companies have supplied equipment to modernize and expand the forest products industry by helping to create large pulp and paper complexes at Vyborg and Svetogorsk. In the Soviet Far East technology transfer has aided in the extensive exploitation of the forest resource, while in the Northwest it has aided in the intensive development of the forest products industry. In East Siberia equipment has been supplied to both the forestry and forest products industries to develop the Ust'–Ilimsk territorial production complex (TPC).

The contrast between the forest industries of the Northwest and the Far East is part of a more general regional variation in the sectoral distribution of technology transfer. Western technology in Siberia and the Soviet Far East has been oriented toward the exploration, exploitation, and transportation of the region's natural resource wealth. In West Siberia imports have aided in the development of the West Siberian oil and gas TPC as well as the construction of transcontinental pipelines and the extension of activities on the Northern Sea Route. In East Siberia imports have been important in the expansion of the Noril'sk metallurgical combine, the development of the aluminum industry at the Sayan TPC, the forest industry at Bratsk–Ust'–Ilimsk TPC, and the chemical industry at Zima and Angarsk. In the Soviet Far East the development of the South Yakutian coal complex, the delimitation of natural gas deposits in the Vilyuy, and oil and gas exploration off Sakhalin Island have all benefited from Japanese credit and technology.[14]

In the European regions, and in the Central and Volga regions in particular, the resource-processing and manufacturing industries have benefited the most from technology imports. In the Volga region the chemical and automotive industries have received the bulk of Western imports. Both the VAZ plant at Togliatti and the KamAZ plant at Naberezhnyye Chelny are located within the Volga economic region. In the Central region the dominance of Moscow is reflected in the higher share of consumer-oriented sectors, such as food production and processing, light industry, and producer and consumer services. The textile, chemical, and automotive industries are also important within the Moscow region.

The literature has tended to focus upon technology transfer as a surrogate for domestic innovation, providing short-term injections of process technologies which enable the rapid expansion of productive capacity. While this is the predominant pattern of technology transfer and economic development in the European USSR, it ignores the pat-

Table 7.3. *Macro-regional dynamics of technology transfer*

Macro-region	Total	1970–75	1976–80	1981–85	1986–89
Europe	75.7	72.5	68.5	66.8	75.7
Siberia	21.4	26.8	29.1	30.1	21.4
Central Asia	2.9	0.7	2.4	3.1	2.9

Source: Project data base.

tern of trade and development in Siberia and the Far East. In these regions imports of products, such as large-diameter pipe, bulldozers, and specialist shipping, have compensated for the inability of Soviet industry to supply the inputs necessary for rapid remote-area resource development. The macro-regional dynamics of technology transfer show an eastward drift over the late 1970s and early 1980s as more imports were required to secure Siberia's resource wealth (Table 7.3). However, in recent years the emphasis has returned to the European regions. The reasons for this geographical shift are to be found in the reforms introduced under perestroika and the creation of new forms of economic cooperation.

East–West trade and regional development: the impact of reform

If, during the 1970s, East–West trade and technology transfer provided an alternative to reform by bolstering a stagnant economy, during the 1990s foreign trade is one of the cornerstones of the reform process. Under the Stalinist system the Ministry of Foreign Trade maintained a monopoly over foreign trade transactions. This monopoly effectively isolated Soviet enterprises from the rigors of the international market place. It also allowed central planners to siphon off foreign currency revenues generated in one sector or region to pay for imports to aid in the development of other sectors and regions. In simple terms, the resource exports of Siberia and the Soviet Far East have been used to finance imports of agricultural products, machinery, and equipment for use in the European regions of the USSR. The reforms introduced under perestroika threaten to undermine this centralized management of export earnings.

The intention of reform in the foreign trade sector is to open Soviet industry to the competitive pressures of the international economy. In doing so it is hoped that Soviet enterprises will respond by producing quality products that can be exported, so reducing reliance upon vulnerable resource exports. This means increasing the volume of exports of manufactured goods from the European regions, while reducing the volume of Siberian oil exported. Since January 1987 a number of reform measures have been introduced to encourage increased foreign trade participation. However, it is worth noting that while the Ministry for Foreign Economic Relations has lost control over the foreign trade activities of the major industrial sectors, so far it retains control over resource exports. At present, clearly, the central authorities are unwilling to relinquish control over export revenues. It is the industries of the European regions, the major beneficiaries of imports, which have benefited from decentralization, while the resource industries of Siberia remain under central control.[15]

The decentralization of the foreign trade system has not been without its problems. Under the previous system the Ministry of Foreign Trade controlled purchases through its foreign trade organizations and these had access to the foreign currency reserves generated by the national economy. Now the industrial ministries and enterprises have the freedom to trade, but have to rely on their own limited reserves of foreign currency. At the same time there is no central accounting system balancing imports and exports. In many instances orders have been placed for Western equipment without the foreign currency to pay for them, or the backing of the Foreign Trade Bank (Vneshekonombank). Over the past six months the Western press has reported numerous instances of late and non-payment of contracts. Soviet officials blame the decentralization of foreign trade rights for the problems of non-payment, rather than a shortage of foreign currency. The truth probably lies in a combination of the two.

Since January 1987, in an attempt to provide access to Western technology and international export markets, the Soviet Union has allowed the creation of joint ventures between foreign companies and Soviet enterprises. There is no doubt that joint ventures have seized the attention of the Western media; however, Western business has been somewhat more cautious. The initial joint venture legislation restricted the level of foreign participation and by the end of 1988 only 193 joint ventures had been registered. In late 1988 modifications were made to allow greater Western participation and control over joint venture activities. By late 1990, 2,100 joint ventures were registered with the Soviet Ministry of Finance. Initially, a list of joint ventures was published by the Ministry of Finance; this was stopped in the spring of 1989 and since then only summary statistics have been made available. Between May 1987 and March 1990 the total value of investment by foreign partners was put at $ 2.3 billion.[16] The average size of joint ventures is rather small, with about 60 percent having a foundation capital of less than 1 million rubles. The most important Western partners have been West Germany, Finland, the United States, Austria, Italy and the United Kingdom, a pattern which follows the previous pattern of Western involvement with one notable exception, the Japanese. Throughout the late 1980s Soviet–Japanese trade continued to decline in significance, reflecting political tensions over territorial disputes and the less than favorable experience with resource development projects in the Soviet Far East.

The data base we have constructed presently contains information on 390 joint ventures. At the end of 1989 there were some 1,000 joint ventures registered. Fortunately, the sectoral distribution of the joint ventures in the data base is roughly comparable with the summary statistics available, suggesting a fairly representative sample. The data in Table 7.1 compare the regional distribution of the 390 joint ventures with that of other forms of technology transfer. The most significant locations for joint ventures are the Central region with 46.1 percent of joint ventures, the Baltic with 10.1 percent, and the Northwest with 8.7 percent. These figures from the data base compare with published data that report Moscow's share at 46.5 percent, the Baltic republics 10.4 percent, and Leningrad 7.3 percent.[17] Unfortunately, summary data are not available by economic region. Nevertheless, it is clear that joint ventures exhibit a somewhat different geography from other forms of East–West trade. The reasons for this are to be found in the nature of joint venture activities.

Comparison of the sectoral distribution of joint ventures and that of other forms of technology transfer (Table 7.4) reveals a considerable difference. Joint ventures tend to be concentrated in light industry, electronics, and service sectors which have not traditionally been the recipients of Western technology. The most popular type of joint venture activity is personal computer production and programing, followed by business and consumer services. Therefore, it is not surprising that that Moscow and Leningrad account for 53.8 percent of all joint ventures. The importance of the Baltic republics (principally Estonia) is somewhat of a surprise, but here joint ventures are predominantly with Scandinavian partners and reflect a desire for greater economic self-sufficiency and increased interaction with neighboring states.

Despite the rapid increase in the number of joint ventures registered, one should not expect a dramatic change in the geography of technology transfer within the Soviet Union. While it is true that by the spring of 1990 over 1,500 have been registered, only 200 were actually opera-

Table 7.4. *Sectoral distribution of technology transfer*

Sector	Total	JVs	Percent	Non-JV	Percent
Metals	173	12	3.08	161	7.60
Oil and Gas	381	4	1.03	377	17.79
Other energy	59	3	0.77	56	2.64
Chemicals	394	35	8.97	359	16.94
Forest	199	23	5.90	176	8.31
Food	150	39	10.00	111	5.24
Transport	195	7	1.79	188	8.87
Machines	148	30	7.69	118	5.57
Automotive	306	9	2.31	297	14.02
Textiles	158	32	8.21	126	5.95
Light industry	89	23	5.90	66	3.11
Electronics	90	42	10.77	48	2.27
Services	81	79	20.26	2	0.09
Other	86	52	13.33	34	1.60
Total	2509	390	100.00	2119	100.00

Source: Project data base.

tional. As yet, beyond the confines of Moscow and Leningrad, joint ventures have had a relatively insignificant impact upon the Soviet economy. There are, however, a number of multi-billion dollar, resource-oriented projects being negotiated for Tengiz in Kazakhstan, and in the West Siberian oil and gas complex; similarly, Fiat is building an automotive plant at Yelabuga in the Volga economic region.[18] In reality these projects should be seen as parts of the traditional pattern of technology transfer. In many respects they resemble the type of compensation agreement that was popular during the 1970s. The emphasis of many joint ventures is upon generating goods and services for export to earn foreign currency. At present a minority are involved in the modernization of Soviet industry. As such, they will do little to promote the goal of economic modernization.

Conclusion

This chapter has presented an overview of our research into the relationship between East–West trade and Soviet regional development. For the most part the discussion has been confined to spatial distribution at the inter-regional scale. From our analysis it is apparent that technology transfer has had a part to play in maintaining the core–periphery relationship between the European USSR and Siberia and the Soviet

Far East. Within each of these macro-regions technology transfer has benefited particular localities such as the Moscow and Leningrad regions and the Volga economic region. In Siberia there is a clear relationship between technology transfer and the creation of territorial–production complexes. Detailed regional studies are now underway to examine more precisely the contribution made by technology transfer to these key regions.

When this project was first conceived, perestroika was barely underway. It is clear that the reform process is changing the nature of the relationship between East–West trade and regional development. At present we are witnessing a period of transition as the Stalinist centralized system is dismantled and the Soviet economy is opened to the international system. Our research has shown how centralized control enabled planners to use foreign trade to focus on high priority sectors and regions. In the future it is likely that decontrol, marketization, and regionalization will reduce the ability of the Soviet Union to use foreign trade to address national economic problems.

Notes

1. The authors wish to acknowledge the support of the Economic and Social Research Council (ESRC grant number: D00232336).
2. We are presently working on a one-year ESRC-funded project entitled "East–West trade and regional development: the impact of Perestroyka."
3. D. J. B. Shaw, "Spatial dimensions in Soviet central planning," *Transactions, Institute of British Geographers*, vol. 10, 1985, pp. 401–12; and Shaw, "Regional planning in the USSR," *Soviet Geography*, vol. 27, no. 7, pp. 469.
4. M. J. Bradshaw and D. J. B. Shaw, "West–East Technology transfer and Soviet regional development: an introduction," Working Paper no. 50, School of Geography, University of Birmingham, 1989.
5. R. F. Miller, "The Soviet economy: problems and solutions in the Gorbachev view," in R. F. Miller, J. H. Miller, and T. H. Rigby (eds.), *Gorbachev at the Helm*, Croom Helm, London, 1987, p. 115.
6. B. Z. Rumer, *Soviet Central Asia: a Tragic Experiment*, Unwin Hyman, London, 1989.
7. J. R. Schiffer, *Soviet Regional Economic Policy: The East–West Debate over Pacific Siberian Development*, Macmillan, London, 1989.
8. G. D. Holliday, *East–West Technology Transfer: A Survey of Sectoral Case Studies*, OECD, Paris, 1984.
9. P. Hanson, *Soviet Foreign Trade Policies in the 1980s*, Berichte des Bundesinstituts für ostwissenschaftliche und internationale Studien, no. 41, Cologne.

10. Most of the journals used to obtain contract information did not come into being until the early 1970s.
11. In the first three-quarters of 1989 the trade activity of joint ventures accounted for less than 0.5 percent of total trade turnover.
12. In some sectors, such as shipping, information on location is not relevant, although we have ascribed ice-breakers for the Northern Sea Route to West Siberia.
13. More data on regional economic performance are being made available and we hope to use this to assess the regional impact of technology transfer.
14. M. J. Bradshaw, "Soviet Far Eastern Trade," in A. Rogers (ed.), *The Soviet Far East: Geographical Perspectives on Development*, Routledge, London, 1990, pp. 239–68.
15. Following a strike threat, the oil and gas trusts in Siberia are now able to retain a proportion of their exports revenue for their own use. Similar concessions were given to coal miners following their strike last year.
16. PlanEcon, "Soviet joint ventures: development through the first quarter of 1990," *PlanEcon Report*, vol. 11, no. 17, 1990, p. 1.
17. Ibid., p. 17.
18. The status of the petrochemical projects in West Siberia remains in doubt. There has been local opposition to the proposals and the original plan for five complexes has now been reduced to two. More recently there have been problems arranging financing for the projects.

8 East–West technology flows: recent developments and perspectives

Jan Maciejewicz

Technology transfer policies of the Central and East European countries can be divided into three basic periods. The first one relates to the extensive and predominant use of foreign trade transactions in acquiring technology. The main forms of technology transfer have been the trade in machinery and equipment and licensing agreements. This period lasted until the mid-1960s and the majority of technology transfer occurred within the region. Technological transactions with firms from the developed market economies were sporadic as compared with intra-CMEA flows.

The second period relates to the following two decades, i.e. until the beginning of the 1980s. It can be characterized by a much more intensive use of acquired technology as well as by an increasing variety of forms and methods of technology transfer. Technology import policies of the Central and East European countries depended considerably upon investment policies and fluctuated over time.

The third period has just been initiated. Technology transfer policies of the Central and East European economies now depend considerably upon the inflow of foreign direct investments which form the major channel of technological borrowing from abroad.

These recent developments will be analyzed below. The chapter concludes with some observations relating to possible future scenarios in the area of East–West technology transfer.

Recent trends in East–West technology flows

Western technology transfer to Eastern Europe was characterized during the past twenty-five years by the predominant use of foreign trade transactions as a principal channel for technology acquisition. Only recently, the increasing role of foreign direct investment is becoming visible. Machinery and equipment have been the principal mode of East–West technology flow until the mid-1980s. The major importer within the CMEA region has been the Soviet Union, whose share in

126   *Jan Maciejewicz*

Table 8.1. *Volume of OECD investment goods exports to Eastern Europe and the Soviet Union, 1971–1987, 1980 prices (percentage change over previous period)*

Country	1971–75[a]	1976–80	1981–85	1986–87
Bulgaria	37	6	53	3
Czechoslovakia	7	16	−17	19
GDR	−1	23	−6	37
Hungary	48	50	3	−3
Poland	184	5	−62	5
Romania	27	6	−67	−38
Total Eastern Europe[b]	48	14	−30	10
Soviet Union	33	65	10	−19

Notes: [a] Over 1970.

[b] Includes estimate of trade between the FRG and the GDR.

Source: ECE, *Economic Bulletin for Europe*, vol. 41, Geneva, November 1989, p. 80.

total imports of machinery and equipment by the seven European CMEA economies from the West accounted for 45 percent in 1970 and increased to 65 percent in 1985. But, in the second half of the 1980s, the Soviet Union reduced dramatically its imports of investment goods from the West.

The changes in volume of OECD investment goods exports to Central and Eastern Europe in 1971–87 are shown in Table 8.1. The major cause of fluctuations illustrated by data contained in Table 8.1 has been the debt servicing problems appearing in the East European economies since the second half of the 1970s. Investment goods imports from the OECD area were, however, important items in overall import policies of the Central and East European economies throughout the whole period analyzed. In the second half of the 1980s, the relative share of machinery and equipment imported from the West in total domestic capital expenditures sharply declined, except for Hungary, as compared with the decade of the 1970s. Thus, bearing in mind the higher average level of technology as represented by imports of investment goods from the OECD area, this fall in relative share of Western machinery in total investment outlays in Central and Eastern Europe may reflect the downward trend in East–West technology flows.

The major source of technology inflows for the East are the EEC countries, accounting for about three-quarters of the total import of investment goods from the West. The Federal Republic of Germany plays a leading role in this respect, supplying half the investment goods being imported by Central and Eastern Europe from the OECD

Table 8.2. *OECD investment goods exports to Eastern Europe and the Soviet Union, 1980–1987, by R & D intensity, percent*

Country		1980	1981–85	1986–87
Bulgaria	A	26	31	36
	B	8	7	5
	C	66	62	59
Czechoslovakia	A	32	31	33
	B	4	4	4
	C	64	65	63
GDR	A	28	27	28
	B	3	3	4
	C	69	70	68
Hungary	A	31	28	29
	B	11	12	13
	C	58	60	58
Poland	A	23	29	29
	B	9	6	9
	C	68	65	62
Romania	A	40	47	55
	B	3	6	5
	C	57	47	40
Soviet Union	A	23	20	22
	B	5	5	4
	C	72	75	74

Notes: [A] High R & D intensive, as defined in the ECE source.
[B] Medium R & D intensive, as defined in the ECE source.
[C] Low R & D intensive, as defined in the ECE source.
Source: ECE, *Economic Bulletin for Europe*, vol. 41, November 1989, p. 88, and own calculations.

countries. Japan, on the other hand, is rapidly increasing its share as technology supplier to the region, especially in the case of the Soviet Union.

As far as the level of sophistication of imported technology is concerned, the available data suggest that the bulk of Western technology exports to the East contain low R&D intensive products (see Table 8.2). Interestingly enough, the largest share of highly R&D intensive technology imports has been recorded during the 1980s in Romania, followed by Bulgaria and Czechoslovakia. In medium R&D intensive products, Hungary was at the top, followed by Poland and Bulgaria. The Soviet Union confined itself largely to low R&D intensive technologies, which accounted for three-quarters of its total imports of investment goods from the OECD countries.

This technological structure of imports from the West reflects to a large extent the pattern of domestic demand in Central and Eastern Europe and shows the importance and magnitude of the necessary restructuring efforts in these economies in the years to come.

Other forms of East–West technology flows were intensively used during the 1970s and then declined in the 1980s. The number of licenses imported from the OECD since 1970 could be estimated at around 3,000, of which one-third were imported by the Soviet Union alone. It was followed by Hungary, Czechoslovakia, and Poland. The direct payments incurred over the period could be estimated at US $3 billion. Most of the acquired licenses were located in the machine-building and chemical industries. As in the case of investment goods the major supplying countries were those in Western Europe.

The position of individual CMEA countries in the import of licenses has been undergoing considerable changes over the period in question. Czechoslovakia seemed to pursue the most stable policy in this area. The Soviet Union decreased its import of licenses only recently while Poland did so in the second half of the 1970s. Hungary still seems to be expanding its imports although already relatively high.

The import of licenses constituted 4–5 percent of the R&D expenditures of industry at the beginning of the 1970s and has increased since 1980 to 8–11 percent.

Another form of technology transfer, i.e. industrial cooperation, developed rapidly in the first half of the 1970s and has remained at the same level since then. The first half of the 1980s witnessed a significant decline in the number of operational industrial cooperation agreements between East and West. The most popular form of those agreements are coproduction and specialization arrangements accounting for about 40 percent of all contracts. They are based on reciprocal supply of goods and services for the end-products or completing each partner's range of products.

The most active participant of industrial cooperation agreements with Western companies has been Hungary, followed by the Soviet Union and Poland. As far as the industrial structure of agreements is concerned, three sectors seem to play a major role: the chemical industry, mechanical engineering and machine tools, and transport equipment industry.

The last form of technology transfer which is to be analyzed in the context of East–West flows relates to foreign direct investment. Western investments in Central and Eastern Europe are of recent origin. Romania, Hungary, and Poland were among the first to introduce legislation allowing for foreign capital inflows. In the second half of the

1980s, foreign investment was accepted in Czechoslovakia and the Soviet Union.

The total number of joint ventures registered in Central and Eastern Europe as of March 1990 amounted to some 3,500: 1,400 in the Soviet Union, and 1,000 each in Hungary and Poland. Other countries of the region are much less attractive for foreign capital. During 1989–91 most of the countries in the region made some major amendments to their laws on foreign investment, facilitating the entry conditions and operational environment for foreign-owned companies. The major objective of these changes has been the stimulation of technological upgrading of their economies and increase of the export potential of countries.

Some 60 percent of established joint ventures operate in the manufacturing sector, while the rest operate in the services sector. Within the former, they are mostly located in the wearing apparel, food, and wood products industries. In the services sector, the majority of joint ventures operate in transport and communication and business services. Thus, the structure of foreign investments in Central and Eastern Europe indicates that this form of external cooperation may not be yielding substantial results from the point of view of technology transfer. Technological links with abroad seem to rely predominantly on organizational and managerial types of technical knowledge and to a much lesser extent on the product and process technology. Therefore, the relationship between Eastern and Western companies engaged in joint ventures is fairly weak and rarely relates to joint research projects or similar undertakings. For instance, in the case of Poland, out of more than 1,000 joint Polish–Western enterprises, only 20 are directly working in the R&D area. This shows the magnitude of potential technology flows between East and West on the basis of foreign direct investment.

However, one should underline that this is only the starting point of this type of external cooperation and successful completion of economic reforms undertaken in some of the East European economies may create better conditions for increased technological cooperation with Western companies.

Economic reforms and prospects for technology transfer: Poland

In the second half of 1989 the Polish government announced a comprehensive economic reform program, aiming at stabilizing the economy and transforming it into a market-oriented one. Thus, the government introduced measures such as liberalization of the price mechanism, a severe limit on increases, and a stable exchange rate for Polish currency as well as sharp control of money supply and high interest rates. All these measures together have led to a substantial decrease in demand as disposable income has been radically decreased (most of it in foreign currencies) through a stable exchange rate of zloty.

The above short description of the mechanism of the Polish stabilization program reflects the possible future implications of the economic mechanism on technological developments in the country. The decade of the 1990s should be a period of fundamental technological change if the country is to catch up with average world standards. The latter objective will apparently be enhanced by the ongoing and planned institutional and structural changes in the economy. Major components of this process are privatization, introducing new competition rules into the economy, the creation of financial markets, and opening up of the economy. In the first half of the 1990s the major elements of a new, market-oriented system will be introduced, while the second half of the decade is expected to yield visible, positive results, including those in the technological development area.

A crucial factor influencing the upgrading and diffusion of technology in Polish industries in the 1990s will certainly be a strong drive to export as a result of the government's macro-economic policy causing a slump in domestic demand. Exports became a major element of the strategy of most industrial and service companies and, because of the competitive external environment, this will exert a strong impact on technological upgrading and diffusion among domestic enterprises. The slump in demand will at the same time be an important element of positive change in the domestic distribution system, in particular with respect to organizational and marketing technology development. Lastly, there is a visible process of increased utilization of various forms of technology transfer from abroad, particularly in the form of sub-contracting and joint ventures.

The role of joint ventures in technology transfer to Polish industry is difficult to determine, as the length of time of their operations in the country is still too short for a comprehensive analysis in this respect. However, the technology factor is often cited by foreign investors as the one leading to a positive decision to be established in Poland. The motivations behind such investment decisions are listed in Table 8.3.

Table 8.3 indicates that foreign capital may be an important source of technology for Polish industry. Organizational and technological factors were pointed out by foreign investors as the factors that affected their decisions to locate their businesses in Poland. In reality, however, this may not mean that increased technology flows to the host country would follow the establishment of foreign companies. In fact, the analysis of

Table 8.3. *Motivations to invest in Poland*

Motivation	Rank
Unsaturated Polish market	2.0
Weak competition on the Polish market	1.9
Low initial value of investment	1.7
Low labor costs in Poland	1.7
Organizational superiority	1.6
Possible high profits	1.5
Strong competition on the home market	1.3
Technological superiority	1.2
Possession of technology particularly suitable for Poland	1.1
Entering neighboring markets from Polish location	1.1
Barriers in direct export on the Polish market	

Notes: 0 – no motivation; 3 – very strong motivation.
Source: M. Malecki, "Motivations to invest in Poland," *Sprawy Miedzynarodowe*, Warsaw, no. 4, 1989.

activities of joint ventures shows that the scope of technology transfer is rather limited. Only a few licensing agreements have been concluded so far and the number of these arrangements is not expected to grow in the close future. Foreign-owned enterprises are usually more effective and better organized than their Polish counterparts and this seems to be the most substantial input of foreign capital to the technological upgrading of Polish industry. In particular, it refers to one aspect of the organization of the production process, i.e. the speed and effectiveness of the decision-making process and lower administrative costs as compared with Polish enterprises.

Prospects for East–West technology flows

International technology flows are determined to a great extent by the general trade developments. Dynamics and structure of East–West commercial and economic relations are determined, *inter alia*, by the pattern of economic reforms in Central and Eastern Europe. The direction of these reforms in most countries of the region seems to be conducive to more dynamic commercial and technological links between East and West. The export drive of Polish enterprises in the course of 1990 seems to confirm this general conclusion. However, this may relate only to a few countries in the region that have already undertaken serious economic restructuring programs. In other countries, this process is still in its initial phase.

The opportunities for increased technology flows between Central and Eastern Europe and developed market economies may also be found in the joint investment activities of the partners. The scale of foreign capital involvement in the economies of the East is still rather limited and the prospects of growth seem to be significant in this area. The capitalization of many investment projects is relatively small and there is a widespread opinion that large capital will soon be attracted to locate in the region. This, in turn, depends considerably upon the general economic and political climate for foreign investments.

The third factor influencing the prospects for East–West technology transfer is the long-term Western assistance programs for the economies in Central and Eastern Europe. It seems that the macro-economic role of this aid is fairly modest (with the exception of the GDR) though it may bring about some positive, indirect results from the point of view of technological upgrading in the region. In particular, it relates to such components of these assistance programs as on-the-job training, review of some sectoral policies, or aid in development of selected sectors of the economy. The major problem here is not only the magnitude of this aid, but also the capacity to efficiently absorb foreign resources. Fundamental changes underway in some East European economies are shifting those countries from basically intra-CMEA type of relations to the intra-European ones. The cost of that shift is still to be paid and the only firm way to generate the necessary resources is the increase of domestic savings.

Lastly, it should be underlined that most of the institutional factors hampering East–West technology flows in the past are now being eased. In particular, this relates to decisions of the COCOM in 1990 to remove some high technologies from the embargo list to Poland, Hungary, and Czechoslovakia. This may give rise, in the near future, to more direct and long-term technological cooperation in fairly new areas, e.g. tele-communications or the computer industry.

9 The opening of the USSR to foreign capital: from concessions during NEP to joint ventures under perestroika

Patrick Gutman

After an extended period of nearly sixty years (1929–87), foreign capital is once again welcome in the Soviet Union. A number of observers draw a parallel between the policy of concessions introduced by Lenin and Krasin at the beginning of NEP and the emergence of equity joint ventures launched by Gorbachev since January 1987 within the framework of perestroika.

By underlining the continuous use of foreign capital, these observers – even unconsciously – give credit to the thesis that history is repeating itself. Methodologically, it is necessary to keep in mind that most of those who draw a parallel between joint ventures under perestroika and concessions at the time of NEP limit themselves to a simple *historical* comparison. Their approach highlights a *descriptive* course of events and underlines the resort to foreign capital without presenting a comparative perspective.

From an analytical point of view, an identical repetition cannot be deduced. It seems important to state *a priori* that repetition of facts does not necessarily imply a similarity of organizational modalities. Only an *analytical* comparative perspective of concessions and joint ventures could lead to a judgment. We will thus examine the two forms of foreign capital in the USSR, using the same analytical criteria in order to demonstrate similarities and differences.

In the first section, I shall try to work out whether the policy of concessions as well as that of joint ventures relate to financial capital export (*exportation de capitaux*) or to productive capital export (*exportation de capital*) according to a distinction put forward by the French economist, Charles-Albert Michalet.

In the second section, we shall compare concessions and joint ventures as different forms of foreign capital in the USSR. In particular, we shall examine both practices as regards "property rights" and organizational modalities.

I   **The similarity of the concessions and joint ventures**

Charles-Albert Michalet showed in *Le Capitalisme mondial* (1976 and 1985) that, by asserting the supremacy of money capital over productive capital, Lenin did not enable us to fully comprehend the current situation as to the internationalization of the process of production. Indeed, in his historically dated analysis of imperialism, Lenin relegated to a position of secondary importance what is in fact the increasingly predominant form of the internationalization of capital, i.e. the delocalization of production which brings about a transfer of the site of value creation.

In fact, the distinction introduced by C. A. Michalet between money capital and productive capital – following Marx's cycle of capital – makes it possible to go beyond the Leninist interpretation by showing that "money capital export does not exhaust the process of imperialism. By only considering this aspect of the internationalization of capital, one misses out the main thing. Indeed, whereas capital is money, it does not follow that all money is capital."[1]

Such a distinction between "exportation de *capital*" versus "exportation de *capitaux*" is difficult to express in English since the singular and the plural forms of the term "capital" are strictly identical. In French, C. A. Michalet can play with the two different forms. In the first case (exportation de *capital*), the emphasis is put on productive capital and the expression then refers to a transfer of the means of production to a foreign location. In the second case (exportation de *capitaux*), the accent is put on massive financial capital exports in accordance with Lenin's interpretation in *Imperialism, the Highest Stage of Capitalism* (1917).

Taking up the distinction made by Michalet, we shall try to assess whether concessions and joint ventures, separated by a time-span of sixty years, entailed a massive money-capital import into the USSR, as during the Tsarist period or whether, on the contrary, they are in fact nothing more than a productive capital import.[2]

Looking at concessions under NEP and joint ventures under perestroika, one can observe a clear link between strong domestic capital constraint and the resort to foreign capital. Unable to obtain commercial credits, much less financial loans, in the beginning of the twenties, the Soviets used the concession mechanism to attract *new* capital. Similarly, though in a different context, joint ventures allow for an increased degree of liberty as regards the management of domestic capital constraint as well as the external one (foreign debt). In this sense, joint ventures can be considered as a way of preventing an excess-

ive increase of the debt. In such a perspective, the question is to substitute foreign direct investment for international credit.[3]

But, apart from the appearance of similarity in the aims – to generate
a massive import of money-capital in the Leninist sense – it remains to
be seen whether both concessions and joint ventures have achieved or
are achieving their goal.

As to concessions, Boris Eliacheff noted in 1926 that foreign capital
invested in the USSR had reached 60 to 70 million gold rubles.[4] He
added that such an amount was insignificant compared to the import of
capital before the Revolution which amounted to billions of gold
rubles.[5] Using Soviet sources, Joseph Watstein indicates that in 1927 the
cumulative foreign capital of the most important thirty-nine concessions
amounted to $30 million, that is to say, less than 1 percent of the overall
capital invested in related sectors. Furthermore, Alec Nove points out
that the sixty-eight concessions still in operation in 1928 represented
only 0.6 percent of the industrial production.[6]

Thus, it is clear that the concessionary policy failed in its primary task,
to attract a massive import of capital. What about joint ventures under
perestroika?

First of all, and from a methodological point of view, a comparison
between concessions and joint ventures is somewhat problematic as the
latter have only been in existence for three and a half years, and thus, a
comparison in terms of capitalization might seem to be premature.
Nevertheless, we are going to draw a parallel as most of the concessions
were established during a five-year span: 1922–26 (see Table 9.1).

Bearing this in mind, it seems that joint ventures – as the former
concessions – do not massively attract foreign capital. The figures provided by the Economic Commission for Europe in the *East–West Joint
Ventures News Letter* as well as those by *Plan Econ Report* show that
foreign capital in joint ventures at the end of the first term of 1990 is
approximately $2 billion. Furthermore, it seems that the evolution of
foreign capitalization is quite contradictory.

On the one hand, the relative importance of the foreign share within
the global statutory capital of joint ventures established in the USSR has
gradually increased since 1987: 34.8 percent for that year, 38.7 percent
in 1988, and 43.3 percent in 1989 (for the first nine months). But, on the
other hand, a steady and uninterrupted decrease of the average foreign
share in each joint venture can be observed: from 241,304 rubles
($388,240) in 1987 to 150,416 rubles ($247,976) in 1988 and to 96,355
rubles ($151,084) during the first nine months of 1989.[7]

The increasing number of joint ventures (23 at the beginning of 1988,
700 in June 1989, 936 in October 1989, 1274 by early 1990, and 1,572 as

Table 9.1. *Statistical data on concessions (number of concessions and percentage*

Nationality of applicants for concessions, 1922–1 July 1927

Nationality of applicant	1922	1923	1924	1925	1926	1927	Total
German	124	216	99	54	216	52	761
British	40	80	33	17	35	14	219
American	45	45	35	28	42	6	201
French	29	53	19	24	36	11	172
Others	100	213	125	130	177	54	799
Total	338	607	311	253	506	137	2,152

Nationality of the holders of concessions, 1922–1926

Nationality of the Concessionaire	1922	1923	1924	1925	1926	Total	Percent of concessions to applications
German	6	12	3	7	11	39	5.5
British	3	6	7	6	1	23	11.2
American	4	5	1	3	2	15	7.7
French		1		2	2	5	3.1
Polish		1	1	2	3	7	9.7
Austrian		2			3	5	7.7
Japanese				4	1	5	4.7
Concessions with mixed capital (Soviet and foreign)		4			1	5	9.4
Others	3	14	14	6	4	41	8.0
Total	16	45	26	30	28	145	7.7
Percent to the total request	5.4	7.3	3.3	11.8	5.5		

Source: S. Chase, R. Dunn, R. G. Tugwell, eds. *Soviet Russia in the Second Decade*, William and Norgate, London 1928, pp. 346–48.

of 1 April 1990) demonstrates that foreign investors tend to set up a venture in order to get a foothold in a growing Soviet market. However, foreign investors do not neglect the risk factor at a time of great difficulties for perestroika. In fact, foreign entrepreneurs are cautious and

Spheres of activity of applications for concessions submitted to the central concessions committee, 1922–1 July 1927

Branch of national economy	1922	1923	1924	1925	1926	1927	Total
Manufacturing industry	66	126	73	80	269	66	680
Trade	71	152	95	65	112	22	517
Mining	63	89	37	29	30	7	255
Agriculture	46	87	34	16	15	1	199
Transport and communications	39	46	24	17	17	3	146
Timber	24	34	17	15	13	7	110
Fishing and hunting	7	11	6	12	13	3	52
Others	22	62	25	19	37	28	193
							2,152
Total	338	607	311	253	506	137	

Main branches of economy in which concessions were granted, 1922–1926

Branch of National Economy	1922	1923	1924	1925	1926	Total	Percent of concessions to applications
Trade	4	14	10	6	2	36	7.4
Timber	1	4	1			6	6.4
Agriculture	3	5		2		10	5.1
Fishing and hunting		3	1	1	1	6	12.2
Mining	4	3	5	9	4	25	10.2
Manufacturing industry		7	6	6	13	32	
Transport and communication	4						5.5
		5	2	1		12	8.5
Building				2	1	3	6.0
Technical aid		1	1	2	5	9	13.6
Others		3		1	2	6	5.5
Total	16	45	26	30	28	145	7.7

select sectors of low capitalization (services, engineering, etc.) or activities which generate direct hard currency revenues (tourism, restaurant, and hotel management). The question is how to steady earnings as soon as possible. Such an attitude is geared toward a minimization of risks. It is unlikely that the growth of joint ventures could make a massive contribution of foreign capital in the present context of the Soviet economy.

After four years of foreign direct investment in the USSR (1987–90), it can be said that neither joint ventures under perestroika (up to now) nor the concessions of NEP have been able to generate massive inflows of capital in Lenin's wording in *Imperialism, the Highest Stage of Capitalism*. Instead, they can be considered as a capital export mechanism in the sense put forward by C. A. Michalet, that is to say, as an export of technical means of production which allows a delocalization of the process of production.

As such, concessions and joint ventures play a qualitative role by introducing into the economy and disseminating modern fabrication processes, technical standards, and Western norms of production as a transfer of technology mechanism. Antony Sutton has particularly underlined this aspect for the concessionary policy.[8] If NEP's concessions and perestroika's joint ventures follow the *historical* line of foreign capital under Tsarist Russia, they break with the latter as far as they fall into "exportation de *capital*" as opposed to "exportation de *capitaux*."

In fact, concessions missed their first objective: to encourage a massive flow of capital. Presently, joint ventures seem to evidence the same trend. This similarity of concessions and joint ventures, with an interval of sixty years in between, to a certain extent gives credit to the thesis that history is repeating itself. However, this common characteristic, in relation to the problematic "exportation de capitaux" versus "exportation de capital" does not necessarily imply identical ways of involving foreign capital.

II   Concessions as opposed to joint ventures

For the study of concessions, we shall concentrate on the "pure" form of concessions, that is to say, type 1 of Antony Sutton's typology. This author identifies the three following types:[9]

> the "pure" concession (or type 1) was an agreement between the USSR and a foreign enterprise whereby the foreign firm was enabled to develop and exploit an opportunity within the USSR under the legal doctrine of *usufruct*, i.e. without acquiring property rights;
>
> the "mixed" company concession (or type 2) generated a corporation in which Soviet and foreign participation were on an equal basis (at first 50:50 but later 51:49), with a Soviet

chairman of the board who had the deciding vote in cases of
dispute;

whereas the first two types are clearly recognized as concessions
by Sutton himself, the technical-assistance contract (or
type 3) has not usually been designated as a concession,
except in the USSR.

In our view, technical-assistance contracts do not form part of the
concessionary policy. Sutton recognizes that these can be excluded from
the analysis, even though he takes them into consideration since he
focuses on technology transfer. As to the "mixed" company concessions, their small number (between twenty and thirty according to different sources)[10] and especially their main commercial function (as
intermediaries in foreign and domestic) trade render them totally atypi-
cal with regard to the principles and functioning logic of "pure"
concessions.

Focusing on the latter – without denying the existence of a few
"mixed" company concessions under NEP – we just follow the views of
several authors on this matter.[11] This enables us to have a precise
approach to the essence of the mechanism of concessions: this is a
delegation strategy and not a *partnership* strategy, and in this we oppose
Sutton's extensive approach of the concessionary policy.

Property rights

To revert to a restrictive definition of concessions is strongly justified
since the adoption of the concessionary policy is based on an ideology
aimed at preserving the ownership of the means of production by the
Soviet state in conformity with the spirit of the proletarian revolution.

The Soviet government was compelled by the need for capital to
encourage foreign activities on its territory through concessions as it was
impossible to get capital without capitalists. However, the presence of
the class enemy is barely tolerated and Soviet legislation is geared
toward its minimization in two ways.

First, the concession contract has a derogatory characteristic in relation to common law. Arsène Stoupnitsky underlines that "in spite of the
importance given by the Soviet government to the concessions contract
as a means to attract foreign capital, there does not exist a general
regulation for such type of contract."[12] Second, the concession contract
is "only a contractual agreement between the state and a private
individual who is granted the right to conduct business on state
property."[13]

Thus, the concession is in essence a strategy of delegation and not of partnership. Furthermore, the concession does not grant any "property rights", it only gives the right of use. Consequently, it deals with *usus fructus* ("pure" concessions of NEP) instead of *abusus fructus* (equity joint ventures under perestroika).

This essential characteristic is emphasized in the treatise on Soviet civil and commercial law:

> In examining the notion of concession in the Soviet law, we will realize that the concessionary right does not amount to ownership. For example, a concessionary in State property does not have the right to transfer it to a third party; in other words, he is not free to dispose of his concession (article 55, note). However, the Soviet law grants this right to owners, otherwise, the lack of this right would take away the substance of ownership. Under such conditions, article 55 on the property right of concession is illusory and inexact. All state assets mentioned in articles 53 and 55 could be granted as concessions but they can never be appropriated.[14]

On the contrary, foreign partners involved in equity joint ventures under perestroika have the opportunity to become majority shareholders. Thus, this constitutes a decisive institutional gap in terms of "property rights." There is a change of strategy from concessions to equity joint ventures with the opportunity granted to foreign capital, in theory and in practice, to manage the joint corporation as a majority shareholder.

This is a significative breakthrough undertaken by perestroika so as to ensure a managerial revolution. It reflects the change of mind with regard to direct foreign investment: the USSR's ideological perception of direct foreign investment as *exportation de capitaux* dates back in history to Lenin's statement in *Imperialism*. At present, there is a pragmatic approach of direct foreign investment as *exportation de capital*. It has lost its ideological dimension and is seen as an opportunity to benefit from a training effect.[15]

Compared to "pure" concessions, there is a striking change, from a mechanism without "property rights" (*usus fructus*) to one with "property rights" (*abusus fructus*). Even taking into consideration type 2 ("mixed" company concessions) there are two features showing the progress made under perestroika: (a) from a conception relevant to "New Forms of Investment"[16] – "mixed" company concessions under NEP – there has been an evolution toward a conception relevant to majority direct investment (equity joint ventures) and from 26 October 1990 to wholly owned subsidiaries; (b) the state is not necessarily any longer the obligatory partner with the right of casting votes as was the case with "mixed" company concessions at the time of NEP.

Due to the "regulated demonopolization" of foreign trade,[17] the

Soviet partner in equity joint ventures can be, for example, a cooperative. Thus, the state not only abandons a part of its rights over the means of production to foreign capital, but it does so to the benefit of decentralized Soviet agents!

Last but not least, the upheaval in terms of "property rights" can be interpreted as the road to privatization. In fact, it is clear that the possibility granted to the foreign partners to become majority shareholders in the statutory ·capital of joint ventures by the decree of 2 December 1988 was the last step toward the wholly owned subsidiary.

The decree finally passed on 26 October 1990 – in the air for several months[18] – which allows foreign capital to acquire Soviet firms directly and wholly, represents a radical move forward in terms of principles. Indeed, in terms of property rights granted to foreign capital, perestroika goes much further than NEP, even if the presidential decree does not go as far as to grant land and underground property. The decree only grants *usus* of underground and land as was the case under NEP with the mechanism of concession. This last point explains the return of the concession formula, especially for the exploitation of raw materials (petroleum, diamonds etc.).[19]

From now on, a subsidiary is going to be either the result of the establishment of a new company (as was the case for joint ventures) or the purchase of an existing one (take-over). In the second case, it is privatization by means of foreign direct investment without any obligation to set up a joint venture with a local partner. Direct investment in the USSR is therefore no longer a mere mode of operating in a foreign country – as between 1987 and 1990 – but it also becomes a privatization mechanism in the framework of the transition toward a market economy. Thanks to the junction established between privatization and foreign direct investment, the multinationalization strategies in the USSR now fall into the mergers–acquisitions operations as in Eastern Europe.[20] We can even imagine that foreign direct investment might contribute to partially solve the debt problem through the "debt–equity–swap" mechanism. Thus, there would be a triple interaction between foreign direct investment, privatization, and debt. Such a direction would indicate that the USSR is willing to substitute foreign direct investment coupled with privatization to an "international credit economy."

Organizational modalities

From an analytical and theoretical point of view, NEP concessions and perestroika joint ventures are both alliance strategies. They are part of the "contractual economy," this intermediary road between "pure market" and "pure internalization." But, even if they both pertain to the "contractual economy," they have, however, different characteristics.

While concessions were granted the *usus fructus*, i.e. the right to exploit, they were not given "property rights." They correspond to a strategy of delegation to foreign capital by the central authority that for certain reasons is not in a position to entrust domestic agents with specific activities. In concessions, the foreign operator works by himself, fulfilling a task that, most of the time, would not have been possible without him because of lack of capital and/or appropriate technology. From this point of view, the concessions are not a policy of "second best." However, the bargaining power of the foreign operator was very narrow: the rules of the game were already established by the administrative authorities (Central Concessions Committee) and all concessions except those of minor importance had to be ratified by the Council of People's Commissars.

On the contrary, equity joint ventures under perestroika grant "property rights" to foreign capital and originate a joint activity. They have thus a completely different perspective from the concessions of the NEP. A strategy of *delegation* has changed to a strategy of *partnership*.

But, the joint venture shows a partial loss of "property rights" by the central government or its representatives that benefits the foreign operator. The latter observes at the same time that his bargaining power becomes more important compared to the concessions regime. As shown by Svejnar and Smith,[21] even if the host government were to determine unilaterally the distribution of accounting profits in the formal contract setting up the venture, the partners would still divide the actual profits in proportion to their true bargaining power so long as at least one input (transfer) price is subject to bargaining. According to Egon Neuberger: "Thus, if relative bargaining power, rather than the contractually set profit shares, determines the actual division of net profits, we can explain why transnational corporations enter into joint ventures under varying and often seemingly adverse conditions in term of their contractual share of profit."[22]

Joint ventures as compared to concessions mean a withdrawing in Soviet prerogatives on both "property rights" and power. Nevertheless, joint ventures have been chosen because as an organizational outfit they are supposed to allow for a better transfer of technology than other forms of presence in the market as explained by Egon Neuberger in the following terms:

There are four basic options available to a government or firm: (a) a licensing agreement covering only current technology tends to have the lowest cost in terms of fees and restrictions: (b) one covering both current and future technology is likely to have more restrictions; (c) a joint venture in which the recipient of the technology is the dominant partner; this option has a higher cost than a licensing agreement since it requires giving up some equity but it generally provides a higher level of technology transfer since the provider of the technology has a much stronger incentive to make its most advanced technology available and the technology transfer effective than is true under a licensing agreement; and (d) a shared management joint venture, one in which both partners participate in the management on relatively equal terms; this has the highest cost in terms of both the equity which has to be given up and the difficulty involved in management (and therefore in the probability of failure) but it also results in the highest level of technology transfer because the incentive for the technology provider is as high or higher than when he is a passive partner, and there is generally a greater participation of personnel from the technology provider with the consequent transfer of the very important intangible technical know-how."[23]

As a result, the choice of joint ventures and now wholly owned subsidiaries reflects the Soviet will to move from a mere technology transfer – with all the absorption and assimilation problems going with such a transfer – to the opening of the "technological package" in order to encourage a "learning by doing" effect, to profit by Western management techniques, and to diffuse Western standards of production.

It also means that the Soviet Union has decided to move from an *inter-firm* cooperation toward an *intra-firm* cooperation, looking for a higher degree of internalization. This explains to a large extent the decree passed on 26 October 1990 which allows foreign capital to have wholly owned subsidiaries.

Conclusion

It is clear that from NEP to perestroika, an important transformation took place in the Soviet perception of foreign capital even if, for years, it remains an "exportation de *capital*" instead of an "exportation de *capitaux*," as opposed to the Tsarist period between 1870 and 1917. Perestroika reflects the substitution of an ideological approach by a pragmatic one in the use of foreign capital. It is already possible to be a majority shareholder but it will also soon be possible for foreigners to be sole owners of Soviet firms. In this sense, Lenin's conception has been completely reviewed in the light of the "world economy."

However, we face a paradox: up to now, perestroika goes further than

NEP in terms of "property rights" granted to foreign capital whereas NEP went further than perestroika in the transition toward a market economy. In fact, joint ventures have today a number of particular advantages which depart from the general rules but operate within an economic framework where the systemic mechanisms have not yet really changed.

As strange as it may seem, at the end of September 1991 – i.e. nearly a year after the completion of our contribution and a month after the putsch attempt – the political and economic evolution taking place in the USSR does not challenge the main lines of our analysis.

From a factual point of view, the cumulative inflow of foreign capital still remains at a low level: $3.151 billion as of 1 January 1991 according to the statistics of the Economic Commission for Europe of the United Nations. Hence, they keep on reflecting "productive capital export" rather than massive "money-capital export."

From a legal point of view and referring to organizational modes concerning the setting up of foreign capital, the law on foreign direct investment dated 5 July 1991 ratified the measures of the presidential decree dated 26 October 1990 that allowed: (a) a 100 percent foreign stake and (b) a diversification of investments' setting-up modes, the possibility to carry out take-over operations rather than mere greenfield investment now authorizes property rights' *transfers* in favor of foreign capital within the privatization framework.

Also, article 41 explicitly provides for recourse to concessions in order to attract foreign capital, in particular for projects involving raw materials. In this respect, the transfers of competence that are taking place from the all-union to the republic level do not seem to modify the property rights granted to foreign operators: ground and underground will remain the property of host republics.

In conclusion, even if the wording of article 41 is extremely vague and imprecise (making ways for dispensatory set-up), it is clear that the very idea of concessions and the possibility to set them up is now acknowledged as a result of the law on foreign direct investment passed last July.

Notes

This is a revised version of a paper presented at the IVth World Congress for Soviet and East European Studies, Harrogate, 21–26 July 1990 (Panel 33, The present role of NEP in the economic debate).

1. C. A. Michalet, *Le Capitalisme mondial*, PUF, Paris, 1976, p. 85; 2nd edn, 1985.
2. On this matter, see René Girault's works and, in particular, R. Girault, *Emprunts russes et investissements français en Russie*, Sorbonne University Press/Armand Colin, Paris, 1973; and R. Girault, "Décollage économique et nationalisme: le cas russe," *Relations internationales*, Brussels, vol. 4, no. 2, 1982, pp. 241–76.
3. This point is discussed by the Trilateral Commission in its 1989 report on East–West economic relations. See *Le Monde*, 12 April 1989, p. 35.
4. See B. Eliacheff, "Notes sur la Russie – régime des concessions," *Revue d'économie politique*, Paris, vol. 40, 1926, p. 870. Eliacheff's estimates of the foreign capitalization are very near to those of Preobrazhensky in his article "Results of our concessionary policy," *Ekonomicheskaia zhizn*, 22 January 1925, quoted by A. de Goulevitch in his study, "Les Concessions et les sociétés mixtes en Russie soviétique," *Revue économique internationale*, Brussels, vol. 4, no. 2, 1925, pp. 247–48. Hwang Jen's estimates are about the same level: 80 million gold rubles. See H. Jen, *Le Régime des concessions en Russie soviétique*, Librairie Universitaire J. Gambier, Paris, 1929, p. 21.
5. Eliacheff, "Notes sur la Russie," p. 870.
6. J. Watstein, "Soviet economic concessions: the agony and the promise," *The ACE Bulletin*, Tempe, vol. 16, no. 1, Spring 1974, p. 23. A. Nove, *An Economic History of the USSR*, The Penguin Press, Allen Lane, 1969, p. 89.
7. Economic Commission for Europe, *East–West Joint Ventures News Letter*, no. 3, 1989, p. 5, United Nations.
8. A. Sutton, *Western Technology and Soviet Economic Development, 1917 to 1930*, vol. 1, Stanford University Press, 1968.
9. Ibid., p. 8.
10. The majority of authors do not make a distinction between "pure" concessions (type 1) and "mixed" company concessions (type 2) in their global statistics. Even Antony Sutton mixes up types 1 and 2. To my knowledge, only Nesteroff presents global statistics distinguishing these two types. See P. Nesteroff, "La Situation juridique des étrangers en Russie des Soviets et les régime des concessions," *Revue de droit international privé*, Paris, vol. 22, 1927, pp. 37–43.
11. For example, one can name Krimmer for whom the "mixed" company concessions are not really pertaining to the concessionary policy. See A. Krimmer, *Sociétés de capitaux en Russie impériale et en Russie soviétique*, Imprimerie J. Aloccio, Tunis, 1934, p. 417.
12. A. Stoupnitsky, "Droit international privé soviétique," in A. de Lapradelle and J. P. Niboyet (eds.), *Répertoire de droit international*, vol. 7, Sirey, Paris, 1930 p. 89, paragraph 21.
13. Ibid., p. 103, paragraph 94.
14. B. Eliashevich, P. Tager, and B. Nolde (eds.), *Traité de droit civil et commercial des soviets*, Librairie Générale de Droit et de Jurisprudence, Paris, vol. 3, 1930, p. 11.
15. On this point, see P. Gutman, "Sociétés mixtes à l'Est et dynamique des flux réciproques d'investissements directs Est–Ouest: nouvelles perspec-

tives," in W. Andreff (ed.), *Réforme et échanges extérieurs dans les pays de l'Est*, L'Harmattan, Paris, pp. 201–2.

16. In his typology of "New forms of investment," Charles Oman includes minority-owned joint ventures, so that "mixed" company concessions under NEP can be considered as a typical New Form of Investment. See C. Oman, *New Forms of International Investment in Developing Countries*, OECD, Paris, pp. 14, 15 (French edn).

17. On this matter, see N. Simon, "Approche: démonopolisation encadrée," *Le Moniteur du commerce international*, Paris, no. 872, 12 June 1989, pp. 82–90.

18. As early as April 1990, Valentin Pavlov, the Soviet Minister of Finance, declared to Interfax (Moscow) that foreign investors might very soon be allowed to purchase shares in state corporations, particularly in the machine-building industry and the consumer goods sector. See *Le Monde*, 6 April 1990, p. 31.

19. See M. Lavigne, "L'URSS dans la crise," *Problèmes économiques*, Paris, no. 2189, 5 September 1990, p. 31.

20. See P. Gutman, "From joint ventures to wholly owned foreign direct investment: new perspectives in Eastern Europe and Soviet Union," in P. Friedensen, B. Wilpert, and X. Iakovleda (eds.), *East–West Joint Ventures: Problems and Prospects*, Campus Verlag, Frankfurt-on-Main, 1992 (forthcoming).

21. J. Svejnar and S. C. Smith, "The economics of joint ventures in centrally planned and labor-managed economies," *Journal of Comparative Economics*, San Diego, vol. 6, no. 2, June 1982, pp. 168–69.

22. E. Neuberger, "Joint ventures in Eastern Europe: theoretical considerations, survey of facts and lessons for China," Research Paper no. 315, Suny-Stony Brook, February 1989, p. 16. A French translation appeared in *Revue d'études comparatives Est–Ouest*, CNRS, Paris, vol. 21, no. 1, 1990, pp. 5–26.

23. Ibid., p. 16.

10   Current joint venture law and its impact on the Polish economy

Jozef Misala

Poland belongs to the forefront of the CMEA countries introducing democratic social changes and radical systemic transformations, which are reflected, *inter alia*, in regulations concerning foreign capital investments. The aim of this chapter is to provide an outline of foreign direct investments in Poland and to suggest points for further discussion.

The first part gives a description and evaluation of the development of foreign capital investments in Poland, covering the period between 1976 and the end of 1988. The second part presents an outline of the institutional conditioning of development of those investments in 1989 and in 1990. The third part concentrates on the development of foreign capital investments in Poland and their economic significance in new conditions. Finally, the fourth part presents fundamental economic problems which are widely discussed at present and some general conclusions.

1   Development of foreign capital investments in Poland to the end of 1988

1.1   *Consecutive stages and outline of conditions*

The development of foreign capital investments in Poland until the end of 1988 can be divided into the following stages: (a) foreign small-scale enterprises (FSSE), 1976 to 1982; (b) transitory period, 1983–86; and (c) of two binding laws on the operation of foreign capital, which ended in 1989. This division is justified both from the legal and economic point of view.[1]

The first stage of operation of foreign capital in the Polish economy was initiated with the resolution of the Council of Ministers of 14 May 1976 in which the possibility of investing in Poland was declared. However, this declaration was limited. First, in spite of the necessity of opening up the Polish economy, the relevant opportunities were limited in a subjective sense, i.e. it was only the representatives of Polonia

(Poles settled abroad) who were allowed to invest in Poland (even with 100 percent of equity capital). Second, investment and operation possibilities were confined to the sphere of small-scale production (especially handicraft). The basis for operation of the so-called Polonian enterprises (defined by the law of 6 June 1982) were permits issued by local authorities, specifying in detail the kind of production and the maximum level of employment.

Adoption of the law by the Sejm (Polish parliament) on 6 June 1982, and more precisely its coming into effect, started the second stage of operation of FSSE in Poland, clearly reflected in the growth in numbers. However, already in July 1983, by the force of an appropriate resolution of the Council of Ministers the requirements binding FSSE became much more stringent. For instance, the rate of corporate income tax was increased from 50 percent to 80 percent and the obligation to resell 50 percent of foreign exchange revenues (net) was replaced with an obligatory resale of 50 percent of export revenues irrespective of the value of imports. Finally, in January 1985, the so-called ceiling of minimum foreign exchange investment outlays was introduced, i.e. the minimum account value of $US 50,000 of declared outlays was regarded as a necessary condition for issuance of a permit for the establishment of a FSSE. Apart from that, an obligation was imposed on foreign investors to place on foreign exchange deposit an equivalent of the declared value to make sure they fulfill their commitments. As I. Nawrocki points out:

in the result of growing descrepancy between publically expressed expectations of the authorities and deteriorating real conditions of operation of foreign enterprises in the years 1983–1986, the climate of unwillingness of the authorities and a part of the society towards those enterprises actually arisen did not contribute to overcoming psychological barriers to the inflow of foreign capital ... Moreover, distortions of the profile of FSSE operation increased which made shaping of a structure adequate to the needs of the national economy difficult.[2]

The third stage of operation of foreign capital in Poland opened with an adoption of another law by the Sejm on 23 April 1986. By its force foreign capital was given access to the so-called state-owned and cooperative sectors of the economy, which means, with several exceptions, access to the entire national economy. At the same time, apart from FSSE, the law provided for another form of foreign investment in Poland, namely joint venture companies including those with capital which did not belong to the so-called Polonia. This meant a considerable broadening of the scope for investment in Poland, which was made accessible to virtually any foreigner. However, provisions regulating the setting up and operation of FSSE differed from those pertaining to

Table 10.1. *Share of FSSE in employment and total value of Poland's foreign trade turnover, 1977–1988 (percent)*

Year	Number of FSSE	Share in total employment	Share in turnover with payment in area I		Share in turnover with payment in area II	
			Imports	Exports	Imports	Exports
1977	3	0.0	–	–	–	–
1978	12	0.0	–	–	–	–
1979	30	0.0	–	–	–	–
1980	76	0.0	–	–	0.0	0.0
1981	154	0.1	–	–	0.0	0.0
1982	252	0.1	0.0	0.0	0.0	0.0
1983	491	0.1	0.0	0.0	0.1	0.1
1984	633	0.2	0.0	0.1	0.4	0.3
1985	683	0.3	0.0	0.1	0.5	0.4
1986	695	0.4	0.0	0.2	0.6	0.5
1987	688	0.4	0.1	0.2	0.6	0.7
1988	764	0.4	0.2	0.3	0.7	0.8

Source: I. Nawrocki "Kapital zagraniczny w polskiej gospodarce w latach 1976–1989" [Foreign capital in the Polish economy in the years 1976–1989], *Handel Zagraniczny* [Foreign Trade], no. 415, 1989; GLIS, 1989.

typical joint venture companies, which was rightly seen as an example of unwillingness of the then economic authorities to take advantage of the FSSE experience in foreign capital cooperation and of the lack of a clear concept of future prospects.[3]

1.2   Economic effects

Until the end of 1988 the economic effects of the operation of foreign capital in Poland were minimal, which is partly reflected in data presented in Table 10.1.

In the first stage of FSSE operation, during which their number amounted to 252, their impact on the development of the Polish economy was absolutely insignificant. They marked their existence only in the so-called transitory period (increase in number from 491 to 695 and share in total Polish foreign trade turnover accounting for 0.6 percent), and especially after 1986 (increase in number to 764, and 0.7 percent share in relevant turnover). In 1988 employment in FSSE was already estimated at 71,000 which accounted for 0.4 percent of those employed in the entire national economy, with the share in the value of overall industrial output in Poland amounting to 1.4 percent. Their activity contributed to an increased supply of goods (especially consumer products) on the domestic market. On the other hand, however, they did not live up to the expectations of law makers as far as inflow of modern technologies and management practices is concerned.[4]

Until the end of 1988 the significance of the economic activity of joint venture companies established in Poland under the provision of the law of 1986 was also limited. Since it had come into force the Ministry for Foreign Economic Relations issued fifty-two appropriate permits, but only some forty enterprises undertook economic activity. The value of the initial capital of companies which obtained a permit amounted in 1988 to 9.7 billion zlotys (an equivalent of some $US 23 million at the 1988 official rate of exchange). Their total employment was estimated at 6,700. The major role was performed by partners from the FRG (17 companies), the USA (7), the USSR, the Netherlands, and Great Britain as well as Austria (5 companies each), Switzerland (4), and Sweden (3). Some companies were also joined by partners from other countries, such as Finland, France, Yugoslavia, Belgium, Denmark, and Hungary.[5]

Until the end of 1988 the biggest number of joint ventures registered in Poland operated in the food and agricultural sector (15), computer industry and hotel trade (5 each), construction and building materials (4), electronics and metallurgy (3 each), film making and publishing (3), chemical industry, wood industry, and furniture manufacturing (2 each). In the case of most of these enterprises the value of exports to the market economy countries accounted for as much as 60 to 80 percent of their total value of sales.[6] Nevertheless, the share of those exports did not exceed the level of 0.1 percent of total Polish exports.

2   Legal conditions since 1 January 1989

On 23 December 1988 the Polish parliament adopted the new law on economic activity with the participation of foreign parties (effective since 1 January 1989) thus making another step toward the opening of the Polish economy to investment cooperation. On 16 January 1989 the Foreign Investment Agency was set up and in August 1989 the first noncommunist government was formed; finally, in December of that year, the Sejm adopted a radical economic program and laws setting out provisions for its implementation.[7]

As a result of essential political changes in the country in December 1989, the whole economic system of Poland underwent the process of a far-reaching transformation. These changes were aimed primarily at replacing the centralized system based on a model of "state ownership" economic management with a market-oriented economy, with special emphasis placed on private entrepreneurship. Among the changes implemented in December 1989 the most significant was the introduction of the limited (so-called internal) convertibility of the zloty, the elimination of exemptions and tax preferences in the form of export subsidies, and the setting of almost all economic subjects on an equal footing. Bearing in mind especially the realization of the last task and the so-called internal convertibility in December 1989, the Sejm amended the law in force since January 1989. The law concerning economic activity carried out with the participation of foreign parties with amendments from December 1989 is referred to here as the new (current) law on joint ventures in Poland.[8]

2.1   Basic provisions of the new law on joint ventures

The new law setting out the present provisions that regulate foreign capital investment in Poland is the outcome of many years of endeavors aimed at the increased attractiveness of undertaking economic activity by foreign investors and the gradual introduction of a uniform legal order regulating capital investment made in Poland. This law also regulates past investments made under the provisions of the law of 1982 (on investment in small-scale production), and the law of 1986 on joint venture companies without subject-type limitations. Therefore, the law of December 1989 states that owners of FSSEs have the right to transform their enterprises into joint venture companies operating under the provisions of the new law (upon meeting the appropriate requirements and obtaining the appropriate permit), or they can continue their activity in accordance with the law of 6 July 1982, counting on the fact that there will be no chance to extend their operation period and, what is more important, to set up a new FSSE. This means that FSSEs operating within the formula of ten-year permits, as a rule extended for a further twenty years, will cease to exist in the Polish economy by the years 2010–20. Thus, the problem of duality of foreign investment in Poland will be settled, with a high likelihood that the bulk of FSSEs will be transformed into joint venture companies.[9]

An essential novelty of the law of 23 December 1989 is the establishment of the Foreign Investment Agency whose task is to coordinate foreign capital cooperation. The idea behind it was to set up foundations for a long-term capital cooperation policy involving foreign capital investment in Poland as well as the stabilization of this policy. A provision exists in this law under which foreign investors have the right to participate in various associations on a voluntary basis (instead of their compulsory association in named chambers of industry and commerce, which was provided for in earlier regulations). It is also important that issuance of a permit for the establishment of a joint venture company is accompanied by competent preparation of the appropriate documents. Such a task is more and more often commissioned with consulting companies, the number of which are growing in Poland. Apart from an appropriate application to the agency it is necessary to submit a competently designed draft of a company's founding act, a competent feasibility study of proposed company, and documentary evidence as to the legal and financial status of the prospective shareholders.[10]

The power to issue permits for conducting business activity in manufacturing, commerce, consulting, etc., by a joint venture company rests with the President of the Agency. A permit is to be issued when the business activity ensures in particular: (a) the introduction of modern technologies and organization methods into the national economy; (b) the provision of goods and services for export; (c) improvement in the supply of modern and high quality products and services to the domestic market; and (d) environmental protection. A permit is denied whenever the conduct of the business activity is unjustified due to: (a) the threat to the economic interests of the state and the requirements of environmental protection; and (b) state security and defense interests and the protection of state secrets.

The law gives foreign parties the right to conduct any kind of economic activity in Poland, even their own, still, in some fields of activity the issuance of a permit may be made subject to the participation of a Polish shareholder in a company (e.g. in forwarding and transport companies). Contributions to a company's equity capital may be made both in money (in zlotys obtained by foreign investors after the sale of foreign currencies to a foreign exchange bank), and in kind (provided that they are transferred from abroad or acquired for zlotys obtained through the documented exchange of foreign currency). The law also provides that the contribution of foreign shareholders should not be less than 20 percent of the equity capital, but not less than 25 million zlotys – equivalent to $US 50,000. Those provisions are an attempt to prevent the establishment of joint ventures with fictitious participation of foreign parties, or parties with capital so small that it deprives the foreign contribution of economic significance in accordance with the basic provisions of the law.

The law sets forth the conditions for economic activity conducted in Poland in the form of a limited liability company, a joint stock company (in accordance with the pre-war Commercial Code of 1934), as well as a single partner limited liability company, which constitutes a supplement of its kind to the Commercial Code of 1934. This supplement is another example of the law makers' efforts to make investment in Poland more attractive, as a single foreign investor may acquire the status of a legal person and thus get more secure property rights.

The law contains some further provisions favorable for joint ventures set up in Poland. First, companies are exempt from corporate income tax during the first three years of their business activity, and an additional period of up to three years may be granted if they engage in sectors preferred by the government (including, *inter alia*, food processing, pharmaceutical, chemical, electronic industries, construction, tourism, and manufacturing of packages, specified in a separate resolution of the Council of Ministers).[11] After the expiry of the exemption period joint venture companies are obliged to pay corporate income tax at the rate of 40 percent, which can be reduced upon presentation by the companies of appropriate export increments and donations for socially beneficial purposes.

A company has the sole authority to decide on the object and volume of output, within the limits of the permit. It may freely choose its trade partners and workers at home and abroad. It is also free to set the prices of its goods and services. A company may sell goods and services on the domestic market provided it obtains a foreign exchange license. However, it is obliged to sell all export revenues to a Polish bank, and at the same time has the right to purchase in this bank foreign currencies necessary for import. A company may freely distribute the after-tax profit. It will, however, deposit 8 percent of the after-tax profit with the reserve fund, as soon as the reserve fund reaches 4 percent of the company's costs in a fiscal year.

Another substantial benefit seems to be that the foreign investor is, like the Polish partners, entitled to a dividend from the company's after-tax profit. The foreign currency dividend may be paid from the surplus of export earnings over import outlays. The foreign currency profit may be used to increase the company's equity or freely transferred abroad, while the zloty profits may either be converted into foreign currency and – with the permission of the Ministry of Finance or a special permit – transferred abroad or be spent on the domestic market.

The foreign partner's profits are subject to income tax. In the case of foreign investors domiciled in a country with which Poland has no agreement on the avoidance of double taxation the rate of income tax is 30 percent. In other cases taxes vary from 5 to 15 percent.

Foreign investors or companies do not pay any customs duty on their contribution in kind imported into Poland. Items received after the dissolution of a company can also be exported duty free. Foreign investors may request the Minister of Finance to issue them with special, additional guarantees of compensation payments for losses resulting from nationalization, expropriation, or other such administrative measures. Moreover, Poland is going to conclude bilateral agreements on investment protection with many countries of the world.

2.2   *The economic program: an outline*

Compared with the legal provisions, the actual conditions (rate of economic growth, degree of stability of the economy, directions of structural transformations, etc.) are obviously more important, although it must be borne in mind that they are a direct consequence of adopted systemic and institutional solutions. Therefore, the economic program of the Polish government should be regarded as facilitating the development of direct foreign investment, as it contains, *inter alia*, many endeavors, the implementation of which can contribute to inflow of foreign capital to Poland.

The economic program of the government in office consists of two parts. On the one hand, it includes measures aimed at fast stabilization of the economy (especially checking inflation and restoring equilibrium in the domestic market), and on the other hand, it fosters measures aimed at changing the socio-economic system, and more precisely, providing conditions for developing a modern market economy in Poland, similar to that of West European countries.[12]

A radical and ambitious program of economic stabilization was initiated in January 1990. Simultaneously with measures aimed at stabilizing the economy, the government program insisted on the necessity of bringing about fundamental systemic changes: (a) a transformation of the system of ownership bringing it closer to that in the West; (b) a gradual introduction of a market mechanism, especially liberalization of price setting with a stable exchange rate and an active anti-monopoly policy; (c) a reform of state finance, including a comprehensive reform of the banking system and new principles of monetary and credit policy (with the introduction of a value added tax); (d) the introduction of a capital market; and (e) the creation of a labor market. Besides, it was stated in the program that "conditions for full, external convertibility of the zloty will arise only when the economy has been stabilized and, especially, when the balance of payments equilibrium has been restored" and, that:

broadening of the scope for foreign capital investment should contribute to more intense competition. Foreign investors will be able to buy shares of Polish enterprises, and set up enterprises with exclusive participation of foreign capital.

Foreign exchange transfer pertaining to the share in a company's profits will be regulated by the provisions of foreign exchange law and by bilateral agreements on investment protection.[13]

3   The development of foreign capital investment in Poland under new conditions

3.1   *Extent, dynamics, and structure*

A considerable increase in the number of foreign capital ventures was the main proof of essential changes in the conditions influencing their development after 1 January 1989. The data revealed by the Foreign Investment Agency shows that, up to 31 July 1989, 305 appropriate permits were issued, up to 30 September 1989, 491 permits, and up to the end of March 1990 as many as 1,145 permits.

An analysis of the permits issued until the end of March 1990 shows that the activity of companies with the participation of foreign parties in Poland was dominated by partners from the FRG (especially those from West Berlin). From the point of view of numbers the significance of joint venture companies established in Poland with the participation of partners from Sweden, Austria, the USA, Great Britain, France, the Netherlands, and Italy was also considerable.

The significance of the so-called multinational companies, i.e. those involving capital from three or more countries, was also remarkable from that point of view. It should be added that until the end of March 1990 among the cofounders of joint venture companies applying for permits to undertake business activity in Poland, there were, *inter alia*, partners from Liechtenstein (11 cases), Australia (10), Finland (9), Israel (8), Spain (5), Greece (5), Lebanon (4), Syria, Turkey, Yugoslavia, Luxembourg, Panama (3 cases each), Singapore (2), Malaysia, Jordan, Libya, Japan, Thailand, Portugal, Tunisia, Hong Kong, and Egypt (1 case each).

Partners from the FRG were predominant in the provision of equity to joint venture companies operating in Poland, denominated in zlotys at the rate of exchange of US $1=9,500 zloty, introduced on 1 January 1990. However, their domination over other countries (especially Sweden, Italy, Austria, and the USA) was less conspicuous than in the case of the approach presented in Table 10.2.

The vast majority of joint ventures registered in Poland until the end of March 1990 were involved in more than one branch of the economy. Obviously striving at foreign trade expansion, food processing, wood processing, and the manufacture of building materials were the most

Table 10.2. *Joint ventures in Poland, by country, March 1990*

Country	No. of companies	Share (percent)
FRG	404	35.3
Sweden	101	8.8
Austria	74	6.5
USA	73	6.4
West Berlin	65	5.7
Great Britain	49	4.3
France	49	4.3
Holland	48	4.2
Italy	47	4.1
multinational	46	4.0
Switzerland	29	2.5
Belgium	27	2.4
Canada	24	2.1
Denmark	22	1.9
other	87	7.4
Total	1,145	100.0

Source: E. Sadowska-Cieślak (ed.), *Spolki z udzialem kapitalu zagranicznego* [Companies with the participation of foreign capital], Instytyt Koniunktur i Cen Handlu Zagraniczego [Foreign Trade Research Institute], Warsaw, 1990, mimeo.

frequently selected branches, which from a macro-economic point of view cannot be regarded as an optimal solution for Poland.

3.2   *Impact on economic development*

The coming into force of the new law on economic activity in Poland definitely opened up a new stage of development, but at an initial stage its economic effects were not very impressive. Despite a considerable increase in the number of permits for economic activity with the participation of foreign partners, the amount of the equity capital of joint ventures registered in Poland accounted for only a fraction of domestic capital by April 1990. This also refers to foreign exchange contributions which at the end of March 1990 amounted to $US 186.6 million. At the same time Poland's gross indebtedness *vis-à-vis* the capitalist countries amounted to $US 39.2 billion, and indebtedness *vis-à-vis* the countries until recently referred to as "socialist" amounted to $US 6.6 billion.

The number of joint ventures registered in Poland until the end of March 1990 (1,145) is not significant either, when we compare it with the overall number of private enterprises (agriculture excluded). The

Table 10.3. *Geographical structure of joint venture companies in Poland by value of equity capital revaluated at rate of exchange of 1 January 1990, 1$US = 9500 zl (March 1990)*

Country	Total value of partners' equity (millions of zlotys)	Share in percent
FRG	729,951.7	21.4
Sweden	334,830.5	9.8
Austria	174,249.8	5.1
USA	178,876.6	5.3
West Berlin	181,640.5	5.3
Great Britain	96,785.1	2.8
France	67,494.8	2.0
Holland	277,423.5	8.2
Italy	317,890.8	9.3
multinational	304,788.3	9.0
Switzerland	60,004.0	1.8
Belgium	11,225.8	3.3
Canada	37,847.8	1.1
Denmark	42,919.3	1.3
other	497,749.9	14.3
Total	3,403,659,3	100.0

Source: as in Table 10.2 and own calculations.

Central Statistical Office estimates their number at some 800,000. Nevertheless, joint ventures being established in Poland constitute a part of the private sector which is clearly gaining in importance in Poland. In 1989 the share of the private sector (including agriculture) in the national income produced accounted for 20.3 percent as compared with 18.1 percent in the preceding year.[14]

At the end of March 1990, 1,145 foreign partners declared investment in the form of joint ventures in Poland of an amount of some $US 186 million, which means that equity capital at the moment of filling an application for a permit amounted on the average to $US 163,000. Thus, the extent of foreign capital investment in Poland was not considerable and there were virtually no cases of large-scale engagement of foreign enterprises of world renown. On one hand, there were many foreign investors just meeting the minimum requirements as to their contribution to the equity capital and, on the other, a small number of companies with capital of several million dollars. E. Sadowska-Cieślak was right to claim that the majority of joint venture companies established in Poland in 1989 were set up by domestic and foreign individuals.[15] These

Table 10.4. *Amount of real contributions to joint venture companies equity capital made by foreign partners in Poland (March 1990)*

Country	No. of companies	Equity capital in millions of zlotys	Equity capital in thousands of $US	Equity capital per 1 company millions of zl	000s of$US
FRG	404	49,694.5	42,612.3	123.0	105.5
Sweden	101	26,740.6	19,740.3	264.8	195.4
Austria	74	34,034.4	8,913.6	459.9	120.5
USA	73	10,919.8	10,618.0	149.6	145.5
West Berlin	65	14,048.7	13,026.9	216.1	200.4
Great Britain	49	5,058.6	5,669.2	103.2	115.7
France	49	5,554.2	3,487.6	113.4	71.2
Holland	48	20,339.6	16,762.7	432.7	349.2
Italy	47	23,597.7	10,459,2	502.1	222.5
multinational	46	38,559.5	15,445.6	838.3	335.8
Switzerland	29	5,985.6	4,199.2	206.4	144.8
Belgium	27	5,272.3	4,713.2	195.3	174.6
Canada	24	6,195.5	2,259.3	258.1	94.1
Denmark	22	7,014.6	1,726.1	318.8	78.5
other	87	36,092.4	26,967.8	414.9	310.0
Total	1,145	289,108.0	186,601.0	252.5	163.0

Source: as in Table 10.2 and own calculations.

were mainly small and medium-size companies often managed by citizens of Western countries, of Polish origin, holders of consular passports generally investing a small amount of capital. This situation did not change considerably in the meantime.

Joint ventures established in Poland after 1 January 1990 have a relatively small number of employees and their share in the total foreign trade turnover of the country is insignificant. It is estimated that in 1989 joint ventures operating in Poland employed some 0.5 percent of the labor force and that the value of their foreign trade turnover accounted for some 2 percent of the total value of Polish exports and imports. The main foreign trade partners are a few other countries (Sweden, Austria, and Italy). Their commodity structure is by no means satisfactory as joint venture exports are dominated by relatively low-processed goods, such as food and agricultural products or wood-and-paper industry products.

4 Conclusion

The economic effects of foreign capital investment in Poland to date are highly unsatisfactory. The amount of capital flowing into Poland has been limited usually, and located very often in sectors the development of which was not a priority. Because of that, capital inflow did not contribute to a substantial increase in labor productivity and economic efficiency. For many different reasons that is no wonder.

The economic program of the government in office, enjoying the support of the IMF authorities, is obviously a factor which should facilitate the inflow of foreign capital to Poland, which is even more evident in view of the fact that in 1990 the implementation of the program brought about many positive effects (e.g. checking inflation, stabilization of the national currency rate of exchange). On the other hand, however, the implementation of this program did not bring about, since it simply could not do so, such a radical change in the economic situation which would attract an inflow of vast amounts of capital to Poland as well as an inflow of the most advanced technologies and management methods. Moreover, the falling rate of inflation and the strengthening of the private sector have so far been accompanied by economic recession, which is extremely difficult to correct. Those problems are at present the subject of lively discussion among Polish economists, politicians, and entrepreneurs. Their evaluation of the present and prospective economic condition of the country, which is the major factor influencing the inflow of foreign capital, may differ considerably.

Intensive discussions over the law of December 1988 and its amendments since December 1989 are also taking place. In the majority of views the current law marks a certain progress over previous laws, but still is not free of shortcomings in the legal–organizational and economic fields. Indirect evidence for that can be the fact that in 1989 only a dozen or so FSSEs took advantage of the opportunity to transform themselves into joint venture companies. FSSEs are not very interested in exports (only half of them export their goods for convertible currencies), or in transferring their profits abroad. As E. Sadowska-Cieślak[16] points out, "most of FSSEs in fact are owned by Polish individuals, although they are registered as companies run by foreigners or holders of consular passports."

There are many shortcomings in the present Polish legislation on the operation of foreign capital in the legal–organizational sphere. Generally speaking, the conditions offered to foreign partners are still, despite some generosity, e.g., in the form of a general exemption from taxation during the first three years of activity, rather stringent and not fully coherent. This can be seen in the following provisions: (a) any property changes within a joint venture (new shares) require a special permit issued by the President of the Foreign Investment Agency, and his decisions cannot be appealed, which is a bureaucratic practice; (b) the law excludes joint venture companies from participation in the gradually emerging capital market in Poland, which is incompatible with the principle of equal status of all economic subjects; (c) obtaining a permit for the foreign capital activity in Poland requires filling in many different documents (including those which concern the economic and financial sphere, expected profits, etc.) which are not always prepared thoroughly and competently, and their examination by the agency often lasts several months; (d) regulations concerning transfers of foreign exchange profits abroad are still too strict, and it must be borne in mind that the possibility of these transfers is, apart from the condition of the national economy, the most important factor determining the inflow of foreign capital. It should also be added that in spite of the fact that a feasibility study is required by the agency (which is hard to understand, especially in the case of domestic and foreign individuals who, in setting up a company, put their assets at risk), this has not managed so far to prevent permits being issued to at least partly fictitious companies (whose owners benefit from taxation exemption), as well as to companies with clearly unadjusted assets of Polish state-owned companies, or to companies whose foreign partners introduced obsolete machinery instead of modern technology.[17]

Discussions on the purely economic conditions of operation of foreign capital in Poland are also taking place at present. It is pointed out, *inter alia*, that Poland is a country quite well endowed with qualified and relatively cheap labor. At the same time the country is situated relatively close to the markets of present and prospective investors. Poland is a country undergoing a process of essential systemic and economic change. Nevertheless, the binding law and its executory provisions are not optimal from the point of view of maximizing the economic effect of joint venture activity. Let us remind the reader that in addition to the regulations mentioned above, even in 1990 one still had to apply for a permit in order to set up an account with a foreign bank, to export or import goods related to the activities of a joint venture, and to sell goods in Poland for foreign exchange. This clearly exerts an unfavorable impact on economic effects, which is even more evident when it is realized that the speed at which Polish banks perform their operations is so far rather unacceptable for foreign investors and that there is always a chance of being denied a permit. So far being granted a one-year visa is not always a sufficient prerequisite for Polish banks to act as intermediaries in obtaining foreign credits by co-owners of joint ventures, and sometimes it is even not enough to be granted domestic credits. Finally, it should be pointed out that foreign investors encounter difficulties involved with lack of international agreements on protection and promotion of foreign investment in Poland, and that Polish banks are often reluctant to guarantee credits for companies with the participation of foreign parties, especially new companies with relatively small equity capital. Such an attitude can only be justified by the occasional attempts to establish the so-called fictitious companies.

Poland is today a country consciously offering foreign capital considerable opportunities which, as can be expected, will be constantly growing. The reason for this is not only existing needs, but also the provisions of the government's economic program (including privatization trends), and often expressed opinions that the 1988 law on companies with the participation of foreign parties should be urgently amended. It is difficult to foresee future provisions in detail, still it is self-evident that the amended law should not make the conditions under which foreign investors work more difficult; and a better adjustment to the conditions of the market economy is needed. If this be so, one can expect in the legal–organizational sphere that the procedure of issuing permits for companies with the participation of foreign capital should be lifted (registration procedures should be maintained), along with a change of the scope of activities of the Foreign Investment Agency, shifting it toward strategic problems, promotion of operation of foreign capital in Poland, etc. On the other hand, in the economic sphere, apart from possible endeavors aimed at liquidating the negative impact of the shortcomings listed above, it cannot be ruled out that in the future operating conditions of both foreign and domestic investors will be set on an equal footing. Obviously, this should be accompanied by a change in attitude of owners of foreign capital (and not only) toward investment in Poland.

Notes

Note of the Editor: A new law on stock companies with foreign investment was approved by the Polish *Sejm* on 14 June, 1991. This law further liberalized the conditions for foreign direct investment in Poland. See postscript to next chapter by Horst Brezinski.

1. See A. Gordos, "Economic ventures in socialist countries with Western participation," *Acta Oeconomica*, vol. 20, no. 4, 1978; J. G. Scriven, "Joint ventures in Poland," *Journal of World Trade Law*, vol. 14, no. 5, 1880; I.

162   *Jozef Misala*

Nawrocki, "Foreign enterprises in Poland; ten years of experience," *The CTC Reporter*, no. 24, 1984, and "Kapital zagraniczny w polskiej gospodarce w latach 1976–1989" [Foreign capital in the Polish economy in the years 1976–1989], *Handel Zagraniczny* [Foreign Trade], no. 4/5, 1989.

2. Nawrocki, "Kapital zagraniczny," p. 10.
3. Ibid.
4. Nawrocki, "Foreign enterprises in Poland."
5. MFER, *Information on Foreign Investments in Poland as of December 1988*, Ministry of Foreign Economic Relations, Warsaw, 1989.
6. Ibid.
7. D. K. Rosati, *Poland: New Business Opportunities for Western Companies*, Discussion Papers, Foreign Trade Research Institute, Warsaw, no. 9.
8. *Ustawa z dnia 23 grudnia 1988 r. o dzialalnosci gospodarczej z udzialem podmiotów zagranicznych* [The Law of 23 December 1988 on Economic Activity with the Participation of Foreign Parties], Ministry of Foreign Economic Relations, Warsaw, 1989.
9. Nawrocki, "Kapital zagraniczny."
10. *Ustawa z dnia 23 grudnia 1988 r.*
11. "Uchwala Rady ministrow z 16.02.1989" [Resolution of the Council of Ministers of 16 February 1989], published in *Monitor Polski*, no. 4, item 12, 1989.
12. L. Balcerowicz, "Program gospodarczy. Glowne zalozenia kierunki" [Economic programme. Main foundations and directions], in *Rzeczpospolita*, Warsaw, December 1989.
13. Ibid., p. 5.
14. *Trybuna*, no. 54, 17 April 1990, Warsaw.
15. E. Sadowska-Cieślak (ed.), *Spolki z udzialem kapitalu zagranicanego* [Companies with the participation of foreign capital], Instytut Koniunktur i Cen Handlu Zagranicznego [Foreign Trade Research Institute], Warsaw, 1990, mimeo.
16. Ibid., p. 178.
17. Ibid. and Sadowska-Cieślak (ed.), *Funkcjonowania spolek z udzialem podmiotów zagranicznych; stan faktyczny i propozycje zmian w ustawie* [Functioning of the joint ventures in Poland; facts and recommendations concerning the present law], Instytut Koniunktur i Cen Handlu Zagranicznego [Foreign Trade Research Institute], Warsaw, 1990.

11 Joint ventures in Poland: interests and experiences of Western firms

Horst Brezinski

In our days, joint ventures stand for magic in international business. This holds particularly true for business with Eastern Europe and the Soviet Union. Yet, setting up a joint venture is only one of several alternatives which enterprises may choose in order to expand their international economic relationship. Such opportunities may consist of foreign trade, cooperation in specific areas of business, direct investment abroad, or joint ventures with foreign partners. Compared to these alternatives, joint ventures require a more complex mechanism of coordination.[1] Being a partner in a joint venture means engaging in legal as well as economic obligations. Decisions are no longer so flexible because the consensus of all partners is required. On the other hand, specifying, by contract, the activities of the individual partners may be difficult because foreign partners cannot be fully controlled and evaluated. Transaction costs of, and within, joint ventures consequently are usually higher than in other forms of international business.

This chapter attempts to analyze the motivational determinants for Western companies to engage in joint ventures with Polish enterprises and asks for the conditions which might cause Western partners to consider joint ventures with Polish partners to be superior to other forms of market transaction or direct investment. The author further asks what the prospects are that cause Western investors to engage in the development and performance of such joint ventures in Poland.

In the absence of the exact number of joint ventures operating in Poland the analysis was based on questionnaires submitted to 336 joint ventures of West German, Austrian, British, Swedish, and Swiss companies with Polish partners founded prior to 1 October 1989. Only joint ventures which were in operation by the end of 1989 were included in the sample. As Figure 11.1 shows, these countries represent 65.1 percent of all foreign joint venture partners in Poland and by this form of international business contribute 49.8 percent of the foreign capital in that country (Figure 11.2). Sixty-two joint ventures (18.5 percent)

164   *Horst Brezinski*

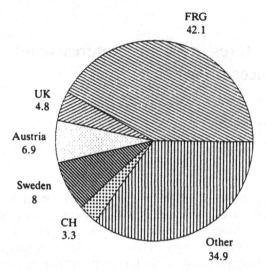

Figure 11.1 Joint ventures in Poland, foreign partners (number), 1
October 1989

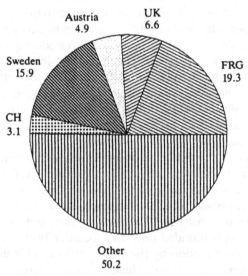

Figure 11.2 Joint ventures in Poland, foreign partners (capital), 1
October 1989
Source: UN–ECE, *East–West Joint Ventures News*, no. 4

responded. Since experts cautiously estimate that only 30 percent of potential joint ventures in Poland function properly, it can be assumed that our rate of return to the questionnaires constitutes over 60 percent of the total of those joint ventures that truly operate.

Our analysis also attempted to identify potential areas of conflict, which might increase the transaction costs mentioned above, the main interests the Polish partners share in joint ventures, and the various obstacles which in the opinion of the Western partners might impair such cooperation. From this conclusions may be drawn concerning the future of the joint ventures in question and their contribution to the further development of the Polish economy, an economy, which, at this time, is in the process of transformation from a socialist to a democratic market economy.

Finally, our empirical analysis may provide hints at how to improve the current joint venture policy. This, in turn, might contribute to the national economic development, the economic structure, and to the systemic changes in the Polish system.

1   Characteristics of joint ventures in Poland

In 1986 a new law on foreign investment envisaged the liberalization of foreign direct investment. (See the contribution by J. Misala in this volume.) The Polish government tried to ensure that macro-economic targets would be met by carrying out the following objectives for joint ventures:

      introduction of modern technological and organizational solutions into the national economy;

      supply of goods and services for export;

      improvement of the supply of quality products and services for the domestic market;

      measures of environmental protection.[2]

In the beginning this new law on foreign investment did not attract many investors. By the end of 1988 only 52 permissions were issued to set up joint ventures.[3] The revised versions of the law of 23 December 1988 and of 28 December 1989 envisaged a substantial liberalization of provisions governing joint ventures. As a consequence, the number of joint ventures rose sharply in 1989 and 1990, from 52 (end of 1988) to 515 permissions by 1 October 1989[4] and to 1,950 by 1 October 1990.[5] Figure 11.1 illustrates that more than 42 percent of the Western enterprises which asked for permission to set up joint ventures by 1 October 1989 originated in West Germany and West Berlin; Swedish firms submitted 8 percent of the applications, Austrian companies filed 6.9

percent, British enterprises numbered 4.8 percent, and Swiss businesses amounted to 3.3 percent.

This ranking order of Western partners with Poland in terms of applications changes dramatically, however, when considering the financial contribution which the individual Western nations make toward the total equity capital provided by the joint ventures. Foreign companies signed up a mere $US 79.4 million in which the West German share was only 19.3 percent, while the Swedes held 15.9 percent. This points to a peculiar characteristic. Far more than 30 percent of all joint ventures were set up by former Polish citizens who now live in the West and who dispose of small amounts of capital only. Big enterprises, on the other hand, were relatively reluctant to engage in joint ventures immediately. Preparing for a joint venture obviously takes a long time because the risk is high and obtaining the necessary information to calculate the prospects of foreign investment in a country like Poland, a country in transition, takes time. Multinational companies and other important Western firms hardly considered setting up joint ventures before the amendment of the joint venture law at the end of 1988 and the real democratization of Poland in the summer of 1989. Instead, it seems that the expected flow of foreign capital into the country began in the second half of 1990.[6]

As a result it appears quite natural that by October 1989 a considerable number of the Western joint venture partners (40 percent) had invested only capital funds of 50–99 million zlotys in their partnerships. Over 250 million zlotys were invested in only 13 percent of the joint ventures (Figure 11.3). Most of the Western partners made use of the opportunity of holding the majority share in the venture, a practice possible after 1 January 1989. Only 14 percent of the joint ventures set up between January and October 1989 did not use this opportunity. Consequently, in October 1989, 77.7 percent of all joint ventures had majority shareholders in the West.

In 1989 the regional distribution of joint ventures in Poland reflected a strong preference for Warsaw (22.1 percent) and Poznan (7.5 percent) (Figure 11.4) with a tendency toward deconcentration when comparing the 1988 situation, when the share of Warsaw was 30.7 percent. This coincides with the observation that most Polish enterprises interested in joint ventures are located in the districts west of Warsaw.[7]

Figures 11.5 and 11.6 reflect the joint venture structure in Poland by economic sectors and industries. It seems evident that joint ventures were mainly set up in the field of manufacturing and not so much in services as in most other East European countries.[8] Figure 11.6 reveals that joint ventures are under-represented in manufacturing industries

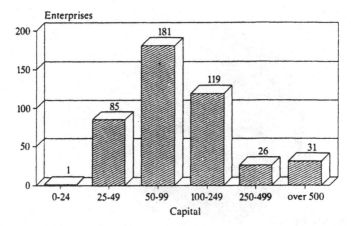

Figure 11.3 Western joint ventures in Poland, capital investment, 1 October 1989 (millions of zloty)

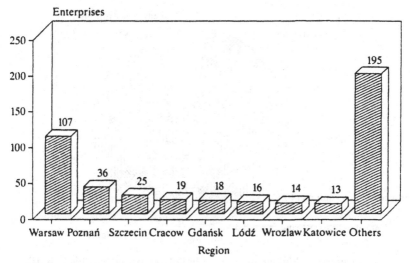

Figure 11.4 Western joint ventures in Poland, regional distribution, 1 October 1989 ($n=443$)

that use high technology. Activities concentrate above all on labor-intensive industries, in particular on metal-processing, construction, wood and food processing, textiles, other consumer goods, tourism, and trade. A look into the register of the Polish agency for foreign investment, however, reveals that the majority of the joint ventures involved applied for up to nine different fields of activity. A similar trend can be

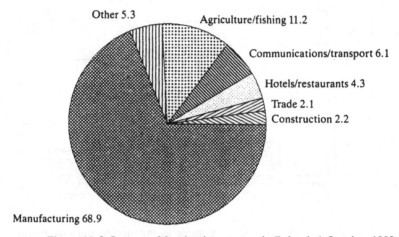

Figure 11.5 Sectors of foreign investment in Poland, 1 October 1989
Source: *UN–ECE, East–West Joint Ventures News*, no. 4

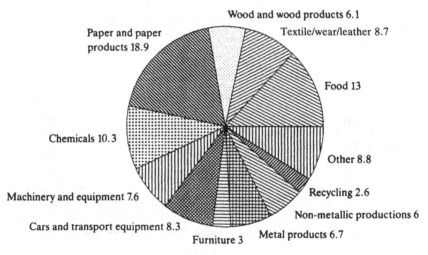

Figure 11.6 Foreign investment in Poland, manufacturing industries, 1
October 1989
Source: *UN–ECE, East–West Joint Ventures News*, no. 4

observed with the Polonia enterprises group which had concessions for
at least three or four different sectors of economic activity.[9] Yet, this
does not mean that the Polish joint ventures aim at diversification right
from the beginning. In general, they concentrate on one field. The
bizarre trend in applications can only be explained by the costs involved
in setting up a new application for a new and different economic

activity. Any change in the type of economic activity requires explicit permission by the administrative authorities; this may set in motion an entirely new process of application which may turn out to be a very time-consuming endeavor. Therefore, Polish joint venture partners try to define, from the beginning, likely areas of potential and profitable economic cooperative activity. This ensures greater flexibility and the avoidance of transaction costs.

Of the joint ventures where interviews were conducted, 60 percent expect a turnover of 1 to 5 million DM during the first three years; 22.5 percent expect sales of over 20 million DM during that period of time. In only 10 percent of the joint ventures investigated do these sales represent more than 70 percent of the turnover of the Western partner's enterprise, in 35 percent of cases the sales of the joint venture amount to 11–30 percent of the Western partner's firm, and in another 35 percent the joint venture turnover is 5–10 percent of the Western companies' receipts.

Contrary to practice in the Polonia firms the newly set up joint enterprises do not contain a fixed period of joint venture contract; 68 percent of the Western enterprises engaged did not insist on a limited period of operation under the contract. Problems of leaving the enterprise and of potential "sunk" costs seem to be of minor importance. This underlines the long-term interests Western partners have in such joint ventures, which reflects a strong belief and confidence in the successful transformation of the Polish economy and society. But what really determines Western investors to set up joint ventures with their Polish counterparts and what compensates them for the expected higher transaction costs of such joint ventures?

2   Factors offsetting higher transaction costs of joint ventures in Poland

The establishment of a joint venture in Poland generally leads to higher transaction costs than are implied in a full direct investment or cooperation in foreign trade. Moreover, the risk of setting up a Polish joint venture seems to be higher than that of investment activities other than joint ventures. Moreover, it would be expected that Western enterprises engaging in joint ventures in Poland had gained some previous experience in other trade relations with Polish enterprises. Surprisingly, however, 35 percent of the joint venture enterprises of the West under study here have had no previous contact with Polish firms. Only 35 percent had foreign trade relations, a mere 22 percent had already acquired some experience in the form of cooperative activities, and no more than 8 percent were already engaged in direct investment in Polonia enterprises. The fact that over one-third of the Western enterprises engage in joint ventures, despite their lack of such experience, can only be explained by the relatively high number of former Polish citizens, now in the West, who have at least some knowledge of the Polish economy and society and do not lack linguistic capabilities as well as a social network in Poland. In addition, there are a number of strong motivational determinants which seem to offset the higher risk and costs of transaction in the eyes of those who engage in Polish–Western business ventures.

All companies interviewed claim that the low labor cost represented a very strong incentive; 80 percent of the enterprises stated that access to the Polish market was important. Being a producer in Poland, it is much easier to bypass trade frictions and restrictions stemming from currency problems.[10] Sixty-five percent of the firms also said that joint ventures provide better access to East European markets. This argument, of course, is likely to lose ground with the transformation of the East European foreign trade systems. In the future all enterprises in the East will have to establish direct foreign trade links.

Apart from these three major determinants (cost of labor, bypassing trade friction, access to markets), 38 percent of the informants name the availability of free production capacities, 33 percent quote the low cost of raw materials, 28 percent expect a sufficient supply of skilled labor or of raw materials, 21 percent mention the low real estate prices, and 19 percent the low cost of energy. Less frequent arguments are nationalistic motivations,[11] and the low cost of research and development. Opportunities of extending product and technology life-cycles or the availability of technology, often quoted in literature, proved to be irrelevant.[12]

Nearly 90 percent of the joint ventures studied intended to export as well as serve the Polish market. The desire to export appears plausible as long as the Polish currency is not fully convertible. The transfer of profits, on the other hand, causes minor problems only. Although the political and social situation in Poland is still unstable – conditions detrimental to the rise of joint venture activities[13] – the motivation of Western firms was mainly confirmed by the announcement of the liberalization of Polish foreign direct investment laws of 1988 and 1989 and the changes in taxation. These changes were judged as favorable by more than 40 percent of the enterprises and as justified by 37.5 percent. Nearly 70 percent of the enterprises regarded the existence of a special agreement to protect foreign investment unimportant. The majority of enterprises trusted the Polish government and believed in the success of the joint ventures even during the period of transition. Sixty percent said that the projected economic reforms in Poland would have a positive impact on their joint ventures, and only 20 percent feared negative repercussions, at least in the short run, from rising prices for inputs, labor, and real estate. The drop in Polish GNP (reduced by more than 30 percent during the first half of 1990), rising unemployment, and the loss of the Soviet market added to the negative prospects. On the other hand, more than 80 percent of the interviewees regarded the creation of free trade areas and/or special economic zones as useful, whereas 15 percent did not see that the establishment of such areas would have any relevant impact on their decision. Merely 5 percent expected negative consequences from the stronger competition for skilled labor.

All in all the informants expected that the introduction of a market economy in Poland would remove some of the obstacles which cause the rise in transaction costs and that such an economy would provide stronger incentives for a better economic performance. In view of the anticipated improvements of the legal, political, and economic and social conditions joint ventures have increased in number and will continue to do so. But the question remains open, as to why a majority shareholding in the joint ventures is necessary. Why do Western enterprises not establish 100 percent direct foreign investments in Poland? Of course, compared to other forms of foreign trade and economic cooperation, which offer entry to and continued operation in the market, a supply of raw materials and energy, access to technology, available labor as well as limited liability and flexibility, and more flexible contractual relationships,[14] joint ventures provide a greater involvement in and better control of the East–West enterprise, a stronger voice in management, exclusivity in the market, better quality control of products, capital appreciation, access to the balance sheet, investment guarantees, and long-term commitment, as well as protection from changes in legislation. These arguments are even more valid in the case of the Western company holding the majority of the shares. On the other hand, compared to a full direct investment, partners in joint ventures benefit from the knowledge of their copartners in terms of local regulations, the domestic market, and lower cash requirements in the start-up process.[15] Consequently, East–West joint ventures are characterized by activities which demand specific and varying capabilities from their partners.[16]

Although the advantages and incentives promote strong interest in joint ventures and their superiority over other forms of international economic activities, there are a number of obstacles which have to be overcome.

3   Elements impeding joint ventures and increasing transaction costs

Obstacles may arise from conflict of the diverging expectations of the partners in the joint venture. The Polish partners have a micro-perspective and are interested in supplying the domestic market and, to a lesser degree than their Western partners, in exports (75 percent); 75 percent are interested in acquiring capital, 30 percent desire technology and management know-how, and 35 percent expect technical know-how. These interests show a strong coincidence with those of their Western partners. Few Polish partners are looking for short-term profits. Consequently, it is not surprising that only 12 percent of the Western enterprises complain about their Polish partner. Major problems in setting up joint ventures are seen in the lack of infrastructure such as telecommunications, transport facilities, and insufficient wholesale structures. Over 90 percent of the enterprises complained about such difficulties. More than 50 percent were dissatisfied with the lack of business knowledge, 40 percent with the poor quality of Polish production, and the lack of convertibility of the Polish currency. About one-third were aware of the deficiencies in education and in skills of workers and of the different mentalities. About the same number criticized the still prevailing bureaucracy and peculiar government regulations. They felt insecure about the frequent and unforeseeable changes in the legal domain. Fifteen percent mentioned the poor quality of the machinery and 20 percent spoke of difficulties with customs, and the language barrier. COCOM regulations were seen as an obstacle by less than 5 percent of the enterprises.

Apart from this criticism, nearly all Western companies complained about the inefficiency of the Polish banking system and the unfavorable prospects of credit financing. The Polish banking system is still far from Western market-type banking and the solvency of a customer has hardly any impact on interest rates for credit. Finally, Poland still lacks a true and adequate capital market.

4   Conclusion

What are the likely prospects of joint ventures in Poland? Of the Western companies polled, 20 percent declared that their expectations had been fully met, 70 percent indicated that their expectations were at least partially met. Only 10 percent were dissatisfied and half of them intended to dissolve the joint venture. This proves that transaction costs are obviously not seen as being too high when compared to those of other forms of market activities. This may also be due to the coincidence of interests and advantages with those of the Polish partners. The joint ventures have stabilized cooperation between the Western and the Eastern partners and there have been a number of synergetic effects concerning capital and inputs of labor and raw materials. Both partners benefit from exports to third countries. The Polish partner has learned that it is not the latest technology but the most usable one that is required.[17] Most modern does necessarily mean most useful. Moreover, the Polish partners have realized that it is easier to raise productivity together with Western partners by adopting' the Western style of management which leads to a reduction in bureaucracy at the enterprise level and to more discipline on the part of the workers.[18]

Over 60 percent of the Western enterprises which were part of the foregoing study plan to increase their investment in Poland. The faster Poland continues in its process of economic, social, and political tranformation, the faster their plans will materialize. Apart from improving infrastructure, the main task of the Polish government is in monetary economics. Establishing a functioning capital market and the convertibility of the Polish currency are indispensable. In this context the new amendment of the law on direct foreign investment dated 28 December 1989, which excluded Western enterprises and joint ventures from keeping a hard currency account, proved to be a boomerang. As long as the Polish zloty is threatened by a possible devaluation, joint ventures are likely to suffer from losses caused by such a devaluation. In addition, they will incur additional costs by being forced to exchange their hard currency revenues into zloty and to convert these again for the financing of imports. The cost of these transactions are estimated at 5 percent of the revenues. Thus, it did not come as a surprise that several Western investors who had wanted to invest $600 million in 1990 in Poland canceled their joint venture plans.

There is no doubt that the Polish goverment will have to accelerate the process of transforming the economy. It has been successful in stabilizing the currency and bringing down the rate of inflation. However, the creation of new institutions is lagging behind schedule. A speeding up of the reforms could contribute to dissolving the old command economy monopolies and establishing market-type competition. This, in turn, would make it easier for Western enterprises to engage in joint ventures with Polish enterprises. This would also give Western enterprises a better chance of exiting from the market when desired, thus reducing the risk implied in an engagement in the Polish economy.

Finally, the Polish government will have to do away with the old bureaucracy in order to facilitate decision making. According to members of the Polish government some of the obstacles still prohibiting or impairing joint ventures may be removed in 1991 when an amendment to the old law will be passed. Thus, it anticipates installing an unlimited transfer of profits, allowing companies to have foreign currency accounts, and simplifying the procedure of registering joint ventures. Another disadvantage already eliminated is the prohibition on Western companies buying land for business purposes. This provision has been revoked by the end of 1990.

From the macroeconomic point of view, joint ventures may not contribute very much to the Polish GNP, exports, employment, and technology transfers. Yet, they can demonstrate how enterprises may operate in a real market economy.

Postscript

Since the completion of this article in late 1990, major changes in joint venture legislation have been enacted which aim at a further liberalization of foreign investment opportunities in the country. These changes include:

> complete freedom of foreign investors of repatriating their profits;
>
> permission for foreign investors to invest in Poland without first applying to the Foreign Investment Agency. Now authorization is only required for those cases in which a permit had already been required before, e.g. in such fields as mining, industry, transport, power stations etc. In addition, such permits are necessary for enterprises engaging in Polish companies operating harbours or airports, active in real estate, in concession-free defense industry, and wholesale business in imported consumer goods. Also, permission by the minister of industry is required when state-owned enterprises intend to invest part of their capital in joint ventures.
>
> cessation of the permission requirement regarding minimum values of foreign investments. Debt-to-equity-swaps are now allowed.
>
> guarantee of tax exemptions for only those investors who invest more than two million ECU (about 2.5 million US $). Exemptions will be valid only until the end of 1993. Such preferential treatment is also to be given for the implementation of new technology transfer, investment in regions of structural unemployment, or exports of more than 20 per cent of goods and services produced. Maximum income tax reduc-

tions are not to exceed the value of funds originally invested
by the foreign investor.

limitation of exemptions from customs duties to capital goods
needed to start production.

The new legislation does away with a number of barriers of entry for
foreign investors. Thus, the internal convertibility of the zloty and the
unrestricted repatriation of profits facilitate market entry. However,
opportunities for tax reductions have been subjected to precise and very
strict conditions, which appear to be among the most rigid in Eastern
Europe. The tax exemptions aim especially at providing assistance to
foreign investors in their attempt to privatize the Polish economy.

The discussion about and the enacting of the new legislation has had a
positive impact on the quantitative development of joint ventures. By
the end of September 1991, their number had increased to 3,512.
Capital invested, however, has not exceeded half a billion US dollars.
There seems to be an increase in regional joint-venture concentration,
33.7 per cent of joint-venture applications were made for the region of
Warsaw. The eight most industrialized regions of the country account
for over 72 per cent of all applications for starting joint ventures. The
policy of the Polish government and the revised legislation have
definitely proved to be positive in the joint-venture development. Yet,
the overall stagnation of the Polish economy, the break-down of the
markets in East Europe, and the insufficient implementation of institutional changes have prevented a true and substantial contribution by
foreign investors to the transformation and recovery of the Polish
national economy. Despite the repeated attempts to facilitate a more
intense foreign financial participation, a number of potential foreign
investors have still been dissatisfied with the situation. In particular,
small and medium-sized companies feel treated unfairly because tax
exemptions are unavailable to them. But, since investments require
some time before they can be put into operation and become effective,
first results of this legislation may probably not be expected before the
second half of 1992. Yet, concluding, it seems that Poland is heading in
the right direction.

Notes

The author is indebted to Hermann Fink for his helpful comments in revising
this contribution.
  1. Rolf Weder, "Joint Ventures als Weg der Internationalisierung," *Neue
Zürcher Zeitung*, 19 August 1989.

2. This last point was not included before 1988 when the law on foreign direct investment was changed.
3. See contribution by Jozef Misala in this volume.
4. *East–West Joint Ventures News*, no. 4, 1990, p. 7.
5. Ibid., no. 6, 1990, p. 8.
6. E.g. "Philips gründet Joint Venture in Polen," *Süddeutsche Zeitung*, 17 April 1990, and "ABB in pact with Poland on second joint venture," *Financial Times*, 13 July 1990.
7. In this respect the situation in Poland differs completely from that in the Soviet Union, where 46.5 percent of the joint ventures are located in the Moscow area. See PlanEcon, *Soviet Joint Ventures*, vol. 6, 1990, no. 17, pp. 18f.
8. Klaus-Jürgen Kuss, "Gemeinschaftsunternehmen in Polen," in Klaus Langefeld-Wirth (ed.), *Joint Ventures im internationalen Wirtschaftsverkehr*, Heidelberg, Verlag Recht und Wirtschaft, 1990, p. 389.
9. Peter Friedrich, "Technologietransfer mit Hilfe von Joint Ventures in Polen: Möglichkeiten, Chancen und Probleme," in Clemens Burrichter and Zbigniew M. Klepacki (eds.), *Wissenschaftlich-technische Zusammenarbeit in den gegenwärtigen Ost–West Beziehungen*, Erlangen, Institut für Gesellschaft und Wissenschaft, 1988, p. 131.
10. Miroslaw Bieszki and Herbert Rath, "Foreign capital investment in Poland – emerging prospects for German–Polish joint ventures under the new law," *Management International Review*, vol. 29, 1989, no. 4, p. 48.
11. E.g. "I am born Polish. This is my duty."
12. Bieszki and Rath, "Foreign capital investment in Poland," p. 48.
13. László Csaba and András Inotai, "Joint Ventures in den Ost–West-Wirtschaftsbeziehungen," in Hanns-Dieter Jacobsen, Heinrich Machowski, and Dirk Sager (eds.), *Perspektiven für Sicherheit und Zusammenarbeit in Europa*, Bonn, Bundeszentrale für politische Bildung, 1988, p. 344.
14. UNCTAD Secretariat, "Joint ventures with the participation of enterprises of the socialist countries of Eastern Europe," Geneva, 20 June 1986, p. 24.
15. Economic Commission of Europe, *East–West Joint Ventures*, New York, United Nations, 1988, p. 4.
16. Rolf Weder, "Internationale Unternehmungskooperation: Stabilitätsbedingungen von Joint Ventures," *Aussenwirtschaft*, vol. 45, 1990, no. 2, p. 278.
17. Marian Malecki, "Technology transfer to Poland through foreign Polonian enterprises," in Jan Monkiewicz and Roland Scharff (eds.), *Reform, Innovational Performance and Technical Progress – The Polish Case*, Erlangen, Institut für Gesellschaft und Wissenschaft, 1990, p. 131.
18. "Was ausländische Investoren in Polen erwartet," *Süddeutsche Zeitung*, 14 November 1989.

Part III

Liberalization: entry into the international markets

12 Perestroika and the new international economy

Erik P. Hoffmann

Because of the multifaceted reforms that Mikhail Gorbachev has launched in the Soviet Union, one can only make educated guesses about the structure and performance of the Soviet economy in the 1990s. Because of the Soviet Union's changing trade relations with the United States and Western and Eastern Europe, we are on even shakier grounds if we predict the course of East–West and East–East economic ties. And because there are at least six "perestroikas" (restructurings) taking place in the world economy – the Soviet, American, European, Japanese, newly industrializing countries (NICs), and some less developed countries (LDCs) – we find myriad uncertainties and complexities in the rapidly evolving international political system.

We know, however, that Gorbachev has initiated a revolution in the political, ethical, and work cultures of the Soviet Union and that cultural revolutions do not take root in short periods of time. Basic components of this revolution were broader and deeper citizen participation in decision making, especially in the workplace; greater individual rights and responsibilities, especially economic risks and rewards; and rising mass and group expectations, especially economic, social, legal, professional, avocational, and ethnic needs and wants. Also, Gorbachev has avoided technocratic solutions to economic and social dilemmas. He has placed much greater emphasis on the democratic forms and content of socio-economic modernization than did the industrial and cultural engineers of the Leonid Brezhnev, Nikita Khrushchev, Vladimir Lenin, and especially Joseph Stalin generations.

From the late 1920s to the mid-1980s Soviet leaders repressed the entrepreneurial spirit and forced it into the illegal domestic economy. In contrast, Gorbachev has encouraged creativity, initiative, and risk-taking. For example, small cooperative enterprises, mostly in service industries and agriculture, have been legalized. Also, foreign trade decision making has been decentralized, and joint ventures with 100 percent foreign ownership have been permitted. But a Soviet entrepreneur's

179

newly granted rights to compete on domestic and world markets must be accompanied by the incentives and skills to do so. To date most factory and farm managers have clung to traditional bureaucratic practices and outmoded technologies. And even if the quality of Soviet goods and services were to improve dramatically in the 1990s, the paucity of marketing know-how would put Soviet products at a competitive disadvantage *vis-à-vis* the industrialized West and NICs.

International economic ties were crucial to Gorbachev's efforts to modernize the Soviet economy. The President and Communist Party leader was deeply dissatisfied with Soviet economic growth and productivity, and he tried to increase significantly the quantity and quality of Soviet manufactured goods for domestic consumption and for export. This required the acquisition and adaptation of many kinds of Western technologies. At the same time Gorbachev wanted a more tranquil global environment to provide what he called a "breathing space" for the implementation of "revolutionary" responses to socio-economic "crises" at home.

The domestic economy, society, and polity

Gorbachev's initial approach to economic reform was to attempt to improve the existing system. At first he thought it would be necessary only to correct certain defects in economic planning and management and thereby to "accelerate" the country's social and economic development. Toward these ends the Gorbachev leadership tried to learn more about Soviet society, but "this turned out to be the most difficult task."[1] Accurate economic data was especially hard to obtain, because so many organizations and groups had a vested interest in withholding or not collecting such data. Nonetheless, Gorbachev sought to fulfill the potential of the centralized economy by emphasizing machine-building and on-the-job sobriety rather than consumer goods and agricultural production.

Also, Gorbachev and his colleagues scrutinized international scientific and technical progress at a major conference in June 1985. They affirmed the importance of participating in the microelectronic and information processing "explosion" begun in capitalist countries during the previous decade. But most Soviet leaders, including Gorbachev, initially viewed modern information and communication technologies as substitutes for reform. That is, they wanted scientific and technological innovations to perfect rather than change the basic characteristics of the command-and-control economy. Echoing an often repeated Brezhnev maxim as late as January 1987, Gorbachev affirmed that Soviet economic progress depended on "how skillfully we are combining the advantages of socialism with the achievements of the scientific–technological revolution."[2]

But Gorbachev understood much better than Brezhnev that the Soviet Union's economic competitiveness *vis-à-vis* the advanced Western countries had been declining rapidly since the late 1970s. At precisely the time that the centralized Soviet economy's pathologies were coming to the fore and it was becoming increasingly permeable to external markets and disturbances, many capitalist economies were experiencing a burst of scientific and technical progress. Gorbachev lamented that Brezhnev's "greatest mistake" was underestimating this "powerful upsurge in the development of microelectronics, information science, and biotechnology" and channeling it to military and space projects rather than to civilian products and services and international trade.[3]

In 1988 Gorbachev's closest Politburo colleague, Aleksandr Yakovlev, eloquently summarized the practical and ideological dilemmas confronting Soviet economic reformers. Alluding to the geological movements that produce earthquakes, he affirmed that perestroika needed a "truly tectonic shift" toward scientific and technical progress and consumer goods production. The Soviet Union must strive for "postindustrialization," with its emphasis on information processing, biotechnology, high-quality products, labor productivity, and a sizable service sector. However, the Soviet economy had yet to complete the "industrialization" phase, which is characterized by the mechanization of industry and agriculture and by the creation of a motivated and skilled labor force concentrated in urban areas and service professions. The chief cause of this economic retardation was state ownership of the means of production, according to Yakovlev: "Private ownership divides the individual and society, sets them against each other. But ownership by 'nobody' is equally destructive." He affirmed that citizens must create an "ideology of the socialist owner," which rejects "the dogmatic principle of the inevitable, absolute subordination of the individual's interests to the interests of the state."[4]

Gorbachev, with seminal contributions from Yakovlev, produced a distinctive ideology whose key tenet was that the Soviet Union could become a freer and more prosperous society only if certain preconditions were expeditiously met. Glasnost was a precondition for socialist and intra-party democratization; democratization for perestroika; perestroika for radical economic reform and social justice; and radical economic reform and social justice for an exemplary material and spiritual culture. Gorbachev and his reformist colleagues struggled to make these presuppositions perform motivational rather than manipulative purposes – that is, to have Soviet ideology serve as a "guide to action" (its chief function under Lenin and Khrushchev) rather than as a *post facto* justification (its chief function under Stalin and Brezhnev). And Gorbachev wanted the new content and functions of ideology to spur scientific-technological progress and entrepreneurship, strengthen the soviets (councils) from the national to the local level, and make the Communist Party responsive and responsible to a politically active citizenry.

Gorbachev found it relatively easy to change Soviet official ideology, quite challenging to alter Soviet political culture, and exceedingly difficult to stem urgent Soviet dilemmas such as economic decline, ethnic conflict, environmental decay, and the impending breakup of the federal union. There was considerable tension between old and new predispositions within society, within national and regional policy-making bodies, and within some individual leaders, including Gorbachev. The President's priorities were considerably left of center, but they became increasingly radical as the entire Soviet political spectrum moved leftward. His priorities were continuously debated by the political leadership and citizenry, periodically modified by unexpected events and consequences, reluctantly implemented by many national officials, willfully obstructed by some regional cadres, and vigorously challenged by nascent non-communist parties, oppositionist platforms, and informal groups. Ultra-conservatives viewed Gorbachev's socio-economic reforms as irresponsibly destructive and ultra-radicals viewed them as insufficiently constructive, especially after communist reformers were swept from power throughout Eastern Europe in 1989.

Yet the Gorbachev leadership launched a truly historic campaign to revise basic values, realize individual potential, and restrain the party–state for the purpose of creating a humane and prosperous socialist society. By 1990 Gorbachev well understood that the dismantling of old institutions and ideas can lead to political chaos and economic stagnation. Robert C. Tucker rightly concludes that Gorbachev made a remarkably bold effort "to cut down the swollen state and reinvigorate the spent society, and that it is encountering heavy resistance."[5]

Foreign economic relations

Gorbachev was keenly sensitive to the interconnections between the domestic and international components of perestroika. He viewed arms control, diplomatic, cultural, and commercial ties between the East and the West as prerequisites for his country's socio-economic transformation. His economic program depended on the more productive use of indigenous technologies, the implementation of industrial and agricultural price reforms, and the willingness and ability of Soviet specialists and Western businessmen to expand technology trade. Gorbachev understood that Soviet industries would find it difficult to apply advanced Western technologies effectively and efficiently, especially in the short run. With a reduction in East–West tensions, however, it would be possible to improve Soviet economic performance by transferring scientists and engineers from military to civilian research and development and by converting existing factories from military to civilian production (for instance, in the aircraft, shipping, nuclear energy, and agricultural machinery industries). In other words, even without substantial technology imports or with poor use of these imports, detente could further Soviet economic growth and productivity.

Gorbachev initially looked to Western Europe rather than the United States as a partner in detente. He stressed that all European nations – including the Soviet Union – have many similar interests (for instance, expanded trade and capital flows and nuclear-free zones) and many dissimilar interests with countries on other continents, especially the United States (for instance, trade and capital embargoes and Europe's "bridgehead" role in an East–West nuclear exchange). He maintained that persistent American efforts to impede West European cooperation with the Soviet Union and Eastern Europe should be resisted by all Europeans. Even before 1989 Gorbachev placed much less emphasis on the ideological differences betweeen the socialist and capitalist countries of Europe and much more emphasis on their geographical, cultural, and political bonds. His spokespersons repeatedly claimed that West and East European countries shared "a common home" and "one all-European civilization" and should function as "an autonomous political body," which cooperates to further "pan-European" interests and "the destinies of general peace and international security."

In addition, Gorbachev called for closer ties between Comecon and the European Community and tighter integration of Comecon. Whereas Brezhnev viewed East–West and intra-Comecon trade as mutually debilitating, Gorbachev viewed them as mutually reinforcing. And Gorbachev, learning more from Poland's experience than did Brezhnev, warned about excessive reliance on East–West trade. Gorbachev often argued that the inclination to buy from capitalist markets rather than to make products oneself had considerably harmed the Soviet and East European economies. While calling for more "rational use" of East–West commercial links, Gorbachev gave top priority to "socialist economic integration."

But Gorbachev responded to declining economic growth and productivity by initiating sweeping changes in Soviet foreign trade decision making in 1987. He broke "the state monopoly of foreign trade" and the Ministry of Foreign Trade's monopoly over international economic activities. He reduced Gosplan's involvement in the planning and management of East–West and East–East trade. He encouraged national and republic ministries, industrial and production associations, and enterprises and farms to establish "direct" ties with their capitalist and socialist suppliers and customers. He called for stronger links between Soviet foreign trade organizations and "end-user" firms in the Soviet Union. And he doubled the number of foreign trade organizations, freeing many of them from the dictates of the foreign trade ministry, central banks, and Gosplan.

Gorbachev sought full participation in international trade organizations, including the World Bank, the International Monetary Fund (IMF), and the General Agreement on Tariffs and Trade (GATT). He argued that export-oriented production, international competition, and non-discriminatory trade would enhance the quality of Soviet manufactured goods and processes. But technical, economic, and political impediments modified the scope, pace, and results of Soviet foreign trade reforms. The inconvertibility of the ruble at home and abroad was a serious and persistent obstacle. Even some radical modernizers minimized the importance of international economic activities, while centrists remained cautious and conservatives skeptical. True, the increasing assertiveness of most union republics and major industries gave promise of freer and expanded internal and external trade. However, national and regional authorities increasingly disputed the ownership of the products and materials traded, and the local soviets and environmental groups acquired much greater power to reject specific ventures. As the domestic Soviet polity and economy rapidly disintegrated, few of their segments quickly integrated themselves into the world economy.

Prospects for the 1990s were not good. To be sure, the breakup of the Soviet internal empire could produce positive economic results for many republics or social groups in the long run. But political risk analysts throughout the world were advising business firms to seek profits in countries other than the Soviet Union. And national Soviet leaders were justifiably concerned about the possibility of rampant inflation and widespread strikes as well as the reality of serious shortages of consumer and producer goods. Gorbachev's postponement of radical economic reforms exacerbated all of these problems. Even the authoritative Program Statement of the 28th Communist Party Congress sidestepped the key issues of private property, free markets, unemployment, and bankruptcy. Presuming the desirability for "a phased transition to the market," the document used vague concepts such as "private labor ownership," "state regulation of market relations," and "an effective mechanism of maintaining employment." And it never mentioned the possibility of enterprise bankruptcy.[6]

By 1990 Gorbachev was beginning to abandon core elements of Brezhnev's economic system. The centralized planning and management of industry had been curtailed to allow substantial enterprise rights and responsibilities, and the collectivization of agriculture had been modified to encourage private cooperatives and long-term leasing of land. The Supreme Soviet passed new laws on enterprises, cooperatives, and business taxation and a preliminary statute on joint-stock companies, all of which helped prepare the way for a market economy. But many old structures were intact, and few new structures were in place. For example, the all-union and union-republic ministries remained accountable for the performances of individual enterprises, and many "state orders" continued to determine enterprises' production. Also, there were still more Soviet bureaucrats supervising agricultural production than the total number of American farmers, as independent-minded economist Nikolai Shmelev often observed.

Moreover, Gorbachev's top economic advisors, ultra-radical Nikolai Petrakov and radical Leonid Abalkin, could not agree on a reform strategy with one another, let alone with centrist premier Nikolai Ryzhkov. Gorbachev compounded the confusion by persistently seeking compromises between ultra-radical and centrist reform proposals, while giving increasing weight to the advice of pro-market economist and Presidential Council member, Stanislav Shatalin. And Gorbachev dodged a difficult decision by calling for a public referendum on the crucial but emotionally charged issue of private ownership of land.

Gorbachev was greatly pressured, however, by the Russian and other republic governments that favored full or virtual independence from Moscow and fast acceptance of the individual's right to own, not merely to use, land, capital, organizations, and other instruments of production. Boris Yeltsin's economic advisors had drafted dramatic and detailed guidelines for the Russian Republic that Shatalin's team modified and applied to the country as a whole. Yeltsin publicly affirmed that his republic would implement these ideas regardless of Gorbachev's approval. And this prospect induced a reluctant Gorbachev to collaborate with Yeltsin and propose a truly radical plan of action.

The 500-day plan emphasized inter-republic economic decision making, dismantled most of the national economic ministries, permitted private ownership of 70 percent of heavy industry, enabled a peasant to leave his or her collective farm with a share of its assets, privatized 90 percent of retail trade and construction, encouraged small-scale businesses, affirmed the property right of foreigners as well as Soviet citizens, decontrolled prices of many consumer and producer goods, approved the creation of a stock market, launched a commercial banking system and a republic-based federal reserve, initiated domestic and international currency reform, and substantially reduced the budgets of the military and KGB.

Briefly stated, this comprehensive plan was an unprecedented effort to create a capitalist economy and the sharpest break yet with the Stalinist legacy. Although the Supreme Soviet did not choose between the Shatalin and Ryzhkov plans, parliamentary deputies generally supported the radicals' central idea – namely, that private ownership of the means of production should replace public ownership. Most important, the Supreme Soviet gave Gorbachev emergency powers to select an economic reform plan in September 1990, and he promptly scuttled Shatalin's in favor of Valentin Pavlov's which was even more conservative and imprecise than Ryzhkov's.

The new international economy

The fate of perestroika was being determined in the international as well as the domestic arena. National and republic communist parties, ministries, and parliaments have had to cope with the increasing interdependence and shifting structure of the world economy. For decades Soviet commentators have viewed the United States, Western Europe, and Japan as the three "centers" of capitalism and have stressed the importance of "interimperialist contradictions," especially economic rivalry. In the 1990s this rivalry was intensifying, because the United States, Western Europe, and Japan were becoming the cores of large regional economic blocs with freer internal trade and greater motivation and capability for external protectionism. Clashes between competing superblocs would have global economic, military, and political reverberations.

The emerging relationships among huge regional trading blocs and the Soviet, East European, and Chinese economies are worth pondering. On the one hand, if economic and political reforms in the postcommunist and socialist countries fail to overcome intractable cultural, bureaucratic, fiscal, and scientific–technological obstacles, the neighboring capitalist countries may abandon efforts to initiate industrial joint ventures and revert to "colonial" ties (for instance, raw materials, semiprocessed goods, and unskilled labor in exchange for high technology, services, and food). On the other hand, if the post-communist and socialist countries move beyond import substitution and force their aging and inefficient factories to compete successfully in world markets, their high-quality products and processes will enable them to participate as more equal members of their respective regional economic blocs. These blocs will then include capitalist, post-communist, and socialist countries – the Soviet Union and Eastern Europe linked with Western Europe and China linked with Japan and the NICs of Asia. And with common economic "homes" and common economic rivals, the diverse countries in the same geographical area are more likely to find common interests in political, military, environmental, and even territorial issues.

Large trading blocs may homogenize the present-day capitalist, post-communist, and socialist economies, and the Soviet Union and China may well become capitalist countries. Pressures for cooperation within the superblocs are considerable, even if power is unequally distributed inside a bloc. But internal cohesion increases a bloc's bargaining power and can be used to intensify competition with other blocs. All three superblocs have begun to compete in the Soviet Union, Eastern Europe, and China as well as in diverse countries throughout the world. The possibility of confrontation is heightened by the allure of huge untapped markets in countries with archaic information and telecommunications technologies, lagging transportation and service infrastructures, and insufficient consumer goods. For example, American multinational corporations might vie for enormous Soviet markets with the West Germans and Japanese, and this would quite probably benefit the Soviet economy.

The nature, pace, and effectiveness of perestroika were the key variables. Soviet leaders were discarding the command-and-control economy at both the national and republic levels and were disseminating more and better economic data than ever before. Also, Gorbachev's policy and institutional changes were designed to increase foreign influences on planning and management, on the direction and speed of technological advances, and on the quality and assortment of manufactured goods. But by early 1990, according to *PlanEcon Report*, less than 200 joint ventures were operational of the 1,542 registered, and most were "small, seriously undercapitalized, and focused on supplying services rather than involved in manufacturing as the authorities had hoped." In addition, "as the Soviet economy slid into chaos, Western enthusiasm for new joint ventures appeared to be declining."[7] Thus, the Soviet Union was struggling to establish long-term and mutually advantageous commercial ties with its potential European and Asian trading bloc partners. It was not at all certain that many Soviet republics and enterprises would be coopted rather than exploited by their more industrialized neighbors and would contribute to and benefit from the "the new stage of the scientific–technological revolution."

Conclusion

The concentration of political, economic, and military power in regional commerical blocs could make rivalry among the blocs more confrontational and more likely to spill over into non-economic issues. But greater international trade usually promotes political and military accommodation rather than assertiveness. This generalization would seem likely to hold in the 1990s with the present or comparable leadership in the major capitalist, post-communist, and socialist countries. Particularly welcome have been the cooperative relationships established by Gorbachev, Wojtech Jaruzelski, and Vaclav Havel with conservative Western leaders as well as the Soviet and East European governments' development of the theory and practice of mutual security. Also, many Soviet and East European officials are keenly aware of interconnections between domestic and foreign policy making, policies, and performance. And leaders and citizens in the former Soviet bloc are increasingly applying global, international, and Western criteria and standards to reevaluate and redirect their collective and individual initiatives.

The Soviet Union has made a little progress toward membership in the World Bank, IMF, and GATT, modest progress in joint ventures, considerable progress in garnering credits from different Western sources, and enormous progress in working constructively through the United Nations. With further progress in these spheres communist and non-communist reformers can enhance growth and productivity in the industrial, agricultural, and consumer goods spheres. Internal problems and external opportunities are pressuring the Soviet Union to participate actively in the increasingly competitive but increasingly regularized international markets. And all of these developments give Soviet national and republic leaders a larger stake in the well being of the world economy and in the marketization of their nation's and republic's civilian economies.

Capitalist countries can strengthen international security by facilitating the integration of post-communist and socialist countries into the international economy. This integration, whatever its forms, will be very difficult. Even with an amelioration of global problems, a relaxation of regional tensions, more East–West commercial, diplomatic, and arms-control agreements, major changes in Soviet and East European policy-making institutions and processes, and the domestic and international convertibility of currencies, the Soviet Union and most of Eastern Europe have just begun multifaceted cultural transformations and market-oriented economic reforms.

The successful modernization of the Soviet and East European countries could create political, economic, and military risks and costs for capitalist countries, traditional alliances, and new regional trading blocs. But the unsuccessful modernization of the former Soviet bloc would generate much more disruptive and deviant behavior within and among these societies. The stronger national and regional governments would be more tempted to initiate assertive foreign policies in selected geographic and issue areas. Also, segments of populations and newly created countries would be more likely to vent their frustrations by exacerbating international tensions or by trying to mobilize support from world public opinion. And bitter ethnic and economic rivalries inside a disintegrating nuclear superpower would destabilize the entire international system.

Western governments and citizens as well as multinational and transnational organizations can influence these developments at the margins and sometimes closer to the core. East–West accords in the 1990s cannot guarantee a more secure and prosperous international order, but they can help to conceptualize and lay the foundations for such an order.

Notes

1. Mikhail Gorbachev, "Speech to All-Union Student Forum," *Pravda*, 16 November 1989, pp. 1–3, in *Daily Report: Soviet Union, Foreign Broadcast Information Service* (hereafter *FBIS-SOV*), 16 November 1989, p. 64.
2. Mikhail Gorbachev, "Report to the CPSU Central Committee Plenum," Tass, 27 January 1987; in *FBIS-SOV*, 28 January 1987, pp. R10, R41.
3. Gorbachev, "Speech to All-Union Student Forum," pp. 66–67.
4. Aleksandr Yakovlev, "Address to Latvian party activists," *Pravda*, 12 August 1988, p. 2, in *FBIS-SOV*, 12 August 1988, pp. 41–42.
5. Robert C. Tucker, *Political Culture and Leadership in Soviet Russia: From Lenin to Gorbachev*, New York, Norton, 1987, p. 194.
6. "28th CPSU Congress Program Statement: Toward a Humane Democratic Socialism," *Pravda*, 15 July 1990, pp. 1, 3, in *FBIS-SOV*, 16 July 1990, Supplement, pp. 20–21.
7. "Soviet economic performance during the first half of 1990," *PlanEcon Report*, Washington, DC, vol. 6, nos. 27–28, 13 July 1990, pp. 3–4ff.

13 From decentralization to liberalization of foreign trade: the experience of Poland

Krystyna Szymkiewicz

On 1 January 1990 Poland entered a new era. Having rejected the option of "improving" or "perfecting" its past economic system, the country embarked upon a very radical program (known as the "Balcerowicz Program") to transform its economy into a market economy. Since the lessons which can be drawn from the application of this program can be very instructive, this chapter will analyze in turn:

the reforms in the field of foreign trade introduced in Poland before 1 January 1990;

the principles underlying the functioning of foreign trade since that date;

the initial results of the liberalization of foreign trade, and the problems relating to trade with CMEA countries.

1 Toward the centralization of foreign trade decision making, 1982–1989

Since 1982, the central plan has become indicative in the part which concerned trade with countries using convertible currencies. (The methods for planning trade with CMEA countries has not changed.) Thus, the data of the central plan should have only guided enterprises in their choice of imports and exports leaving them to take definitive decisions in an autonomous way, taking account of their own objectives.

According to the law of 26 February 1982,[1] import and export authorizations could henceforth be granted to economic actors other than the import–export organizations which depended on the Ministry of Foreign Trade. The latter could provide an authorization, called a "concession," to physical or legal persons for the import or export of specified goods and services.[2]

As far as instruments of decentralization are concerned, it should be noted that the Polish reform of 1982 authorized exporting enterprises to dispose freely of a part of their profits in hard currency deposited in a special account, called a hard currency savings account (ROD in

Polish). The maximum rate of savings was 50 percent of profits and the actual rate was on average in the order of 20 percent (reduced administratively to 16 percent in 1987). The ROD were generally considered to be the most important economic instrument introduced by the reform.

The existence of the ROD led to the creation in 1983 of an internal hard currency market. The sales of currencies held in ROD accounts were at first sporadic and strictly regulated. They were to become much more frequent after May 1987. The authorities of before October 1989 (when the government of T. Mazowiecki took office) hoped that the expansion of this market would, in time, permit the fixing of a genuinely market-related exchange rate for the zloty, thus leading to its convertibility.

From the middle of 1987 an attempt was made to redefine the responsibilities of the different actors in foreign trade. At the same time, efforts continued with a view to improving the monetary and financial mechanisms.[3]

1.1   A new international framework

In accordance with the law of 23 October 1987 moves were made to reform the central administration. The former Ministry for Foreign Trade was replaced by a Ministry for Foreign Economic Cooperation. The areas of competence of this ministry were expanded but the size of its staff was reduced and its internal organization simplified. It had to become a less bureaucratic institution, losing the function of monitoring the application of the Plan and concentrating on the preparation of a global strategy and of the rules for its implementation.

Approximately one year later, on 23 December 1988, the Diet adopted two very important pieces of legislation: the Law on Economic Activity, and the Law on Economic Activity involving Foreign Capital.[4] The first provided for free access to foreign trade for all physical and legal entities and guaranteed them equal treatment. Any economic actor could henceforth either engage in direct contracts with foreign partners or import and export goods using specialized intermediaries. No special authorization was needed for foreign trade except for a certain number of products and services, a list of these being maintained by the Ministry for Foreign Economic Cooperation. The first list, established on 30 December 1988, contained five large groups of products under imports and twenty-eight under exports (raw materials exported in large quantities, and products subject to quotas in the American and EEC markets).

The second law is presented in detail by J. Misala in Part II of this volume. It is sufficient here to recall that its initial version introduced a special provision to stimulate production for export. The rate of tax on profits was fixed at 40 percent with a possibility of 0.3 percent reduction in taxes for each percent of the value of the goods exported. A new version of this law, adopted by the Diet on 23 December 1989, reduced the rate of tax to 30 percent and at the same time dropped the tax incentives for exports.

From 1 January 1989 a reform of the Polish banking system was initiated which was radical in its objectives. The key issue was abandoning the system of a single bank and replacing it with a two-tier system, along with the creation of a network of commercial banks. Thus, the Narodowy Bank Polski (NBP) retains the classic role of a central bank, while many commercial banks are engaged in the financing of economic activity. On 1 January 1989 the Polish government had already permitted the creation of nine commercial banks. Thus, at this time, sixteen banks were functioning in Poland, four of which were authorized to conduct exchange operations: the Central Bank, the Commercial Bank, Bank Polska Kasa Opieki, and the PKO Bank.[5]

1.2   *Monetary and financial mechanisms*

Having become a member of the IMF in 1986, Poland undertook to introduce progressively the mechanisms of a market economy. Accordingly, efforts have been made to reduce subsidies (and eventually to eliminate them), to create a set of customs tariffs and, above all, to arrive at a market-related rate of exchange.

Thus, it was decided to end the traditional form of subsidy for exports which was to pay producers the difference between the external and internal prices. This was replaced by subsidies calculated as a percentage of the exchange rate. On 1 January 1988 a single agricultural subsidy was introduced which provided a 50 percent rate for exports to CMEA countries and a 20 percent rate for those to hard currency countries. On 1 July 1988 the subsidy rates were fixed for industrial products exported to hard currency countries. Thirty-one groups of products were identified, on which the rates varied from 5 percent to 25 percent of the value of the exports, expressed in terms of the "transaction price" (external price converted into zlotys at the official rate of exchange). In accordance with the rules of GATT, such subsidies must be temporary and must help to direct production toward profitable sectors.

A new set of customs tariffs entered into effect on 1 January 1989. On 1 January 1976 Poland had introduced a customs tariff on imports but

because of the centralized planning of trade, this tariff could not serve as
a protection device, and merely functioned as a fiscal mechanism. The
classification of goods in the new tariff conforms to the harmonized
system for the identification and labeling of goods which was approved
in 1985 by the Customs Cooperation Council in Brussels. Its introduction thus enables Poland to use a "common language" with the Western
countries which use the same system. It should be emphasized that
Poland is the first East European country which also uses a customs
tariff in its trade with CMEA countries.

The "active exchange rate policy" operated by successive governments has proved a very interesting and highly controversial experiment. It has involved frequent changes in the official rate[6] or, to be
more precise, a progressive devaluation of the zloty in terms of the
dollar or the transferable ruble. Independently of major devaluations
carried out on several occasions since 1982, Polish currency since April
1987 has continuously been devalued by minor adjustments. Very small
changes have been made every two or three weeks and sometimes,
every week.[7] This process has resulted in a depreciation of the zloty
which, as J. Ch. Asselain[8] has noted, represents a kind of historical
record.[9] The aim was to correct the rates in parallel with the increase of
internal prices in such a way that 80 percent of Polish exports would
become profitable. This policy proved relatively successful in 1987. But
during 1988 and 1989 the devaluation of the zloty was less than the rate
of inflation and therefore the exchange rate did not stimulate exports
enough.

The adoption, on 15 February 1989, of the Law on Possession and
circulation of Hard Currency[10] would seem to be an act of major significance. It deregulated completely exchange of hard currency between
individuals, and, under certain conditions, authorized enterprises to
conduct foreign exchange operations.

On the one hand, a market between individuals was created which
established its own rate of exchange. Individuals could sell or buy hard
currency in banks, and exchange bureaus could be created by enterprises as well as by private persons. On the other hand, there was a
multiplication of sales by auction to various types of enterprises. In 1989
there were four types of such auctions, organized by separate agencies
and using different operating methods:

1. The *Export Development Bank* organized sales by auction for state
enterprises as well as cooperatives and private companies. Joint ventures and companies involving foreign capital (*polonijne*) could participate in such auctions as sellers but not as buyers.

2. The *Pekao Bank SA* auctioned the hard currency coming from

"internal exports" (mainly the earnings of PEWEX shops which sell for dollars in the internal market). This hard currency was allocated exclusively to trading companies which imported for the needs of the internal market.

3. The consultancy company *Investexport* organized the sale by auction of hard currency which was needed to purchase very specific raw materials. The auctions catered for companies which used these materials in their production. In this case, the auction constituted an improved form of central allocation of hard currency. It was better than the classic form of allocation in that it caused enterprises to pay a high price for imports, thus obliging them to make an estimation of the advisability of these purchases. But they still did not have any real choice in the matter!

4. Since 1989 the *Handlowy Bank* had the task of organizing auctions of hard currency needed for the purchase of all the imported supplies foreseen in the Central Plan (raw materials and half-finished products, such as metals, wool, cotton, chemical products, paper, tobacco, etc. – some fifty items in all). Any economic entity could participate in these auctions except joint ventures and companies involving foreign capital.

Each of these auctions represented a different market with its own exchange rate based on that market. In October 1989, when the government of T. Mazowiecki took office, the official rate for the dollar applied to foreign trade was 2,200 zlotys, while the rate on the individual market was around 7,000 zlotys. The rate prevailing at the auctions was closer to that in the individual market than to the official rate. (Before the legalization of the individual market, the rate at auctions resembled that prevailing on the black market.)

1.3   *Assessing the reforms of pre-1990*

If judged by the number of measures taken, the results of these reforms might well appear impressive. When one examines what has actually been achieved, they are much less so. The measures taken have not really resulted in a decentralization of foreign trade decision making. Nor have they initiated a process of restructuring which would lead to a stimulation of foreign trade. The experience of these years has demonstrated that it is impossible to reform a specific economic sector unless the functioning of the economy as a whole is modified.

The institutional changes are not to be underestimated. The state monopoly of foreign trade, long considered an inherent element of a planned economy, has been put in question. The multiplication of actors in trading, and the elimination of the specialization by product of the traditional trade organizations, has opened the way to new initiatives. New phenomena are to be noted, such as links between trading companies and producers, and increased activity in the internal market to find more products for export.

On the other hand, in the sense of changes to the working mechanisms of the system, the results of the reform are much more disappointing, in spite of the often innovative character of the solutions applied. The liberalization of the planning process has been restricted to trade with hard currency countries. But even in the case of trade with this monetary region the freedom of enterprises has been limited because of the central allocation of raw materials and hard currency. In mid-1989, around 60 percent of imports were still being financed in this way.

Some of the measures introduced made no economic sense, such as the agricultural subsidy in trade with CMEA countries, with which the prices were stable. The same can be said for the customs tariff since the rates applied could not modify the planned imports. The growth in sales by auction was expected in time to result in a single rate of exchange. In actual fact, it has multiplied the rates of exchange and made economic planning even more difficult.

2   The liberalization of the foreign exchange and trade system

As opposed to previous governments which considered the convertibility of the zloty as the outcome of their reforms, the team of T. Mazowiecki considered it as a starting point on the road toward a market economy in its stabilization and restructuring program applied since January 1990. In the next two sections we examine the creation of a single rate of exchange for the zloty, and other foreign trade regulators in the new Polish economic system.

2.1   *Internal convertibility of the zloty*

On 1 January 1990 a single rate of exchange was set for the zloty against the American dollar, at a level close to that of the open market at the end of 1989. Fixed at 9,500 zlotys to a dollar, this rate was to stay stable for a period "of at least 3 months"[11] in order to facilitate the adjustment phase of the Polish economy. This rate remained unchanged in 1990. In parallel with the creation of a single hard currency market, Poland had introduced the internal convertibility of the zloty. Total convertibility is foreseen for later, after the economy has stabilized and, above all, after the balance of payments has evened out.

What are the practical consequences of introducing internal convertibility? It means that, inside the country, Polish currency can be freely converted into hard currency, and *vice versa*. On the other hand, the export of hard currency is regulated and the Polish zloty cannot be exchanged outside Poland. In Poland, payment in hard currency is exceptional and requires a special authorization.

In accordance with the law on hard currency of 15 February 1989, amended on 28 December 1989,[12] earnings in hard currency from an economic activity must be sold in their entirety to Polish banks at the official rate. This regulation applies to all economic entities: state and private enterprises, cooperatives, companies involving foreign capital, and joint capital ventures (before 1990 the latter were obliged to transfer to Polish banks only 15 percent of their hard currency export earnings). But, on the other hand, each enterprise which has to make a payment in hard currency can buy it at any time and at the official rate.

The central allocation of hard currency was eliminated at the same time as the hard currency savings accounts and the hard currency auctions. However, an enterprise which has its own savings account in hard currency earned from exports completed before 1990 can use it until the funds are exhausted.

The amended version of the law on hard currency maintains the existence of a separate exchange market for individuals. The rate of exchange used in this market is to be closely watched by the authorities. The latter will intervene when this rate stays "for a certain time"[13] at a level that is 10 percent more than the official rate. It is to be noted that the individual market concerns hardly 2 to 3 percent of all exchanges conducted in the country.[14] The Central Bank of Poland (NBP) envisages a unification of the exchange markets, whereby the present salespoints (*kantory*) will not be eliminated but will sell hard currency to individuals at the official rate of exchange.[15]

Individuals traveling abroad have the right, without being required to provide any justification, to take out $500 or the equivalent in other convertible currencies.[16] (Soon it may be perhaps $1,000.) This amount can be increased if the funds come from a hard currency account held in a Polish bank.

One of the measures to strengthen the zloty concerns changes in the regulations governing the shops which sell goods for hard currency. From 1 July 1990 these shops must also accept Polish currency. After 1 January 1991 the zloty becomes the only currency accepted.

2.2   *Regulations governing trade*

The monopoly of the state in foreign trade has been permanently eliminated. Any entity conducting legal economic activity, that is, one which is registered with a local administration (at the *gmina* level),[17] may engage in foreign trade. Someone wishing to conduct trade abroad must also obtain an identification number which is required when completing customs and banking formalities.[18]

Imports and exports of the majority of products have been deregulated. For some of them only an import (or export) license is required. According to the customs law in force, dated 28 December 1989,[19] the customs tariff is the principal regulator of imports although licenses are still needed for some specified products. For exports, licenses are the sole regulator since the customs tariff has been eliminated. It should be added that the current import tariff is applied exclusively to commercial and personal imports.

Import and export licenses are necessary for the following products:

> products for which a trading "concession" is always needed (radioactive material and solid isotopes, military and police products and services, services as an agent or representative on behalf of foreign partners);[20]
>
> products traded in the framework of international agreements which provide for payment in units of account (especially in transferable rubles) or through a clearing account:
>
> products which are allocated for export.

In this last category a distinction is made between external and domestic quotas. Among the former are included European Community quotas (on such products as sheep, fruit, metal products, textiles, shoes), and those imposed by such countries as the United States, Canada, Sweden, Norway, or Finland (textiles, shoes, metal products). In the second case, internal regulations fix maximum export quotas for certain products which are lacking in Poland. The decree of the Ministry for Foreign Economic Cooperation, dated 31 December 1989, listed twenty-two products for 1990 (including oil, coke, paper, copper, silver, sulphur, textiles, cement, meat, butter, sugar). At the same time, the Council of Ministers (which by virtue of the customs law may introduce temporary quotas) decided that in 1990 quotas would also be applied to twenty-four other products, such as petrol, fertilizer, some raw materials, and grain.[21]

In the current system there has been a major liberalization of imports, although exports remain under administrative control to a greater degree. However, the liberalization of exports is continuing. Thus, since August 1990, exports of the twenty-two products belonging to the first group have been freed of all controls. The reduction or elimination of restrictions is also foreseen for the twenty-four products belonging to the second group.[22]

Economic calculations concerning the advisability of imports from hard currency countries now depend on three elements: the rate of exchange, the customs tariff, and the tax on turnover. The latter is levied on all importers, including individuals who return from abroad with so many goods that it may be assumed that they are for resale. It should be noted here that the turnover tax, which is considered as a leftover from the old system, is to be replaced in 1991 by a value-added tax.

In the field of exports, the exchange rate is now the sole criterion of profitability (except for certain products, the export of which was deregulated in August 1990 and the internal prices of which are particularly low; a temporary tax applied to these exports, especially to coal, aims to protect domestic demand). Under the old system, there were special incentives to export such as priority allocation of hard currency for imports or reduction in the profit tax. Neither of these exist any longer.

Initiatives have been taken to improve the current system. A new set of customs tariffs is being prepared. The law concerning joint ventures has been amended in 1991 to authorize Western partners to transfer their profits freely out of Poland. Finally, the establishment is foreseen of a governmental institution, similar to COFACE in France, which will guarantee the loans allocated to Polish exports.

3   Trade with CMEA countries: terms and problems

The monetary and credit policy conducted in the framework of the Balcerowicz plan has a double goal: to limit excessive expansion of demand and to reestablish confidence in the zloty. After the first five months of its implementation, it can be said that it has completely achieved its objectives. There is even a fear in some quarters that the reduction of domestic demand has gone too far, with the risk of provoking a deeper and longer recession than that foreseen originally.[23] The reduction of domestic demand has had a direct influence on the evolution of foreign trade: it has stimulated exports and, at the same time, has led to a considerable reduction in imports.

3.1   *The situation in 1990*

In order to cope with reduced sales in the domestic market, many enterprises have sought to sell their products abroad. Accordingly, in February 1990, a major increase in exports was recorded, as much to Western countries as to the East. Finally, in spite of an important drop in exports in January, the average rate of growth calculated over five months (compared to the same period in 1989, using constant prices) was 11.8 percent for exports in convertible currencies and 4.5 percent for those in non-convertible currencies.[24] During the same period, a reduction of imports was recorded, of the order of 27.7 percent from countries using convertible currencies and of 35.2 percent from countries using non-convertible currencies.

As a result of this evolution Poland has achieved important trade surpluses with both areas. The surplus in convertible currencies, which was $1,208.9 million after the first four months of 1990, rose to $1,605.3 million at the end of May (the amount foreseen in the plan at the start of the year was $800 million). The surplus in transferable rubles increased likewise from 1,419.9 million rubles to 1,980.3 million rubles.

Favorable terms of trade (110.6 percent for these five months) have contributed to an increased positive balance with the ruble area, even if for the major part the surplus is due to a reduction in imports. With Western countries, the terms of trade have not been advantageous for Poland. They have, however, shown some improvement, increasing from 98.5 percent at the end of April to 99.1 percent at the end of May 1990.

According to the Central Planning Office, the surplus should amount to 4 million rubles and $3 million at the end of 1990.[25] The increased surplus in convertible currencies constitutes a positive element, making it possible to create some monetary reserves which Poland did not possess at the beginning of the reforms. It will also be used to finance oil imports. On the other hand, the surplus with CMEA countries does not permit increased imports but merely serves to reduce Polish debt (5.8 billion rubles at the end of 1989).

This rapid debt elimination carries a risk of inflation, which is why the government decided to intervene, from 1 June 1990, with a view to restraining exports and stimulating imports (this paradoxical provision, peculiar to centrally planned trade, will disappear on 1 January 1991). The rate of the transferable ruble was also diversified in June 1990: a rate of 2,100 zlotys to the ruble continued to be applied to planned trade and a rate of 1,000 zlotys to the ruble was fixed for unplanned trade. At the end of July 1990 the latter rate was reduced to 500 zlotys.

The elimination of the transferable ruble, as from 1 January 1991, will open a new chapter in the reciprocal trade between CMEA countries. The problem of a surplus in non-convertible currencies will be resolved, but other problems will appear.

3.2   Trading conditions after 1991

The first elements of information on this subject were to be found in the Polish press in July 1990. They are summarized here, starting with Poland's most important trading partners.[26]

USSR

During 1991 and 1992 trade with this country will be conducted in the framework of dollar clearing agreements. After this period the use of clearing agreements is to be reduced considerably in favor of trade in convertible currencies. For a part of the goods covered by clearing agreements deliveries will be obligatory. On the import side, these include oil, gas, and electric power; on the export side, certain raw materials and basic consumer goods. The central planning bodies of the two countries have the task of specifying the latter. Other products will be included on the lists of products to be exchanged. The role of clearing agreements is to be steadily reduced.

The balances of clearing accounts will be paid in dollars. A technical credit will be extended to 5 percent of trade, estimated at around $500 million. Up to $200 million, the interest rate will be low. For the remaining $300 million, the rate prevailing on the international market will be applied. Every six months, any balance which exceeds the ceiling of this credit is to be paid in convertible currency.

World prices are to be applied throughout as from 1991. Since mid-1990 the Polish and Soviet governments have been advising enterprises to conclude their agreements for 1991 in convertible currencies on the basis of world prices.[27]

Czechoslovakia

From 1 January 1991 trade will be conducted in convertible currencies and on the basis of world prices. During a period of transition (1991–92), machines and equipment as well as construction and assembly contracts will be sold using clearing accounts. The lists of goods are only to be indicative. As with the USSR, the payment of the balance is to be made in three stages: credit at low interest, credit at standard interest, and payment of the remainder in convertible currencies. Experts from the two countries were to prepare before the end of July 1990 the draft payment agreements which would enter into force at the beginning of 1991.

East Germany

The move to payments in convertible currencies will take effect on 1

January 1991; thus transferable rubles will only be used until the end of 1990 (with the exception of non-commerical payments). Poland announced its readiness to use convertible currencies, from 1 July 1990, at the non-commercial rate of 3.96 DM for 1 transferable ruble. A specific method of payment was being arranged for construction contracts.

Hungary

Trade will be conducted in convertible currencies from 1 January 1991. The prices and terms of sale were to be determined by the enterprises concerned. Draft payment agreements were to be prepared before the end of August 1990, and an overall trade agreement was to be ready in September 1990. The two countries were to strive for a reciprocal trade balance at the end of 1990. Poland proposed that any eventual surplus should be settled by a delivery of goods during the first half of 1991.

Bulgaria

From 1 January 1991 payment in convertible currencies will also be the rule for trade with this country. A list of goods to be exchanged between 1991 and 1993 will be established. Bulgaria wants deliveries from this list to be obligatory but Poland insists that they should be indicative. The trading partners in the two countries are free to negotiate their contracts and to decide their own terms.

There is a difference of position concerning the usage of the surplus in transferable rubles built up by Poland in 1990. The Bulgarians proposed to absorb it through deliveries of goods during the twelve months of 1991, whereas the Poles stated that such deliveries should be completed by 30 June 1990 and any outstanding balance be paid in convertible currencies.

Romania

In this case also, trade must be conducted using convertible currencies, with the possibility of using clearing accounts during a period of transition.

Other Countries

Mongolia, Cambodia, and Laos have accepted to trade with Poland in 1991 in convertible currencies. Vietnam has requested that, for a transition period, certain raw materials should be traded using clearing accounts, but the rest of her trade will be conducted in convertible currencies. At mid-1990 trade terms with North Korea and Cuba had not yet been revised.

4   Conclusion

The elimination of the transferable ruble is of strategic importance for the foreign relations of the ex-socialist countries in the future. In the Polish case we have seen that, on account of the different trade logic inside and outside the CMEA, all reforms in the sense of decentralization were limited to relations with market economy countries. Now the way is clear for the whole of foreign trade to be governed according to the same rules of the market.

At the moment it is difficult to identify the range of problems posed by the transition to trading in convertible currencies. At the macro-economic level a reduction of trading within the CMEA grouping is expected, and at the micro-economic level there will be some restructuring of enterprises and some of them will even be closed down. In the long term the generalization of trading at world prices and in convertible currencies should facilitate the liberalization of the economic system in all Eastern countries. But, for the moment, an unbalanced progress of the reform process can become a major obstacle to the implementation of the new trade rules.

The most serious cause for concern on the part of the Polish authorities is the future of Polish trade with the USSR. In 1991, Polish importers will have free access to hard currency, whereas those in the USSR will probably still have to request such allocations from the central authorities or from those of the relevant republic. Since 1990, some Polish enterprises have succeeded in signing contracts with their Soviet partners, others have already redirected their sales toward the West, and others are proposing joint ventures with the USSR. There is a risk that some traditional exporters to the Soviet market have not fully realized that 31 December 1990 marks the end of a long period of centrally planned trade.

There are also uncertainties concerning Polish–German trade. In the future Germany will certainly become Poland's most important trading partner (it is already the principal creditor and supplier of advanced technology). But for the moment there are many claims to be settled following the disappearance of the GDR and the sudden termination of numerous contracts during the summer of 1990.

The 14th June 1991 Law on companies with foreign participation is much more liberal that the former texts: Poles and foreign investors are treated equally, there is no need for minimum capital, and all benefits can be exported. On the 1 of August 1991, customs rates were increased from 11 to 14.2 percent. They now classified like those of the EEC countries ('Combined Nomenclature"). After sixteen months of monetary stability, a devaluation of the zloty (16.8 percent) took place on 17 May 1991. Since then the value of the exchange rate of the zloty is fixed in relation to five main currencies: $, Deutschmark, £ sterling, FF and SF. More recently, on 14 October it was decided to revise the exchange value of the zloty regularly. Since February 1991, Poles going abroad have been allowed to take $ 2,000 instead of $ 500.

The results of foreign trade for 1991 seem to be less good than those of 1990. At the end of 1990, Poland registered a surplus of about 3.7 billion. By the end of July 1991, the results of foreign trade were negative and amounted to $ 275 million. Trade between Poland and small ex-socialist countries has diminished, but what is much more important is Poland's relations with the Soviet Union. On the one hand,there is no agreement about mutual debts. On the other hand, the Soviet Union lacks foreign currency and therefore makes very few purchases abroad. Poland was hoping to benefit by about $1.5 billion from exports to the Soviet Union. Unfortunately, after the first six months of 1991, these exports only brought $250 million to the Polish economy.

Notes

1. *Official Gazette* (*Dziennik Ustaw*), no. 7, pos. 59, 1982.
2. K. Szymkiewicz, "Le Commerce extérieur: locomotive de la réforme économique en Pologne," *Le courrier des pays de l'Est*, no. 332, September 1988, pp. 54–55.
3. K. Szymkiewicz, "Le Système du commerce extérieur polonais: vers une nouvelle rationalité économique," *Revue d'Etudes Comparatives Est–Ouest*, March 1990, vol. 21, no. 1, pp. 143–61.
4. The complete texts of these laws were published in a special edition of the newspaper *Rzeczpospolita* on 1 January 1989.
5. By the middle of 1990, fifty-three banks had been registered and twenty-six were already functioning, R. Kowalski, "Narodowy Bank Polski ostrzega" [Central Bank of Poland Issues a Warning], *Rzeczpospolita*, no. 179, 3 August 1990, *Ekonomia i Prawo* supplement, p. ii.
6. The official rate of exchange (applied exclusively to the conversion of foreign trade prices) was fixed by the Central Bank of Poland (Narodowy Bank Polski), following a procedure based on the comparison of the internal and external prices of exported products. In practice, the value of the zloty was determined on the basis of a basket of the main export earnings in hard currencies. Two "basic" rates were fixed in this way: one in transferable rubles for trade with CMEA countries, and another in dollars for trade with hard currency countries.
7. Szymkiewicz, "Le Commerce extérieur," p. 155; T. Wasilewski, "Le Fonctionnement des marchés des changes en Pologne," *Revue d'Etudes Comparatives Est–Ouest*, vol. 21, no. 1, 1990, pp. 88–90.
8. J. Ch. Asselain, "Conditions et perspectives du rétablissement de la convertibilité des monnaies en Europe de l'Est," *Report to the Journées AFSE–GRECO "EFIQ" (CNRS): Etat actuel de la théorie*, organized by the Laboratoire d'Analyse et de Recherche Economiques, University of Bordeaux I, at Bordeaux, 17–18 May 1990, p. 2.
9. At the official rate, the dollar was worth 80 zlotys in January 1982, 2,200 zlotys in October 1989, and 6,500 zlotys at the end of December 1989.

10. *Official Gazette* (*Dziennik Ustaw*), 1989, no. 6, pos. 33. See also "Nowe prawo dewizowe" [New Law on Hard Currency], *Rzeczpospolita*, no. 44, 21 February 1989, p. 4.

11. Polish government memorandum on economic policy, *Rzeczpospolita*, no. 299, 28 December 1989, p. 3.

12. *Official Gazette* (*Dziennik Ustaw*), 1989, no. 6.

13. *Rzeczpospolita*, no. 299, 28 December 1989, p. 3.

14. T.E., *Rzeczpospolita*, 30 November 1989, p. 1.

15. P. Aleksandrowicz, "Pieniadz na dluzszej smyczy" [Money on a Longer Leash], *Rzeczpospolita*, no. 165, 20 July 1990, *Ekonomia i Prawo* supplement, p. 1.

16. Decree of Finance Minister, dated 31 December 1989, *Handel Zagraniczny*, no. 12, 1989.

17. Since the 1970s Poland has been composed of forty-nine administrative units called *wojewodztwa*, subdivided in *gminy* (of which there were 2,121 at the end of 1988).

18. These numbers are allocated by the regional Statistical Offices (of *wojewodztwo*).

19. *Official Gazette* (*Dziennik Ustaw*), no. 75, pos. 445, 1989.

20. Decree of Minister for Foreign Economic Cooperation, 21 December 1989.

21. I. Lewandowska, "Jac handlowac z zagranica. Bez niespodzianek na cle" [How to conduct foreign trade: avoiding surprises at the customs], *Rzeczpospolita*, no. 146, 26 June 1990, p. 4.

22. L. Balcerowicz and W. Baka, "Dokument dla Miedzynarodowego Funduszu Walutowego. Drugie polrocze: trudna walka z inflacja" [Document for the IMF. Second half of the year: difficult fight against inflation], *Rzeczpospolita*, no. 211, 11 September 1990, *Ekonomia i Prawo* supplement, p. iii.

23. According to a study by the Central Planning Office (CUP) undertaken on the basis of the economic results obtained between January and April 1990, by the end of the year the continuation of this trend would produce a decrease of 20 percent in national revenue compared with 1989 (instead of the 5 percent foreseen at the beginning of the year).

24. M. Misiak, "Gospodarka po maju. Niska produkcja" [The Economy at the End of May. Low production], *Zycie gospodarcze*, no. 25, 24 June 1990, p. 11.

25. P.A., *Rzeczpospolita*, no. 200, 29 August 1990, *Ekonomia i Prawo* supplement, p. 1. The actual figures for 1990 were slightly higher.

26. The information contained in this paragraph is derived mainly from an article by D. Walewska, "Handel w RWPG po 1 stycznia 1991 roku. Z kim, za ile?" [Trade with CMEA after 1 January 1991. With whom, and to what extent?], *Rzeczpospolita*, no. 153, 4 July 1990, *Ekonomia i Prawo* supplement, p. ii.

27. D. Walewska, "Handel z ZSRR. Bez mitow i emocji" [Trade with the USSR. Without myths and without emotion], *Rzeczpospolita*, no. 114, 18 May 1990, pp. 1, 2.

14 Between two fires? Foreign economic relations of Eastern Europe: past, present, and future(s)

Istvan Salgo

Eastern Europe finds itself, from a foreign economic relations aspect, between two fires. On the one hand, the countries of the region have to handle, actually or potentially, the distressing burdens of tensions accumulating in their relationship with the West, manifested in their debt position.[1] On the other hand, the decomposition of CMEA relations and their uncertainties are provoking, not without reason, serious concern in these countries, most of them just passing the basic phase of political transition. It is obvious, nevertheless, that the collapse of the old system, as far as the economy is concerned, was not a consequence basically of external shock effects but of an accumulation of internal problems, even if external factors did contribute greatly to this process.[2]

We shall focus here on the region now termed East-Central Europe (the former six, more and more to be called the five and the ex-GDR).

The breakdown of CMEA relations is taking place in a period when at the same time the internal system of conditions for integration into the world economy has not yet been established. This is, however, no wonder: the rigid rules of CMEA relations have been a basic hindrance to any opening toward the world economy while problems arising from the lack of this have been serving for quite a time as an ideological arsenal for maintaining the cooperation system. This is true even if we consider that restrictions in Soviet fuel deliveries, along with the increasing problems of convertible currency debts, have had an impact on the economic policy of most of the small CMEA countries beginning from the end of the seventies and have led to a deliberate restriction of economic growth, which was slowing down anyway. From this time, though, it was but the economy-stabilizing effect of the CMEA which was ebbing away in contrast to processes of the later period, especially in the latest years, when CMEA relations became unambiguously de-stabilizing for the economies of these countries.

We shall survey the features of foreign trade characterizing the small

East European CMEA countries in their main relations. We shall analyze the changes which have taken place in these fields in the latest period and the changes underway, including their efficiency. We shall then look at the outlets which might be available from the present "double squeeze" at the moment of the writing of this paper, in summer 1990, at the tensions that these outlets involve and at the implications which may be concluded from these changes for the Soviet economy. Let us first recall the main features of the traditional system.

When judging the role in foreign trade of the traditional centrally planned economy one has to set out from the fact that, similar, to other systems, this is basically determined by the entity of the economic system.[3] It follows logically from the claims of the traditional planned economy to control the totality of socio-economic processes that impacts of the external markets are not allowed to exercise their effect on the internal economy, by means of state institutions and direct state intervention. At the same time, meeting this demand in practice and curing tensions resulting from the given functioning of the economy have always required, even if to various extents in the individual countries and in individual periods, the existence of foreign trade relations. The duality referred to above has, on the one hand, resulted that although foreign trade could not be chased out from the economy, its active role was strongly pushed to the background by economic policy and, respectively, by the way of operation of the economy.

All these qualitative characteristics are reflected in real processes. As for autarchic inclinations, the specifics of the system are not reflected in the low share of foreign trade in gross domestic product but in the low ratio of current account items to the indicator of national performance (i.e. in the extremely low role, in international comparisons, of items beyond commodity turnover).[4] According to the data of CEPII (France) the foreign economy intensity indicator of the East European small countries discussed in the previous approach, with a value of 17.8 percent in 1986, exceeded only those of the large countries of the world economy, in which country group the Soviet Union with its rate of 6.1 percent proved to be the least open, immediately following China.[5] Another strong systemic feature is that the share of the countries of this region in world trade is low and showing a decreasing trend.

The subordinated role of foreign trade, the autarchic character and mechanisms of economic management, a remarkable weakness of dynamic fields and forms of international economic relations (e.g. services, direct foreign investment) are equally characteristic for relationships maintained in all directions. At the same time substantial differences, too, can be observed in both the way of handling the two main relations and in the parameters of connections maintained.

In contradiction to trade with market economy countries, CMEA relations are based from an institutional point of view on an international extension of the domestic management system. Accordingly, trade is conducted on the basis of agreements between state management organs. This system has been based on a number of essential pillars considered to be constant. One of these is that increments of mutual deliveries of goods can efficiently contribute to economic growth of the member countries. Another that the demand for fuel and raw materials from member countries is to be ensured by the Soviet Union, in exchange for processed products. A further assumption is that trade should be performed through a specific mechanism of cooperation based on bilateral agreements.

1   Tensions and attempts at handling them

Notwithstanding that in the countries discussed centralized foreign trade became (by insulating centrally planned economies somewhat from external disturbances and by ensuring imports needed for domestic plan fulfillment) one of the most successful fields of direct planning, the system as a whole has made foreign trade highly inefficient and rigid. In this sense directly planned management of the economy became the victim of its own success.[6] This again has led to numerous changes in the approach to the world economy and in the foreign trade system. Despite the differences among countries, a common feature is found in the way of handling external tensions in the relations with market economies.

In the framework of perfecting and reforming the foreign trade mechanism, the following changes took place.[7] On the one hand, decentralization affecting both foreign trade management and the enterprise sector in the organizational–institutional system of foreign trade has been introduced. On the other hand, some links between external and internal prices have been established. Finally, in stimulating exports and restricting imports, implementation of an array of economic instruments has been gradually gaining a major role, even if this took place with contradictions.

Nevertheless, these changes have been limited. Foreign trade was decentralized with numerous built-out barriers. Monopolistic positions remained even in the countries most advanced in this field. Although the separation between external and domestic prices has been weakened, hardly any progress was made in forming an internal price system based upon a significant exchange rate linking domestic and external prices. As for handling export and import processes, means of administrative and informal control, even if to a different extent in various countries, continued to play an outstanding role, sometimes getting even stronger.

Chances for opening toward the world economy have been severely deteriorated by the fact that so far no significant change has taken place in the system of connections maintained in the CMEA sector. Up to the landslide of 1989, despite all internal criticism expressed regarding the mechanism of the CMEA, stronger interests were tied to maintaining the existing system.

Finally, the measures taken so far in the interest of economic adaptation (adjustment) to the world market and of smoothing out external economic tensions were treated basically as specific matters of regulating foreign trade. The linkage between various reform policies and the external economy was a weak one.[8] As a consequence, the basic contradiction between the weakness of export capabilities and significant import demands could not be changed in essence. Hence the conditions for solving the debt problem could not be created.

On the basis of all the above, a categoric no is the answer to whether earlier reforms have improved the external economic position of the countries of the region, even if with various qualifications for various countries.[9] This is demonstrated by the factual survey of the situation emerging at the end of the eighties in the two main relations, beginning with relations with the West.

Naturally a further analysis is needed to determine what new factors contributed to the worsening of performances in foreign trade in 1989, with a decrease in the volume of East European exports for the first time in twenty years. Spectacular or less spectacular failures of the old system, earlier standards or rules suddenly being questioned, or their gradual erosion have been affecting and will continue to affect external economic performances, as well as decisions of economic policy made in the context of various political changes.[10] In view of these conditions it is not surprising that the unfavorable trend of world economy marginalization of East European countries is continuing, and that their share in world exports is further decreasing (see Table 14.1).

This development in exports and imports has reduced the trade balance surplus of the countries under review from $US 3.0 billion in 1988 to 2.4 billion in 1989, while the negative balance of invisibles surged to $US 4.5 billion, a value unseen since 1982.[11] As a consequence, the balance of payments of the region (current account) turned negative and produced a deficit of $US 2 billion. As compared to the year of 1988 this means a deterioration of 2.3 billion, surpassed by these countries for the last time in 1973–74 only (then the current account

Table 14.1. *Share of the small East European countries in the value of world exports (in percentage)*

1970	1980	1985	1986	1987	1988	1989[a]
6.1	4.1	4.7	4.6	4.3	3.9	2.8

Note: [a] January–September.
Source: Economic Survey of Europe 1989–1990, UNO–ECE, New York 1990, calculated on these data.

Table 14.2. *Gross debt volume of Eastern Europe in convertible currencies ($US billion)*

	1981	1984	1985	1986	1987	1988	1989[a]
Bulgaria	3.2	2.2	3.7	5.1	6.3	7.9	9.5
Czechoslovakia	4.6	3.1	3.5	4.5	5.3	5.7	6.9
GDR[b]	13.4	11.3	14.4	15.7	11.9	19.5	21.2
Hungary	8.7	8.3	11.8	15.1	17.7	17.3	20.6
Poland	25.9	26.9	29.8	33.6	38.8	39.2	41.0
Romania	10.2	7.2	6.6	6.5	6.0	2.8	1.0
Total	68.0	59.5	69.8	80.3	93.0	92.4	100.2

Notes: [a] Including intra-German debts.
       [b] projected.
Source: Financial Market Trends, no. 45, OECD 1990.

deficit increased from $US 2 billion to 4.8 billion) although due to exchange rate problems consequences from such a comparison can be drawn but cautiously.

The convertible currency debt of the East European countries continued to grow in 1989: its net value has exceeded $US 80 billion and the gross value – 100 billion (see Table 14.2). At the same time the magnitude of the debt alone does not provide sufficient basis for qualification. Namely, for evaluating the situation one needs various relative indicators, an analysis of debt service capability of the region or of the countries, and of the general directions of economic policy measures.

At the other side of foreign trade relations, in the CMEA trade of East European countries, serious problems already noticeable before have erupted in the course of the year 1989.

Economic growth in the countries of this region is slowing down steadily: according to UN data the annual growth rate of Net Material Product had been in the range of 4.9 percent to 8.7 percent in the period

Table 14.3. *Average annual growth rate of trade of East European countries among themselves and with the Soviet Union, 1987–1989 (on the basis of the value in transferable rubles of trade turnover in percent)*

	Exports			Imports		
	1987	1988	1989	1987	1988	1989
Eastern Europe	4.3	5.4	−2.1	−4.2	5.1	−1.2
Soviet Union	3.2	3.2	−2.2	−4.3	−6.5	−5.2

Source: Economic Survey of Europe 1989–1990, UNO–ECE 1990, p. 143.

of 1970 to 1978, and in the period of 1979 and 1989 only of 1.7 percent to 4.1 percent for the whole region. Considering that especially in domestic relations foreign trade contributes to economic growth basically in an extensive way and not from the aspect of efficiency, this situation indicates that cooperation is playing a decreasing role. The exhaustion of the possibilities of a wasteful management based on using up all reserves is primarily occurring through the shrinking delivery capabilities of the Soviet Union. The purchasing potential of the small East European countries is decreasing steadily and significantly.

A new phenomenon of the year 1989, however, is that the trend of export of East European countries has been revised: their value has decreased both in trade among themselves and with the Soviet Union. For this reason the value of mutual trade started to decrease in contradiction to earlier years (see Table 14.3).

The situation is even more unambiguous if approached in a structural projection. Namely, it is evident that the performance capability of the Soviet economy having been shattered, the regional model and practice based on a complementary, Soviet-centered exchange of goods is being questioned. The situation is made worse by the fact that in the course of the eighties when signs of this became obvious, the small member countries turned their efforts to maximizing fuel and raw material imports from the Soviet Union, i.e. to maintaining this continuously deteriorating situation, doomed in advance.[12]

Growth and structural problems are a source of further tension as well, on the grounds of the natural bilateral cooperation system. While trade and current account balances of the East European countries deteriorate in relations with convertible currency accounting countries, the latter balance even becoming negative, an opposite phenomenon is experienced in intra-CMEA relations. In East European trade with the Soviet Union the surplus of these countries amounted in 1987 to 0.6

billion transferable rubles, in 1988 already to 3.8 billion, and in 1989 to 4.5 billion. It may be assumed as probable by all means that as a whole the small countries were net exporters to the Soviet Union. This is a serious burden for these countries in various ways. These claims appear in an accounting transferable unit but mean an extended, permanent, and non-transferable extension of net income produced by the small countries. During all this time Eastern Europe was a net importer of resources in convertible relations, i.e. part of its convertible assets have been exposed in a very disadvantageous way.

Within the given system no remedy can be found. Intergovernment handling of CMEA relations is completely incompatible with economic transformation of the countries of the region, a restriction of the role of the state, and the extension of market conditions.[13] This explains why, since 1989 in quite a number of East European countries, administrative measures taken to reduce ruble exports[14] might temporarily improve the balance but are incapable of providing a permanent solution to these problems.

2   In the squeeze of constraints

East European countries have reached the last decade of the millenary with a serious historical legacy. In a year of change in political systems they have to reckon with unfavorable economic prospects. In the sphere of external economic relations the exchange of goods with the Soviet Union could not reach even the level of contracts. It is still questionable how economies surviving recession can mobilize resources for increasing convertible currency exports.[15] At the same time, conditions for change are qualitatively more favorable than in the course of the previous years. The new domestic political situation provides in principle adequate space to liquidate earlier structures and to perform necessary reforms. In addition, political changes meet some favorable international economic conditions: among others, a deepening of internationalization and acceleration of the West European integration process.[16]

Taking advantage of such an opportunity means meeting a number of conditions. These include how far requirements of economic reforms and opening toward the world economy can be met. A reform remaining autarchic would be unable to handle tensions in the two main relations. As a counterpart an opening performed without an internal reform would lead to chaos due to the persistence of weak behavior of the economic subjects.[17]

A reform opening toward external markets contains a number of elements but its two main pillars are undoubtedly a transformation of the property structure and a consistent opening toward the world economy. This requires not only a number of institutional conditions (e.g. the establishment of the institutions of capital markets, its technical infrastructure, personnel conditions, etc.) but also quite a number of partial reforms. Opening toward the world market includes reforming the relations maintained with the CMEA members in connection with property reform, the elaboration of unambiguous rules for direct foreign investment, ensuring freedom for foreign trade activities, liberalization of exports and imports, and formation of conditions for convertibility, etc.[18]

Although these questions arise in every country, the answers are different due to the real economic situation of each country, and to the institutional legacies. It can be stated, therefore, that while the remarkable differences which prevailed until the last year in the attitude of various countries to reforms have been swept away, the region has so far not been homogenized regarding the way of handling the transition and sequencing it.

The reform of CMEA trade is a typical case. The need to abolish trade based on intergovernment agreements has been formulated in the latest years above all in Hungary, the forerunner of reform processes. If reform of the CMEA as a whole cannot be reckoned with, then, considering the growing internal functional disturbances of the internal management and regulation system of the CMEA connections, and also the fact that this system cannot be adjusted to the requirement of marketing, Hungary has to find an independent solution for handling its CMEA connections. Though transformation of the trade system of the CMEA cannot be performed in one stroke, the efficiency of measures aiming at liberalizing the economy would become highly questionable if a significant part of this trade continued further on to be handled within an intergovernment framework.[19]

An overall consensus, however, exists only in the statement that the present situation is untenable. On the other hand, it is also excluded that in the short run an overall full-range, market-based system be established.[20] Between the two extremes, however, quite a number of solutions may arise which otherwise would include tensions in any case. One group of proposals is based on the general concept that transition to the market economy should take place starting from the dual character of these economies.[21] In this spirit a gradual transition is needed for the transformation of the CMEA trade which is based on a constantly shrinking centralized sphere, funtioning on the basis of the present rules and on a constantly widening decentralized sphere, resting on enterprise agreements.[22] Others start from the fact that both the real economy situation and the institutional requirements of the reform demand a radical change. This would clearly be a transition to convertible currency accounting, doing away with one of the most serious obstacle so far prevailing to a world economy integration, namely that the three markets – world market, CMEA, domestic market – are separated.[23]

The dispute has been settled due to the fact that beginning in 1991, East European trade with the Soviet Union is to be conducted in hard currency.

Nevertheless, the circumstances, conditions, and technical modalities of the new system are not yet clear.[24] For instance, it is not yet obvious what trade carried out at world market prices (current prices) in convertible currency would mean: convertible currency accounting, a clearing or barter system, or a combination of these. On the other hand, a high uncertainty surrounds the question as to what extent the internal Soviet economic management and foreign trade control conditions will allow for an efficient system of settlements. Finally, one does not know what would be the cost implications and in which fields.

It is, however, clear enough that changing over to the new system would involve costs emerging even in the external economy sphere for the East European countries. What is more, this would occur in a way similar to other costs, not all at once but lasting for several years. Debt management is a case in point. Namely, if these countries trade among themselves with a convertible currency accounting, they have to expect a deterioration of the terms of trade in the exchange of goods remaining, and this has to be covered by some source.

Naturally, one of the key issues of the transition would be what the Soviet Union would be ready to accept as compensation of losses thus emerging. It can, nevertheless, be taken for granted that this would not be a full-scale compensation. Thus whether to offset the loss of Western export revenues to cover additional Soviet purchase demands, or whether to offset increased Soviet convertible currency incomes, the East European countries will have to find funding. The amount of this can hardly be estimated, but some guidance may be obtained for orientation from Soviet estimates stating that East European countries would have to contemplate some $US 6–10 billion of losses resulting from this change-over.[25] If this conservative estimate were to be drawn by these countries in totality from international capital markets, then, compared to the 1989 data of the OECD the share of these countries would increase from the average of 1 percent (as of the latest years) to 2.4 percent of the overall credit extensions by the OECD.

All this emerges when demand for external resources due to realization of reforms is increasing anyway. Thus it is not superfluous to think about modalities and conditions for debt relief, rejected at the beginning of the eighties but gaining ground more and more since.[26] The West may consider aiding the Soviet Union in relation with liberalization of trade with East European countries, and supporting regional cooperation, ultimately promoting the homogenization of world trade.

Such a support should, however, be tied to rigorous conditions. The Soviet Union should have to create internal trade management conditions for a liberalized regional trade. The interests of the Soviet Union should be tied to the realization of short-term gains, i.e. use of external sources. This attraction can be ensured by the Soviet Union shifting to convertible currency accounting in the exchange of goods within the CMEA, even without being forced to perform necessary institutional reforms. At the same time such a condition would enhance the solution already recognized in Eastern Europe, but not fully carried out there either, of linking up internal reforms closely to foreign trade policy.[27] External resources provided "via" Eastern Europe to the Soviet Union might reduce the danger of seeking to balance the presently deteriorating current account by means of administrative intervention.

Notes

1. The point is not simply the order of magnitude of external debts but meeting debt service obligations even for those countries which otherwise have a rather low debt. In Romania convertible currency imports grew by 42 percent in the first two months of 1990, while exports dropped by one-third as compared to the similar period of 1989 and although according to OECD data the gross external debts at the end of 1989 for this country amounted to $US 1 billion only, according to some Romanian economists, there is serious concern that a situation might arise in which debt service obligations could not be met anymore, Romania, "Interjú Astridel Radulescu-val, a Népgazdasági Intézet munkatársával," an interview with A. Radulescu, staff member of the Institute for National Economy, *Világgazdaság* (economic daily in Hungary, founded by the Hungarian Chamber of Commerce), 12 May 1990.
2. The 1970s have been characterized by an outward projection of internal tensions and the 1980s by external economic tensions turning internal. Quotation from D. Daianu; L. Csaba, "Reformpolitika..." [Reform policy and opening to the world economy in Eastern Europe], *Gazdaság* (Hungarian economic periodical), no. 3, 1989.
3. T. Wolf, "Foreign trade in the centrally planned economy," *Fundamentals of Pure and Applied Economies*, no. 27, Harwood, 1988.

4. Reference is made here to statements of the author's joint study with Mr. Ivan Szegvari, published so far only partly, on the system-specific character of external economic relations of the socialist countries and on its quantifiable and institutional peculiarities.
5. G. Lafay and .G. Herzog, *Commerce international: la fin des avantages acquis, Economica*, 1989.
6. Wolf, *Foreign Trade*, p. 43.
7. I. Szegvári, "Külkereskedelmi irányitás, a szocialista országok reformfolyamata" [Foreign trade management, the reform process of the socialist countries], *Gazdaság*, no. 4, 1990.
8. Csaba, "Reformpolitika," pp. 78–79.
9. In Poland and Hungary steps have been made creating a closer relation between reforms and opening. Due to this convertible currency trade, performances of these two countries as compared to other countries of the region have developed more favorably during the year of 1989, UNO–ECE, *Economic Survey of Europe in 1989–1990*, 1990, p. 231.
10. Besides inefficiency of export campaigns heavily relying on former political channels it should also be mentioned that even the politically and economically equally justified suspension of excessive forcing of exports and restriction of imports (e.g. in Romania) might also lead to a deterioration of short-term performances.
11. UNO–ECE, *Economic Survey of Europe in 1989–1990*.
12. A. Köves, "Impertrestrikciós kényszer és importmaximalizációs törekvések" [Constraint of import restriction and efforts for maximizing imports], *Külgazdaság*, no. 9, 1988.
13. The report of the working group for foreign economic relations of the Hungarian Reform Committee stresses as one of the basic reasons of the weakness in the capability of exports to convertible currency markets the one-sided CMEA-orientation of the Hungarian economy prevailing for forty years (*World Economy*, 1989, p. 14).
14. UNO–ECE, *Economic Survey*, p. 81.
15. Ibid., p. 84.
16. M. Kaser, "East European Reform: synthesis and prospects for external competitiveness," NATO colloquium, 1990.
17. Czaba, "Reformpolitika," p. 104.
18. It is often suggested that East European countries should establish convertibility of their national currency during the first steps of transition. Beyond the fact, however, that the economic content of such a move remains rather obscure, attention has to be drawn to the circumstance that convertibility is not simply a matter of declaration but is a function of several preconditions needed for the functioning of its adjustment mechanism (efficient financial management, market behavior of economic units, liberalization of imports). P. Dembinski, "De l'inconvertibilité au contrôle de change" *Réforme et échanges extérieurs dans les pays de l'Est*, ed. W. Andreff, L'Harmattan, 1990.
19. BIS, 60ème *Rapport Annuel*, Basle, 1990.
20. I. Szegvári, "A jó dollár és a rossz KGST" [The good dollar and the bad CMEA] Figyelö, 3 August 1990.

21. See the description of the economic model provoking an extremely sharp debate in Hungary, the concept of which is based on a steadily shrinking state sector and a steadily expanding private sector, J. Kornai, *The Road to a Free Economy*, Norton and Company, 1990.
22. Szegvári, "A jó dollár és a rossz KGST."
23. G. Oblath, *Áttérés a dollárelszámolásra a szovjet viszonylatú kereskedelemben* [Changeover to dollar accounting in the trade with the Soviet Union], Budapest, Kopint–Datorg, 1990, p. 23.
24. Ibid.
25. M. Lyubsky, "SEV na perepute" [CMEA at the crossroads], *Trud* (Soviet periodical), 4 April 1990.
26. G. Oblath and V. Pásztori, "A kelet–nyugati pénzügyi kapcsolatok" [East–West financial relations], *Figyelö* (Hungarian economic weekly), 26 April 1990.
27. Csaba, "A peresztrojka öt éve" [The five years of perestroika], *Külgazdaság* (Hungarian economic periodical), no. 6, 1990.

Index

Abalkin, Leonid, 78, 185
Afghanistan, 26, 32, 67, 68, 69
agriculture, 9, 10, 42, 66, 192
Andropov, 48, 50, 51
Angola, 69, 71, 93, 94, 96, 99
Arefieva, Elena, 71
Asselain, Jean-Charles, 193
assistance (foreign): of the EEC to the
    Soviet Union and Eastern Europe,
    see EEC; of the GDR to the Third
    World, 86–101; of the Soviet Union
    to the Third World, 66–85; of the
    West to the Soviet Union, 24, 33,
    112
Australia, 155
Austria, 7, 12, 13, 150, 155, 156, 157,
    158, 264

Belgium, 7, 9, 12, 150
Berlin Wall, 23, 26, 30
Brazil, 94, 96
Brezhnev, 48, 50, 51, 179, 180, 181, 184
Bukharin, Nikolai, 79
Bulgaria, 9, 10, 13, 62, 126, 127
Bush, 37

Cambodia, 67, 68, 69, 75, 87
Canada, 48, 155, 156, 157, 158
Central European Payments Union, see
    CEPU
centrally planned economy, 13–16, 20, 61,
    86–87, 183
CEPU, 11, 18–21
Chernenko, 43, 48, 50, 51
China, 186, 187
CIA, 67, 68, 73, 75
CMEA, 16, 17, 19, 32, 33, 34, 190, 198–
    201; assistance to the Third World
    countries, 67, 91, 93, 94; demise of,
    213; developing members, 68, 69,
    74–78, 93, 94; single integrated
    market, 8; Socialist Economic
    Integration, 7

Cocom, 25, 27, 28, 29, 33, 35, 132, 172
Comecon, see CMEA
commodity composition of trade; USSR,
    41–43, USSR–USA, 45–47, GDR–
    Third World, 97
commonwealth of states, 31
communist party of the Soviet Union, see
    CPSU
concessions, see NEP; 133, 138, 139, 140,
    141
Conference for Security and Cooperation
    in Europe (CSCE), 35
convertibility, 18, 19, 151, 154, 170, 173,
    195–96, 214
Council for Mutual Economic Assistance,
    see CMEA
CPSU, 23, 107, 184
Cuba, 67, 68, 69, 70, 73–78, 87, 93, 94,
    95, 96, 97, 99
customs union, 7, 16, 49
Czechoslovakia, 9, 10, 11, 17, 18, 19, 26,
    62, 65, 126, 127, 128, 129

de Maizière, 99
Denmark, 7, 9, 12, 155, 156, 157, 158

East–South trade, 77–80, 95–98
East–West, integration, 7–22; trade, 23–
    35, 119–22, 125–29
EBRD, 34
EEC, agreement with CMEA, 8, 13;
    assistance to Eastern Europe, 34;
    assistance to the USSR, 29;
    association agreements with CMEA
    countries, 8; common agricultural
    policy, 9; member countries, 12;
    single market, 7, 8; trade agreements
    with CMEA countries, 7, 10; Treaty
    of Rome, 7, 8, 10, 11
EEA, 7, 11, 12, 13, 17
EFTA, 7, 11, 17, 48; membership, 12
Egypt, 96, 97, 155
Ethiopia, 69, 93, 94, 96, 99

217

218   *Index*

SELECTED PAPERS FROM THE FOURTH WORLD CONGRESS FOR SOVIET
AND EAST EUROPEAN STUDIES, HARROGATE, JULY 1990

Edited for the International Committee for Soviet and East European
Studies by Stephen White, University of Glasgow

Titles published by Cambridge

Market socialism or the restoration of capitalism?
edited by ANDERS ÅSLUND

Women and society in Russia and the Soviet Union
edited by LINDA EDMONDSON

Soviet foreign policy in transition
edited by ROGER E. KANET, DEBORAH NUTTER MINER and TAMARA J.
RESLER

The Soviet Union and Eastern Europe in the global economy
edited by MARIE LAVIGNE

The Soviet environment: problems, policies and politics
edited by JOHN MASSEY STEWART

New directions in Soviet history
edited by STEPHEN WHITE